JavaScript-mancy: Getting Started

Getting Started With the Arcane Art of Writing Awesome JavaScript For C# Developers

Jaime González García

© 2016 Jaime González García

Contents

Tome I.II JavaScriptmancy and Data Structures

JavaScript Arrays: The All-in-one Data Structure

Organizing Your Data With ES6 Maps

Sets, For When There Can Only Be One

Book I. Epilogue

Tome I.III JavaScriptmancy and OOP: The Path of The Summoner (preview)

References and Appendix

CONTENTS

About The Author

Jaime González García

Jaime González García (@Vintharas[1]) *Software Developer and UX guy, speaker, author & nerd*

Jaime is a full stack web developer and UX designer who thinks it's weird to write about himself in the third person. During the past few years of his career he has been slowly but surely specializing in front-end development and user experience, and somewhere and some time along the way he fell in love with JavaScript. He still enjoys developing in the full stack though, bringing ideas to life, building things from nothingness, beautiful things that are a pleasure and a delight to use.

Jaime works as a Technical Solutions Consultant at Google helping publishers be great. He also builds his own products in his spare time and blogs at barbarianmeetscoding.com (long story that one). He loves spending time with his beloved Malin, drawing, writing, reading fantasy and sci-fi, and lifting heavy weights

---

[1]https://twitter.com/Vintharas

About the Technical Reviewers

Nathan Gloyn

Nathan Gloyn (@NathanGloyn[2]) *Passionate developer, architect and speaker*

Independent software consultant and agile coach, Nathan is passionate about development and a firm believer in agile principles. In his day job he is contractor helping clients to build and deliver working software.

Nathan has successfully bootstrapped agile teams in various companies and has given presentations on technology and agile at a number of events.

---

[2]https://twitter.com/NathanGloyn

Andreas Bäcklund

Andreas Bäcklund (@andbackl[3]) *Consultant, passionate programmer*

Andreas is a consultant, passionate programmer, double master and a lifelong learner.

Andreas enjoys all sorts of tech and has been developing software that runs on everything from ship engines to the cloud. He enjoys working in the full stack because it's rewarding, exciting and challenging, all at the same time.

---

[3]https://twitter.com/andbackl

Prelude

It was during the second age
that the great founder of our order Branden Iech,

first stumbled upon the arcane REPL,
and learnt how to bend the fabric of existence to his very will,

then was that he discovered
there was a mechanism to alter the threads
being weaven into the Pattern,

then that we started experiencing the magic of JavaScript

> - Irec Oliett,
> The Origins of JavaScript-Mancy
> Guardian of Chronicles, 7th Age

Imagine... imagine you lived in a world were you could use JavaScript to change the universe around you, to tamper with the threads that compose reality and do anything that you can imagine. Well, welcome to the world of JavaScript-mancy, where wizards, also known as JavaScriptmancers, control the arcane winds of magic wielding JavaScript to and fro and command the very fabric of reality.

We, programmers, sadly do not live in such a world. But we do have a measure of magic [4] in us, **we have the skills and power to create things out of nothingness**. And even if we cannot throw fireballs or levitate (*yet*), we can definitely change/improve/enhance reality and the universe around us with our little creations. Ain't that freaking awesome?

Well, I hope this book inspires you to continue creating, and using this beautiful skill we share, this time, with JavaScript.

A Story About Why I Wrote This Book

I was sitting at the back of the room, with my back straight and fidgetting with my fingers on the table. I was both excited and nervous. It was the first time I had ventured myself to attend to one of the unfrequent meetings of my local .NET user group. *Excited* because it was beyond awesome to be in the presence of so many like-minded individuals, people who loved to code like me, people who were so passionate about software development that were willing to sacrifice their free time to meet and talk about programming. *Nervous* because, of course, I did not want to look nor sound stupid in such a distinguished group of people.

The meetup started discussing *TypeScript* the new superset of JavaScript that promised *Nirvana* for C# developers in this new

---

[4]"Any sufficiently advanced technology is indistinguishable from magic." Arthur C. Clarke. Love that quote :)

world of super interactive web applications. TypeScript here, Type-Script there because writing JavaScript sucked... JavaScript was the worst... everybody in the room started sharing their old war stories about writing JavaScript, how bad it was in comparison to C#, and so on...

"Errr... the TypeScript compiler writes beautiful JavaScript" I ad-ventured to say... the room fell silent. People looking astonishingly at each other, uncomprehending, unbelieving... Someone had dared use *beautiful* and *JavaScript* in the same sentence.

This was not the first, nor will be the last time I have encountered such a reaction and feelings towards JavaScript as predominant in the .NET community. JavaScript is not worthy of our consideration. JavaScript is a toy language. JavaScript is unreliable and behaves in weird and unexpected ways. JavaScript developers don't know how to program. JavaScript tooling is horrible...

And every single time I sat muted, thinking to myself, reflecting, racking my brains pondering... How to show and explain that JavaScript is actually awesome? How to share that it is a beautiful language? A rich language that is super fun to write? That's how this book came about.

And let me tell you one little secret. Just some few years ago I felt exactly the same way about JavaScript. And then, all of the sudden, I started using it, with the mind of a beginner, without prejudices, without disdain. It was hard at first, being so fluent in C# I couldn't wrap my head around how to achieve the same degree of fluency and expressiveness in JavaScript. Nonetheless I continued forward, and all of the sudden I came to love it.

The problem with JavaScript is that it looks too much like C#, enough to make you confident that you know JavaScript because you know C#. And just when you are all comfortable, trusting and unsuspecting JavaScript smacks you right in the face with a battle hammer, because, in many respects, JavaScript is not at all like C#. It just looks like it on the surface.

JavaScript is indeed a beautiful language, a little rough on the edges, but a beautiful language nonetheless. Trust me. You're in for a treat.

Why Should You Care About JavaScript?

You may be wondering why you need to know JavaScript if you already grok C#.

Well, first and foremost, *JavaScript is super fun to write.* Its lack of ceremony and super fast feedback cycles make it a fun language to program in and ideal for quick prototyping, quick testing of things, tinkering, building stuff and getting results fast. If you haven't been feeling it for programming lately, JavaScript will help you rediscover your passion and love for programming.

JavaScript is the language of the web, if you are doing any sort of web development, you need to understand how to write great JavaScript code and how JavaScript itself works. Even if you are writing a transpiled language like TypeScript or CoffeeScript, they both become JavaScript in the browser and thus knowing JavaScript will make you way more effective.

But *JavaScript is not limited to the web,* during the past few years JavaScript has taken the world by storm[5], you can write JavaScript to make websites, in the backend, to build mobile applications, games and even to control robots and IoT devices, which makes it a true cross-platform language.

JavaScript is a very approachable language, a forgiving one, easy to learn but hard to master. It is minimalistic in its contructs, beautiful, expressive and supports many programming paradigms. If you reflect about JavaScript features you'll see how it is built with simplicity in mind. Ideas such as type coercion (*are "44" and 44 so different after all?*) or being able to declare strings with either single or double quotes are great expressions of that principle.

---

[5]http://githut.info/

JavaScript's openness and easy extensibility are the perfect foundations to make it a *fast-evolving language and ecosystem*. As the one
language for the web, the language that browsers can understand,
it has become the perfect medium for cross-pollination across all
software development communities, where .NET developers ideas
can meet and intermingle with others from the Ruby and Python
communities. This makes knowledge, patterns and ideas spread
accross boundaries like never before.

Since no one single entity really controls JavaScript[6], *the community has a great influence in how the language evolves*. With a
thriving open source community, and openness and extensibility
built within the language, it is the community and the browsers the
ones that develop the language and the platform, and the standard
bodies the ones that follow and stabilize the trends. When people
find JavaScript lacking in some regard, they soon rush to fill in the
gap with powerful libraries, tooling and techniques.

But don't just take my word for it. This is what the book is for, to
show you.

What is the Goal of This Book?

This book is the first installment of the JavaScript-mancy series and
its goal is to provide a great and smooth introduction to JavaScript
for C# developers. If you are a C# developer that has had no or little
experience with JavaScript before then this book will help you get
started. If you have had quite a bit of experience with JavaScript but
it is still frustrating and you don't understand why things behave
the way they do, then this book will boost your JavaScript Fu until
you start enjoying the language.

---

[6]The ECMAScript standard in which JavaScript is based is evolved by the TC39
(Technical Committee 39) composed of several companies with strong interest in JavaScript
(all major browser vendors) and distinguished members of the community. You can take a
look at their GitHub page for a sneak-peek into how they work and what they are working
in

What is the Goal of The JavaScript-mancy Series?

The goal of the JavaScript-mancy series is to make you fluent in JavaScript, able to express your ideas instantly and build awesome things with it. You'll not only learn the language itself but how to write idiomatic JavaScript. You'll learn both the most common patterns and idioms used in JavaScript today, and also all about the latest version of JavaScript: ECMAScript 6 (also known ECMAScript 2015) and even about the upcoming version ECMAScript 7.

> You can use ECMAScript as a synonym for JavaScript. It is true that we often use ES (short for ECMAScript) and a version number to refer to a specific version of JavaScript and its related set of new features. Particularly when these features haven't yet been implemented by all major browsers vendors. But for all intents and purposes ECMAScript is JavaScript. For instance, you will rarely hear explicit references to ES5.

But we will not stop there because what is a language by itself if you cannot build anything with it. I want to teach you everything you need to be successful and have fun writing JavaScript after you read this series. And that's why we will take one step further and take a glance at the JavaScript ecosystem, the JavaScript community, the rapid prototyping tools, the great tooling involved in building modern JavaScript applications, JavaScript testing and building an app in a modern JavaScript framework: Angular 2.

Why JavaScript-mancy?

Writing code is one of my favorite past times and so is reading fantasy books. For this project I wanted to mix these two passions of mine and try to make something awesome out of it.

In fantasy we usually have the idea of magic, usually very powerful, very obscure and only at the reach of a few dedicated individuals. There's also different schools or types of magic: pyromancy deals with fire magic, allomancy relates to magic triggered by metals, necromancy is all about death magic, raising armies of skeletons and zombies, immortality, etc.

I thought that drawing a parallel between magic and what we programmers do daily would be perfect. Because it is obscure to the untrained mind and requires a lot of work and study to get into, and because we have the power to create things out of nothing.

And therefore, **JavaScript-mancy, the arcane art of writing awesome JavaScript.**

Is This Book For You?

I have written this book for you C# developer:

- you that hear about the awesome stuff that is happening in the realm of JavaScript and are curious about it. You who would like to be a part of it, a part of this fast evolving, open and thriving community.
- you that have written JavaScript before, perhaps even do it daily and have been frustrated by it, by not been able to express your ideas in JavaScript, by not being able to get a program do what you wanted it to do, or struggling to do so. After reading this book you'll be able to write JavaScript as naturally as you write C#.

- you that think JavaScript a toy language, a language not capable of doing real software development. You'll come to see an expressive and powerful multiparadigm language suitable for a multitude of scenarios and platforms.

This book is specifically for C# developers because it uses a lot of analogies from the .NET world, C# and static typed languages to teach JavaScript. As a C# developer myself, I understand where the pain points lie and where we struggle the most when trying to learn JavaScript and will use analogies as a bridge between languages. Once you get a basic understanding and fluency in JavaScript I'll expand into JavaScript specific patterns and constructs that are less common in C# and that will blow your mind.

How is The Book Organized?

This is the introductory book to **Part I. Mastering the Art of JavaScript-mancy** which aims to teach you how to write JavaScript with fluency.

We will start by taking a quick walkthrough through all that JavaScript has to offer from types, functions and objects, to data structures, exception handling and regular expressions.

Then we will do a deep dive into JavaScript functions which are more common-place and live more independent lives in JavaScript than in C#. You'll learn different patterns to do defaults, multiple arguments, function overloading in both ES5 and ES6.

We will continue taking a look at objects in JavaScript and at the many improvements that ES6 brings to object literals.

After you've learned more about functions and objects, two core constructs of JavaScript, we will discuss the big gotchas where we C# developers usually get stuck and stumble focusing particularly in the behavior of the this keyword.

We will finish this introduction to JavaScript with a look at some great ES6 features that will improve the readability of your code and at JavaScript data structures: the super useful and polifacetic array, the map and the set.

How Are The JavaScript-mancy Series Organized? What is There in the Rest of the Books?

The rest of the books are organized in 3 parts focused in the language, the ecosystem and building your first app in JavaScript.

After this introductory book **Part I. Mastering the Art of JavaScript-mancy** continues by examining **object oriented programming in JavaScript**, studying prototypical inheritance, how to mimic C# (classic) inheritance in JavaScript. We will also look beyond class OOP into mixins, multiple inheritance and stamps where JavaScript takes you into interesting OOP paradigms that we rarely see in the more conventional C#.

We will then dive into **functional programming in JavaScript** and take a journey through LINQ, applicative programming, immutability, generators, combinators and function composition.

Organizing your JavaScript applications will be the next topic with the module pattern, commonJS, AMD (Asynchronous module definition) and ES6 modules.

Finally we will take a look at **Asynchronous programming** in JavaScript with callbacks, promises and reactive programming.

Since adoption of ES6 will take some time to take hold, and you'll probably see a lot of ES5 code for the years to come, we will start every section of the book showing the most common solutions and patterns of writing JavaScript that we use nowadays with ES5. This will be the perfect starting point to understand and showcase the new ES6 features, the problems they try to solve and how they can greatly improve your JavaScript.

In **Part II. Welcome to The Realm Of JavaScript** we'll take a look at the JavaScript ecosystem, following a brief history of the language that will shed some light on why JavaScript is the way it is today, continuing with the node.js revolution and JavaScript as a true cross-platform, cross-domain language.

Part II will continue with **how to setup your JavaScript development environment** to maximize your productivity and minimize your frustration. We will cover modern JavaScript and front-end workflows, JavaScript unit testing, browser dev tools and even take a look a various text editors and IDEs.

We will wrap Part II with a look at the role of **transpiled languages**. Languages like TypeScript, CoffeeScript, even ECMAScript 6, and how they have impacted and will affect JavaScript development in the future.

Part III. Building Your First Modern JavaScript App With Angular 2 will wrap up the book with a practical look at building modern JavaScript applications. Angular 2 is a great framework for this purpose because it takes advantage of all modern web standards, ES6 and has a very compact design that makes writing Angular 2 apps feel like writing vanilla JavaScript. That is, you won't need to spend a lot of time learning convoluted framework concepts, and will focus instead in developing your JavaScript skills to build a real app killing two birds with one stone (Muahahaha!).

In regards to the size and length of each chapter, aside from the introduction, I have kept every chapter small. The idea being that you can learn little by little, acquire a bit of knowledge that you can apply in your daily work, and get a feel of progress and completion from the very start.

Understanding the Code Samples in This Book

How to Run the Code Samples in This Book

For simplicity, I recommend that you start running the code samples in the browser. That's the most straightforward way since you won't need to install anything in your computer. You can either type them as you go in the browser JavaScript console (F12 for Chrome if you are running windows or Opt-CMD-J in a Mac) or with prototyping tools like JsBin[7], jsFiddle[8], CodePen[9] or Plunker[10]. Any of these tools is excellent so you can pick your favorite.

If you don't feel like typing, all the examples are available in jsFiddle/jsBin JavaScriptmancy library: http://bit.ly/javascriptmancy-samples[11].

For testing ECMAScript 6 examples I recommend JsBin[12], jsFiddle[13] or the Babel REPL at https://babeljs.io/repl/[14]. Alternatively there's a very interesting Chrome plugin that you can use to run both ES5 and ES6 examples called ScratchJS[15].

If you like, you can download all the code samples from GitHub[16] and run them locally in your computer using node.js[17].

Also keep an eye out for **javascriptmancy.com**[18] where I'll add interactive exercises in a not too distant future.

---

[7]http://jsbin.io
[8]https://jsfiddle.net/
[9]http://codepen.io
[10]http://plnkr.co/
[11]http://bit.ly/javascriptmancy-samples
[12]http://jsbin.io
[13]https://jsfiddle.net/
[14]https://babeljs.io/repl/
[15]https://bit.ly/javascriptmancy-scratchjs
[16]
[17]http://www.nodejs.org
[18]http://www.javascriptmancy.com

A Note About Conventions Used in the Code Samples

The book has three types of code samples. Whenever you see a extract of code like the one below, where statements are preceded by a ›, I expect you to type the examples in a REPL.

> ### The REPL is Your Friend!
>
> One of the great things about JavaScript is the REPL (Read-Eval-Print-Loop), that is a place where you can type JavaScript code and get the results immediately. A REPL lets you tinker with JavaScript, test whatever you can think of and get immediate feedback about the result. Awesome right?
>
> A couple of good examples of REPLs are a browser's console (F12 in Chrome/Windows) and node.js (take a look at the appendix to learn how to install node in your computer).

The code after › is what you need to type and the expression displayed right afterwards is the expected result:

```
> 2 + 2
// => 4
```

Some expressions that you often write in a REPL like a variable or a function declaration evaluate to undefined:

```
> var hp = 100;
// => undefined
```

Since I find that this just adds unnecessary noise to the examples I'll omit these undefined values and I'll just write the meaningful result. For instance:

```
1  > console.log('yippiiiiiiii')
2  // => yippiiiiiiii
3  // => undefined        <==== I will omit this
```

When I have a multiline statement, I will omit the › so you can more easily copy and paste it in a REPL or prototyping tool (*jsBin*, *CodePen*, etc). That way you won't need to remove the unnecessary › before running the sample:

```
1  let createWater = function (mana){
2      return `${mana} liters of water`;
3  }
```

I expect the examples within a chapter to be run together, so sometimes examples may reference variables from previous examples within the same section. I will attempt to show smallish bits of code at a time for the sake of simplicity.

For more advanced examples the code will look like a program, there will be no › to be found and I'll add a filename for reference. You can either type the content of the files in your favorite editor or download the source directly from GitHub.

CrazyExampleOfDoom.js

```
1  export class Doom {
2    constructor(){
3      /* Oh no! You read this...
4      /
5      / I am sorry to tell you that in 3 days
6      / at midnight the most horrendous apparition
7      / will come out from your favorite dev machine
8      / and it'll be your demise
9      / that is...
10     / unless you give this book as a gift to
11     / other 3 developers, in that case you are
12     / blessed for ever and ever
13     */
14   }
15 }
```

A Note About the Exercises

In order to encourage you to experiment with the different things that you will learn in each chapter I wrap every single one of them with exercises.

It is important that you understand that there is almost no wrong solution. I invite you to let your imagination free and try to experiment and be playful with your new found knowledge to your heart's content. I do offer a solution for each exercise but more as a guidance and example that as the one right solution.

In many of the exercises you'll see the following pattern:

```
1  // mooleen.weaves('some code here');
2  mooleen.weaves('teleport("out of the forest", mooleen, randalf)');
```

This is completely equivalent to:

```
1  // some code here
2  teleport("out of the forest", mooleen, randalf);
```

I just use a helper function weaves to make it look like *Moolen, the mighty wizard* is casting a spell (in this case teleport).

A Note About ECMAScript 5 and ECMAScript 6,7 within The Book

Everything in programming has a reason for existing. That hairy piece of code that you wrote seven months ago, that feature that went into an application, that syntax or construct within a language, *all were or seemed like good ideas at the time.* ES6, ES7 and future versions of JavaScript all try to improve upon the version of JavaScript that we have today. And it helps to understand the pain points they are trying to solve, the context in which they appear and in which they are needed. That's why this book will show you ES5 in conjunction with ES6 and beyond. For it will be much easier to understand new features when you see them as a natural evolution of the needs and pain points of developers today.

How will this translate into the examples within the book? - you may be wondering. Well I'll start in the beginning of the book writing ES5 style code, and slowly but surely, as I go showing you ES6 features, we will transform our ES5 code into ES6. By the end of the book, you yourself will have experienced the journey and have mastered both ES5 and ES6.

Additionally, it is going to take some time for us to start using ES6 to the fullest, and there's surely a ton of web applications that will never be updated to using ES6 features so it will be definitely helpful to know ES5.

A Note About the Use of Generalizations in This Book

Some times in the course of the book I will make generalizations for the sake of simplicity and to provide a better and more continuous learning experience. I will make statements such as:

> *In JavaScript, unlike in C#, you can augment objects with new properties at any point in time*

If you are experienced in C# you may frown at this, cringe, raise your fist to the sky and shout: *Why!? oh Why would he say such a thing!? Does he not know C#!?*. But bear with me. I will write the above not unaware of the fact that C# has the dynamic keyword and the ExpandoObject class that offer that very functionality, but because the predominant use of C# involves the use of strong types and compile-time type checking. The affirmation above provides a much simpler and clearer explanation about JavaScript than writing:

> *In JavaScript, unlike in C# where you use classes and strong types in 99% of the situations and in a similar way to the use of dynamic and ExpandoObject, you can augment objects with new properties at any point in time*

So instead of focusing on being correct 100% of the time and diving into every little detail, I will try to favor simplicity and only go into detail when it is conductive to understanding JavaScript which is the focus of this book. Nonetheless, I will provide footnotes for anyone that is interested in exploring these topics further.

Do You Have Any Feedback? Found Any Error?

If you have any feedback or have found some error in this book that you would like to report, then don't hesitate to drop me an email at jaime@vintharas.com.

A Final Word From the Author

The goal for this series of books is to be holistic. Holistic enough to give a good overview of the JavaScript language and ecosystem, yet contain enough detail to impart real knowledge about how JavaScript really works. That's a fine line to tread and sometimes I will probably cover too little or too much. If so don't hesitate to let me know. The beauty of a lean published book is that I have much more room to include improvements suggested by you.

There is a hidden goal as well, that is to make it as fun and enjoyable as possible. Therefore the fantasy theme of the whole book, the conversational style, the jokes and the weird sense of humor. Anyways, I have put my heart and soul into this book and hope you really enjoy it!

Jaime, 2015

Tome I. Mastering the Arcane Art of JavaScript-mancy

Introduction

For many years JavaScript has been frowned upon and looked down on by many developers due to its quirky nature, obscure behaviors and many WTFs that populate its hairy APIs and operations.

Frown upon no more! For with modern design patterns, libraries, tools and the long awaited ECMAScript 6 (ES6, ES2015) writing JavaScript is now a pleasure.

Join me at the school of JavaScript-mancy as we travel along the modern landscape of writing JavaScript in 2015 and beyond, as we discover the organic evolution of this beautiful language and its thriving ecosystem, and delve in the latest features/spells/incantations of the JavaScript Arcana.

You my friend, can no longer ignore JavaScript. JavaScript is the most deployed language on earth, a beautiful and expressive language that supports many paradigms and which has a thriving community that continuously expands and improves its ecosystem with patterns, libraries, frameworks and tools. You don't want to miss this train.

But JavaScript, though forgiving and specially conceived to be easy to learn, can be either daunting for us that have a strongly-typed mindset and come from languages such as C# or Java or, more often, laughed at as a toy.

For you who consider it daunting and hate working with it worry not! I will show you the most common misconceptions and all the patterns you need to know to become as fluent in JavaScript as you are in C#.

For you who consider it a toy language, something associated not with real programming but with copy-paste coding or scripting to add flare to websites, I will show you all the different patterns and programming paradigms that JavaScript supports and which make it just as good and powerful as C#.

Let's get started!

Once Upon a Time...

*Once upon a time, in a faraway land, there was a beautiful hidden island with captivating white sandy beaches, lush green hills and mighty white peaked mountains. The natives called it **Asturi** and, if not for an incredible and unexpected event, it would have remained hidden and forgotten for centuries.*

*Some say it was during his early morning walk, some say that it happened in the shower. Be that as it may, **Branden Iech**, at the time the local eccentric and today considered the greatest Philosopher of antiquity, stumbled upon something that would change the world forever.*

In talking to himself, as both his most beloved companions and his most bitter detractors would attest was a habit of his, he stumbled upon the magic words of JavaScript and the mysterious REPL.

In the years that followed he would teach the magic word and fund the order of JavaScriptmancers bringing a golden age to our civilization. Poor, naive philosopher. For such power wielded by mere humans was meant to be misused, to corrupt their fragile hearts and bring their and our downfall. It's been ten thousand years, ten thousand years of wars, pain and struggle.

It is said that, in the 12th day of the 12th month of the 12th age a hero will rise and bring balance to the world. That happens to be today.

12th Age, Guardian of Chronicles

This book has a story in it. It is a story of a fantasy[19] world where

---

[19]For those of you that are not fantasy nerds I have included a small glossary at the end of the book where you can check words that you find strange. You should be able to understand the book and examples without the glossary, but I think it'll be more fun if you do

some people can wield JavaScript to affect the world around them, to essentially program the world and bend it to their will. Cool right? The story follows the step of a heroine that comes to this hypothetical world to save it from evil, but of course, she needs to learn JavaScript first. **Care to join her in her quest to learn JavaScript and save the world?**

The Essential Ingredients Of JavaScript-Mancy

The importance of the fundamentals cannot be enough overstated,
the gathering of the proper ingredients for an incantation,
the carefulness and caring of the preparations,
the timing and intimate knowledge of the rituals,
everything affects the end result.

To practice is to be,
practice as you want to be,
for do you want to be an Artful Wizard, or a mediocre one?

> \- Kely Sompsin,
> Maester of the Guild,
> Fourth Age

An Introduction to JavaScript-Mancy

I expect the reader of this manuscript to be well acquainted with the basics of programming, but I couldn't, in good faith, start the book without some sort of introduction to the arts of JavaScript. This first chapter will therefore take you through the whole breadth of the JavaScript language, albeit in a superficial way. I will show you all the basic features of JavaScript, even those of its latest incarnation ECMAScript 6, and how they differ or are similar to C#. I abhorr starting programming books with page after page on for loops and if statements so I will attempt to be as brief, interesting and entertaining as I can.

If you feel like you are well versed in the basics of JavaScript (and the new ES6 features) then by all means jump over this chapter, but be aware that there's a story happening in the examples, so you might be interested in taking a look. In any case, here we go...

```javascript
/*

And so here are we... at the start of a new adventure,
our heroine sleeping peacefully in the middle of a clearing,
surrounded by the darkness of a moonless night.

We will call her... *stranger* since we do not yet know her name...

*/

stranger.says('hmmm... what?! where!?');
stranger.weaves('Console.WriteLine("lux++!")');
// => Uncaught ReferenceError: Console is not defined

stranger.says('hmm?');
stranger.weaves('Console.WriteLine("lux = lux + 1 !!")');
// => Uncaught ReferenceError: Console is not defined

/*

The stranger curses and looks startled. Well I suppose she looks
startled, it is hard to see a person's expression in the complete
```

```
blackness of a moonless night as you well know...

*/

randalf.says("I'm afraid that is not going to work here...");
randalf.weaves("lux();");
// => A tiny wisp of light appears out of thin air and
//    illuminates the surroundings

/*

Ok, now! THAT, my friend, is what startled looks like!");

*/

randalf.says("Hmm, you are not ready yet...no...no... " +
    "You are going to need to learn some ~~~JavaScript~~~");
```

JavaScript

 Experiment JavaScriptmancer!!
You can experiment with all examples in this chapter
within this jsBin[20] or downloading the source code
from GitHub[21].

JavaScript, as we the guardians of JavaScript-mancy usually call
the arts, is a multi-paradigm dynamic programming language.
The multi-paradigm bit means that JavaScript lends itself well to
different styles (paradigms) of programming like object-oriented or
functional programming. The dynamic part means that... well the
dynamic part is widely disputed even today... but for all intents and
purposes we can say that JavaScript is evaluated as it is executed,

[20]http://bit.ly/javascriptmancy-basics
[21]https://github.com/vintharas/javascriptmancy-code-samples

there's no compilation step in which variables are bound, types are checked and expressions analyzed for correctness. The JavaScript runtime defers all this work until the code itself is being executed and this allows for a lot more freedom and interesting applications like metaprogramming [22].

JavaScript is also **dynamically typed** so a variable can reference many different types during its lifetime and you can augment objects with new methods or properties at any point in time.

I can, for example, summon a minion from the depths of hell using the var keyword and let it be a number:

```
1  > var minion = 1
2  > minion
3  // => 1
```

And I can do some alchemy thereafter and transform the minion into something else, a string, for example:

```
1  > minion = "bunny";
2  // => "bunny"
```

I can keep doing that for as long as I want (as long as I have enough mana[23] of course), so let's make my minion an object:

---

[22]This is a gross oversimplification. If you've read some traditional literature about static vs dynamic programming languages you'll be familiar with the idea that static programming languages like C++, Java, C# are compiled and then executed whereas dynamic programming languages like Ruby, Python or JavaScript are not compiled but interpreted on-the-fly as they are executed. The repercussions of this being that a compiled program cannot be changed at runtime (you would need to recompile it), whereas an interpreted one can, since nothing is set in stone until it is run. In today's world however, JavaScript runtimes like V8 (Chrome) or SpiderMonkey (Mozilla) compile JavaScript to machine code, optimize it, and re-optimize it based on heuristics on how the code is executed.

[23]For those of you not familiar with magic, *mana* can be seen as a measure of *magical stamina*. As such, doing magic (like summoning minions) spends one's mana. An empty reservoir of mana means no spellcasting just as a empty reserve of stamina means no more running.

```
1  > minion = {name: 'bugs', type: 'bunny'};
2  // => Object {name: 'bugs', type: 'bunny'}
```

In JavaScript I don't need a class to create an object. I can just create an object with whichever properties I desire and then later on augment [24] it with new properties to my heart's content:

```
1  > minion.description = 'A mean looking bunny';
2  > console.log(minion);
3  // => Object {name: bugs, type: bunny,
4  //             description: A mean looking bunny}
```

JavaScript Has Some Types

JavaScript supports the following types: Number, String, Object, Boolean, undefined, null and Symbol.

As you may have guessed, JavaScript has a single type to represent all numbers. Which is pretty nice if you ask me, not having to ever think about doubles, and shorts, and longs and floats...

```
1  > var one = 1
2  > typeof(one)
3  // => "number"
4
5  > var oneAndAHalf = 1.5
6  > typeof(1.5)
7  // => "number"
```

There's a string type that works as you would expect any respectable string to behave. It lets you create string literals. Interestingly enough, JavaScript strings support both single (') and double quotes ("):

---

[24] As an article of interest you can augment objects in C# if you use the dynamic keyword with ExpandoObjects

```
1  > var text = "Thou shalt not pass!"
2  > typeof text
3  // => "string"
4
5  > var anotherBitOfText = 'No! Thou Shalt Not Pass!'
6  > typeof anotherBitOfText
7  // => "string"
```

JavaScript also has a boolean type to represent `true` and `false` values:

```
1  > var always = true
2  > var never = false
3  > typeof(always)
4  // => "boolean"
```

And an object type that we can use to create any new custom types:

```
1  > var skull = {name: 'Skull of Dark Magic'}
2  > typeof(skull)
3  // => object
```

JavaScript differs from other languages in that it has two different ways of representing the lack of something. Where C# has `null`, JavaScript has both `null` and `undefined`. Unlike in C#, the default value of anything that hasn't been yet defined is `undefined`, whereas `null` must be set explicitly.

```
1  > skull.description
2  // => undefined
3  > typeof(skull.description)
4  // => undefined
5
6  > skull.description = null;
7  > typeof(skull.description)
8  // => object :)
```

This can get even more confusing because of the fact that there's a third possibility. That a variable hasn't been declared:

```
1  > abracadabra
2  // => Uncaught ReferenceError: abracadabra is not defined
```

The confusion coming mainly from the error message: *abracadabra is not defined.* You can just think about these variables as *undeclared* instead of *not defined* and stick to the previous definition of undefined.

ECMAScript 6 brings a new primitive type, the symbol. Symbols can be seen as constant and immutable tokens that can be used as unique IDs.

```
1  > var crux = Symbol()
2  > typeof(crux)
3  // => symbol
```

Later within the book, we'll see how we can use Symbols to enable new patterns for hiding data in JavaScript.

Everything Within JavaScript Behaves Like an Object

In spite of JavaScript not having the concept of value types or reference types, numbers, strings and booleans behave like C#

value types and objects behave like C# reference types. In practice, however, everything within JavaScript can be treated as an object.

Numbers for instance, provide several useful methods:

```
1  > (1).toString()
2  // => 1
3  > (3.14159).toPrecision(3)
4  // => 3.141
5  > (5000).toLocaleString('sv-SE')
6  // => 5 000
```

And so do strings:

```
1  > "a ghoul".toUpperCase()
2  // "A GHOUL"
```

Interesting right? If a number is a primitive value type, how come it has methods? Well, what is happening is that, whenever we call a method on a number or other primitive type, the JavaScript runtime is wrapping the primitive value in a special wrapper object. So even though 1 is not an object itself, when JavaScript evaluates (1).toPrecision(3) it wraps the value within the Number object on-the-fly. You can test the reverse process and instantiate a number using the wrapper object directly:

```
1  > var number = new Number(1);
2  // => Number {}
3  > typeof(number)
4  // => 'object.'
```

Then unwrap the original value with valueOf:

```
1    > number.valueOf()
2    // => 1
```

Even more remarkable than numbers and strings, **functions behave
like objects**. They have their own methods:

```
1    > var fireBall = function(){ world.spell('A blazing ball of fire mat\
2    erializes from the palm of your hand!');};
3    > fireBall.apply
4    // => function apply(){}
```

And you can even add properties to a function:

```
1    {lang="javascript"}
2    > fireBall.maxNumberOfCharges = 5
3    // => 5;
4    > fireBall.maxNumberOfCharges
5    // => 5;
```

Let's take a quick look at each one of these types and how they work
in JavaScript.

Strings in JavaScript

Strings, like in C#, let you represent text literals.

```
1    > "hi there"
2    // => hi there
3    > "creepy"
4    // => creepy
5    > "stop repeating what I say"
6    // => stop repeating what I say
```

Unlike in C# you can use both single (') and double quotes (") to
create a string. Oftentimes you will see one used to escape the other:

```
1  > "this ain't cool man"
2  // => this ain't cool man
3  > 'you think you are so "funny"'
4  // => you think you are so "funny"
```

Any string has a number of useful methods:

```
1  > "I am tired of you devious REPL".split(' ');
2  // => ["I", "am", "tired", "of", "you", "devious", "REPL"]
3  > "I am tired of you devious REPL".replace('tired', 'ecstatic');
4  // => I am ecstatic of you devious REPL
5  > "I am tired of you devious REPL".indexOf('tired');
6  // => 5
```

ES6 also brings a number of new methods like startsWith, endsWith, repeat:

```
1  > "Stop REPL!".startsWith("Stop");
2  // => true
3  > "Stop REPL!".endsWith("REPL!");
4  // => true
5  > "NaN".repeat(10) + " BatMan!!!"
6  // => NaNNaNNaNNaNNaNNaNNaNNaNNaNNaN BatMan!!!!
7  > "ha! Now I beat you at your own game!"
8  // => "ha! Now I beat you at your own game!"
```

Until recently, there was no such thing as C# String.format nor StringBuilder so most injecting values in strings was done using the + operator or string.concat:

```
1  > var target = 'minion';
2  > "obliterate " + target + " with hellfire!"
3  // => obliterate minion with hellfire!
4  > "obliterate ".concat(target, " with hellfire!")
5  // => obliterate minion with hellfire!
```

Fortunately, ES6 brings *template strings* and a more elegant approach to string interpolation.

Better String Interpolation ES6 Template Strings

The new **ES6 Template Strings** improve greatly the way you can operate with strings. They allow string interpolation based on the variables that exist in the scope where the template is evaluated, thus providing a much cleaner and readable syntax.

In order to create a template string you surround the string literal with backticks and use `${variable-in-scope}` to specify which variable to include within the resulting string:

```
1  > var spell = 'hellfire';
2  > `obliterate ${target} with ${spell}!`
3  // => obliterate minion with hellfire!
```

Template strings also let you easily create multi-line strings.

Where in the past you were forced to make use of string concatenation and the new line character \n:

```
1  > "One ring to rule them all\n" +
2    "One ring to find them;\n" +
3    "One ring to bring them all\n" +
4    "and in the darkness bind them"
5  // =>  One ring to rull them all
6  //     One ring to find them;
7  //     One ring to bring them all
8  //     and in the darkness bind them
```

ES6 Template strings let you write a multi-line string in a more straightforward fashion:

```
1  > `One ring to rull them all
2    One ring to find them
3    One ring to bring them all
4    and in the darkness bind them`
5  // =>  One ring to rull them all
6  //     One ring to find them;
7  //     One ring to bring them all
8  //     and in the darkness bind them
```

Functions in JavaScript

Functions are the most basic building component in JavaScript. As such, they can live more independent lives than methods in C# which are always tied to a class. So, you'll oftentimes see functions alone in the wild:

```
1  > function obliterate(target){
2      console.log(`${target} is obliterated into tiny ashes`);
3  }
4  > obliterate('rabid bunny')
5  // => rabid bunny is obliterated into tiny ashes
```

JavaScript, in a radically different way than C#, lets you call a function with any number of arguments, even if they are not defined in a function's signature:

```
1  > obliterate('rabid bunny', 'leprechaun', 'yeti')
2  // => rabid bunny is obliterated into tiny ashes
```

And even with no arguments at all, although depending on the function implementation it may cause some chaos and some may-hem:

```
1  > obliterate()
2  // => undefined is obliterated into tiny ashes
```

You can use the very special arguments array-like object to get hold of the arguments being passed at runtime to a given function:

```
1  > function obliterateMany(){
2      // ES6 method to convert arguments to an actual array
3      var targets = Array.from(arguments).join(', ');
4      console.log(`${targets} are obliterated into tiny ashes`);
5  }
6  > obliterate('Rabid bunny', 'leprechaun', 'yeti')
7  // => Rabit bunny, leprechaun, yeti are obliterated into tiny ashes
```

Or the finer **ES6 rest syntax** reminescent of C# params:

```
1  > function obliterateMany(...targets){
2      console.log(`${targets} are obliterated into tiny ashes`);
3  }
4  > obliterate('Rabid bunny', 'leprechaun', 'yeti')
5  // => Rabit bunny, leprechaun, yeti are obliterated into tiny ashes
```

In addition to functions working as... well... functions, they perform many other roles in JavaScript and are oftentimes used as building blocks to achieve higher-order abstractions: they are used as object constructors, to define modules, as a means to achieve data hiding and have many other uses.

ES6 changes this complete reliance on functions a little bit as it provides new higher level constructs that are native to the language, constructs like **ES6 classes** and **ES6 modules** which you'll be able to learn more about later in this series. Indeed throughout this series I'll show you both ES5 constructs, the present and the past, and ES6 ones, the present-ish and the future, so you'll feel at home in any JavaScript codebase you happen to work with.

Functions as Values

An interesting and very important aspect of functions in javascript is that they can be treated as values, this is what we mean when we say **functions are first-class citizens** of the language. It means that they are not some special construct that you can only use in certain places, with some special conditions and grammar. Functions are just like any other type in JavaScript, you can store them in variables, you can pass them as arguments to other functions and you can return them from a function.

For instance, let's say you want to create a very special logger that prepends your name to any message that you wish to log:

```
1  > var log = function(msg){ console.log(msg);}
2  > var logByRandalf = function (msg, logFn){
3      logFn(`Randalf logs: ${msg}`);
4  }
5  > logByRandalf('I am logging something, saving it to memory for ever\
6  ', log);
7  // => Randalf logs: I am logging something, saving it to memory for \
8  ever
```

But that was a little bit awkward, what if we return a function with the new functionality that we desire:

```
1  > var createLogBySomeone = function (byWho){
2      return function(msg){
3          return console.log(`${byWho} logs: ${msg}`);
4      };
5  }
6  > var logByRandalf = createLogBySomeone('Randalf');
7  > logByRandalf('I am logging something, saving it to memory for ever\
8  ');
9  // => Randalf logs: I am logging something, saving it to memory for \
10 ever
```

If you feel a little bit confused by this don't worry, we will dive deeper into functional programming, closures and high-order functions later in the series. For now just realize that **functions are values** and you can use them as such.

JavaScript Has Function Scope

Another very interesting aspect of JavaScript that is diametrically opposed to how things work in C# is the scope of variables. JavaScript variables have **function scope and not block scope**. This means that functions define new scopes for variables and not blocks of code (*if statements, for loops*, code between {}, etc...) which highlights once more the importance of functions in JavaScript.

You can appreciate function scope in all its glory in these examples. First if you declare a single function with an i f block you can verify how the i f block doesn't define a new scope as you would expect in C#:

```
1  > function scopeIsNuts(){ // new scope for scopeIsNuts
2      console.log(x); // => undefined
3      if (true){
4          var x = 1;
5      }
6      console.log(x); // => 1
7  }
```

But if we replace the i f block with a new function inner, then we have two scopes:

```
1    > function outer(){ // new scope for outer
2        var x = 0;
3        console.log(x); // => 0
4
5        function inner(){ // new scope for inner
6            var x = 1;
7            console.log(x); // => 1
8        }
9        inner();
10
11       console.log(x); // => 0
12   }
```

ES6 let, ES6 const and Block Scope

ES6 attemps to bring an end to the confussion of JavaScript having function scope with the let keyword that allows you to create variables with block scope. With ES6 you can either use var for function scoped variables or let for block scoped ones.

If you rewrite the example we used to illustrate function scope with let, you'll obtain a very different result:

```
1    > function scopeIsNuts(){ // new scope for scopeIsNuts
2        console.log(x); // => undefined
3        if (true){
4            let x = 1;
5            console.log(x); // => 1
6        }
7        console.log(x); // => undefined
8    }
```

Now the x variable only exists within the if statement block. Additionally, you can use the const keyword to declare constant variables with block scope.

```
1  > function scopeIsNuts(){ // new scope for scopeIsNuts
2      console.log(x); // => undefined
3      if (true){
4          const x = 1;
5          console.log(x); // => 1
6          x = 2; // => TypeError
7      }
8      console.log(x); // => undefined
9  }
```

ES6 Default Arguments

ES6 finally brings default arguments to JavaScript functions, and they work just like in C#:

```
1  > function fireBall(target, mana=10){
2      var damage = 1.5*mana;
3      console.log(`A huge fireball springs from
4  your fingers and hits the ${target} with ${damage} damage`);
5  }
6  > fireBall('troll')
7  // => A huge fireball springs from your fingers and hits the troll
8  //    with 15 damage
9  > fireBall('troll', /* mana */ 50)
10 // => A huge fireball springs from your fingers and hits the troll
11 //    with 75 damage
```

ES6 Destructuring

Another nifty ES6 feature is destructuring. Destructuring lets you unwrap any given object into a number of properties and bind them to variables of your choice. You can take advantage of destructuring with any object:

```
1  > var {hp, defense} = {
2      name: 'conan',
3      description: 'cimmerian barbarian king of thieves',
4      hp: {current: 9000, max: 9000},
5      defense: 100, attack: 400};
6  > console.log(hp);
7  // => {current: 9000, max: 9000}
8  > console.log(defense);
9  // => 100
```

Even when passing an object to a function:

```
1  function calculateDamage({attack}, {hp, defense}){
2    var effectiveAttackRating = attack - defense + getHpModifier(hp);
3    var damage = attackRoll(effectiveAttackRating);
4    return damage > 0 ? damage: 0;
5
6    function getHpModifier(hp){
7      return hp.current < 0.1*hp.max ? 10 : 0;
8    }
9
10   function attackRoll(dice){
11     // do some fancy dice rolling
12     return dice;
13   }
14 }
15
16 var troll = {
17   name: 'Aaagghhhh',
18   description: 'nasty troll',
19   hp: {current: 20000, max: 20000},
20   defense: 40, attack: 100
21 };
22 var conan = {name: 'conan',
23   hp: {current: 200, max: 200},
24   defense: 1000, attack: 1000
25 };
26 console.log(calculateDamage(troll, conan));
27 // => 0
28 // => no troll gonna damage conan
```

ES6 Arrow Functions

Another great feature brought by ES6 are arrow functions which resemble C# lambda expressions. Instead of writing the obliterate function as we did before, we can use the arrow function syntax:

```
1   /*
2   > function obliterate(target){
3       console.log(`${target} is obliterated into tiny ashes`);
4   }
5   */
6   > let obliterate = target =>
7       console.log(`${target} is obliterated into tiny ashes`);
8   > obliterate('minion');
9   // => minion is obliterated into tiny ashes
10  > obliterate('rabid bunny')
11  // => rabid bunny is obliterated into tiny ashes
```

And if you have a function with more arguments or statements, you can write it just like we do in C#:

```
1   > let obliterateMany = (...targets) => {
2       targets = targets.join(', ');
3       console.log(`${targets} are obliterated into tiny ashes`);
4   };
5   > obliterateMany('bunny', 'leprechaun', 'yeti');
6   // => Bunny, leprechaun, yeti are obliterated into tiny ashes
```

We will dive deeper into arrow functions later in the book and see how they not only provide a terser and more readable syntax but also serve a very important function in what regards to safekeeping the value of this in JavaScript. (We've got ourselves a very naughty this in JavaScript as you'll soon appreciate yourself)

OOP and Objects in JavaScript

JavaScript has great support for object-oriented programming with objects literals, constructor functions, prototypical inheritance, ES6 classes and less orthodox OOP paradigms like mixins and stamps.

Objects in JavaScript are just key/value pairs. The simplest way to create an object is using an object literal:

```
1  > var scepterOfDestruction = {
2      description: 'Scepter of Destruction',
3      toString: function() {
4          return this.description;
5      },
6      destruct: function(target) {
7          console.log(`${target} is instantly disintegrated`);
8      }
9  }
10 > scepterOfDestruction.destruct('apple');
11 // => apple is instantly disintegrated
```

ES6 makes easier to create object literals with syntactic sugar for functions also known as *method shorthand*:

```
1  > var scepterOfDestruction = {
2      description: 'Scepter of Destruction',
3      toString() {
4          return this.description;
5      },
6      destruct(target) {
7          console.log(`${target} is instantly disintegrated`);
8      }
9  }
```

And for creating properties from existing variables also known as *property shorthand*:

```
 1  > var damage = 10000;
 2  > var scepterOfDestruction = {
 3      description: 'Scepter of Destruction',
 4      damage, // as opposed to damage: damage
 5      toString() {
 6          return this.description;
 7      },
 8      destruct(target) {
 9          console.log(`${target} is instantly disintegrated`);
10      }
11  }
12  > scepterOfDestruction.damage;
13  // => 10000
```

This works great for one-off objects. When you want to reuse the same type of object more than once you can either use a vanilla factory method or a constructor function with the new keyword:

```
 1  // by convention constructor functions are capitalized
 2  > function Scepter(name, damage, spell){
 3      this.description = `Scepter of ${name}`,
 4      this.damage = damage;
 5      this.castSpell = spell;
 6      this.toString = () => this.description;
 7  }
 8  > var scepterOfFire = new Scepter('Fire', 100,
 9      (target) => console.log(`${target} is burnt to cinders`));
10  > scepterOfFire.castSpell('grunt');
11  // => grunt is burnt to cinders
```

Prototypical Inheritance

Yet another big diffence between C# and JavaScript are their inheritance models. JavaScript exhibits what is known as prototypical inheritance. That means that objects inherit from other objects which therefore are called prototypes. These objects create what is known as a *prototypical chain* that is traversed when the JavaScript runtime tries to determine where in the chain a given method is defined.

Let's say that you have an object that represents an abstraction for any item that can exist in your inventory:

```
1  > var item = {
2     durability: 100,
3     sizeInSlots: 1,
4     toString(){ return 'an undescriptive item';}
5  }
6  > item.toString();
7  // => an undescriptive item
```

And a two handed iron sword that in addition to being an item (and an awesome item at that) has its own specific set of traits:

```
1   > var ironTwoHandedSword = {
2      damage: 60,
3      sizeInSlots: 2,
4      wield() {
5        console.log('you wield your iron sword crazily over your head'\
6   );
7      },
8      material: 'iron',
9      toString() {return 'A rusty two handed iron sword';}
10  };
```

You can take advantage of JavaScript prototypical inheritance to reuse the item properties across many items, by setting the item object as the prototype[25] of the ironTwoHandedSword (and any other specific items that you create afterwards).

```
1   > Object.setPrototypeOf(ironTwoHandedSword, item);
```

This will establish a prototypical chain, so that, if we attempt to retrieve the sword durability, the JavaScript runtime will traverse the chain and retrieve the property from the item prototype:

---

[25]One does not simply change the prototype of an object willy-nilly at runtime since it can affect performance a lot. Instead, you would use Object.create or a function constructor, and if needed, you would augment the prototype as needed.

```
1  > ironTwoHandedSword.durability;
2  // => 100
```

If, on the other hand, you attempt to access a property that exists in both the prototype and the object itself, the nearest property in the chain will win:

```
1  > ironTwoHandedSword.toString();
2  // => A rusty two handed iron sword
```

ES6 exposes the __proto__ property that lets you directly assign a prototype through an object literal:

```
1  > var ironTwoHandedSword = {
2      __proto__: item,
3      damage: 60,
4      // etc...
5  };
6  > ironTwoHandedSword.prototype = item;
```

There's a lot more to prototypical inheritance and the many different OOP paradigms supported by JavaScript. But we'll look into them further later in the series.

ES6 Classes

A new addition to JavaScript you might have heard about and celebrated are ES6 classes. The existence of ES6 classes doesn't mean that JavaScript gets classes just like C# and we're not going to worry about constructor functions and prototypical inheritance anymore. **ES6 classes are "just" syntactic sugar over the existing inheritance model and the way we craft objects in JavaScript.** That being said, it is a great declarative way to represent constructor/prototype pairs.

A JavaScript class looks very similar to a C# class:

```
1  class Item {
2    constructor(durability = 100, sizeInSlots = 1){
3      this.durability = durability;
4      this.sizeInSlots = sizeInSlots;
5    }
6    toString(){
7      return 'an undescriptive item';
8    }
9  }
10 var item = new Item();
11 item.toString();
12 // => an undescriptive item
```

And so does inheritance:

```
1  class Sword extends Item {
2    constructor(durability = 500, sizeInSlots = 2,
3               damage = 50, material = 'iron'){
4      super(durability, sizeInSlots);
5      this.damage = damage;
6      this.material = material;
7    }
8    wield() {
9      console.log(`you wield your ${this.material} sword
10 crazily over your head`);
11   }
12   toString() {
13     return `A ${this.material} sword`;
14   }
15 };
16 var sword = new Sword();
17 sword.wield();
18 // => you wield your iron sword crazily over your head
```

Arrays, Maps and Sets in JavaScript

Up until recently JavaScript had only one single data structure, albeit very verstatile, to handle collections of items: the array. You can create an array using using square brackets [ ]:

```
1   > [1, 2, 3, 4 ,5]
2   // => [1,2,3,4,5]
```

You can mix and match the different elements of an array. There's no type restrictions so you can have numbers, strings, objects, functions, arrays, etc... in much the same way that you can find the most strange items in a kender's [26] pouch:

```
1   > var aKendersPouch = [
2       'jewel',
3       '3 stones',
4       1,
5       {name: 'Orb of Power'},
6       function() { return 'trap!';}
7       ];
```

You can access the items of an array via their indexes:

```
1   > aKendersPouch[0]
2   // => jewel
3   > aKendersPouch[4]()
4   // => trap!
```

You can also traverse the indexes of an array using the for/in loop:

```
1   > for (var idx in aKendersPouch) console.log(aKendersPouch[idx]);
2   // => jewel
3   // => 3 stones
4   // => ...etc
5   // => function() { return 'trap!';}
```

And even better the items of an array using ES6 for/of loop:

---

[26]like a hobbit but with shoes. If curious look up the joyful, corageous and beloved Tasslehoff Burrfoot.

```
1  > for (var item of aKendersPouch) console.log(item);
2  // => jewel
3  // => 3 stones
4  // => ...etc
5  // => function() { return 'trap!';}
```

Arrays have a lot of cool and useful methods that you can use to add/remove or otherwise operate on the items within the array:

```
1   > aKendersPouch.length
2   // => 5
3
4   // add item at the end of the array
5   > aKendersPouch.push('silver coin');
6   // => 6 (returns the current length of the array)
7   > aKendersPouch.push('6 copper coins', 'dental floss');
8   // => 8
9
10  // pop item at the end of the array
11  > aKendersPouch.pop();
12  // => dental floss
13
14  // insert item at the beginning
15  > aKendersPouch.unshift('The three Musketeers');
16  // => 8
17
18  // extract item from the beginning of the array
19  > aKendersPouch.shift();
20  // => 'The three musketeers'
```

And even LINQ-like methods to perform functional style transformations within an array:

```
1  > const isValuable = item => parseInt(item) > 5;
2  > const toGoldCoins = item => parseInt(item) || 0;
3  > const sumCoins = (sum, price) => sum + price;
4
5  > var goldCoins = aKendersPouch
6                       .filter(isValuable) // ES6 analogous to LINQ Wh\
7  ere
8                       .map(toGoldCoins) // analogous to LINQ Select
9                       .reduce(sumCoins, 0); // analogous to LINQ Aggr\
10 egate
11 > console.log(goldCoins);
12 // => 6
```

You will learn a ton more about arrays later in the book.

ES6 Spread Operator and Arrays

The **ES6 spread operator** can also be used to merge or flatten an array within another array:

```
1  > var newRecruits = ['Sam', 'John', 'Connor'];
2  > var merryBandits = ['Veteran Joe', 'Brave Krom', ...newRecruits];
3  > merryBandits;
4  // => ["Veteran Joe", "Brave Krom", "Sam", "John", "Connor"]
```

ES6 Maps and Sets

ES6 gives us magicians two new data structures to work with: maps, a true key/value pair data structure and sets to handle collections of unique items.

You can create a new map using the Map constructor:

```
var libraryOfWisdom = new Map();
libraryOfWisdom.set('A',
  ['A brief history of JavaScript-mancy', 'A Tale of Two Cities']);
libraryOfWisdom.get('A')
//=> ['A brief history of JavaScript-mancy', 'A Tale of Two Cities']\
;
```

You can even seed a map with existing information by sending an array of key/value pairs[27]:

```
var libraryOfWisdom = new Map([
  ['A', ['A brief history of JavaScript-mancy', 'A Tale of ...']],
  ['B', ['Better Dead Than Powerless: Tome I of Nigromantics']]
]);
libraryOfWisdom.get('B');
// => ['Better Dead Than Powerless: Tome I of Nigromantics']
```

In a similar fashion, you create sets using the Set constructor:

```
var powerElements = new Set(['earth', 'fire', 'water', 'wind']);
powerElements
// => Set {"earth", "fire", "water", "wind"}
```

Sets will ensure that you don't have duplicated data within a collection:

```
powerElements.add('water').add('earth').add('iron');
console.log(powerElements);
// => Set {"earth", "fire", "water", "wind", "iron"}
```

JavaScript Flow Control

JavaScript gives you the classic flow control structures that you are accustomed to: if, for, while loops behave much in the same way

---

[27]in reality, it does not need to be an array, but an iterable that produces key/value pairs [<key>:<value>]

in JavaScript than in C# (but for the function scoped variables of course).

In addition to these, JavaScript has the for/in loop that lets you iterate over the properties of an object:

```
1   > var spellOfFarseeing =
2       { name: 'Spell of Farseeing',
3         manaCost: 10,
4         description: 'The spell lets you see a limited' +
5                      'portion of a far away location;'}
6
7   > for (var prop in spellOfFarseeing) {
8       console.log(`${prop} : ${spellOfFarseeing[prop]}`);
9   }
10  // => name : Spell of Farseeing
11  // => manaCost : 10
12  // => description : The spell lets you see a limited
13  // portion of a far away location
```

And the ES6 for/of loop that lets you iterate over collections[28] (arrays, maps and sets):

```
1   > for (var element of powerElements) console.log(element);
2   // => earth
3   // => fire
4   // => water
5   // => etc...
```

Logical Operators in JavaScript

Abstract Equality and Strict Equality

JavaScript equality operators behave in a particularly special way. The operators that you are accustomed to use in C# == and != are

---

[28]for the sake of correctness, you can use the for/of loop not only on arrays, maps and sets but on anything that implements the iterable protocol. We will discuss iterability later within the series.

called **abstract equality operators** and evaluate the equality of expressions in a loose way. If the two expressions being evaluated by one of these operators don't match in type, they'll be converted to a matching type. For instance, in evaluating the abstract equality of 42 and "42", the string will be converted to a number resulting in both values being equal:

```
1   > 42 == '42'
2   ==> true
```

Fortunately JavaScript also provides operators that performs strict equality (=== and !==) which is basically a comparison of two values without the implicit type conversion.

```
1   > 42 === '42'
2   ==> false
```

Implicit Type Conversion Also Know As Type Coercion

This implicit conversion that takes place in JavaScript gives birth to the concept of *truthy* and *falsey*. Since any value can be evaluated as a boolean, we say that some values like an array [] or an object {} are truthy, and some other values like empty string ' ' or *undefined* are falsey. In the examples below we use the !! to explicitly convert values to boolean for clarity purposes:

```
1   > !![]
2   // => true
3   > !!{}
4   // => true
5   > !!""
6   // => false
7   > !!undefined
8   // => false
9   > !!null
10  // => false
11  > !!0
12  // => false
```

This allows for a terser way to write if statements

```
1   > if (troll) // as opposed to (troll != null && troll != undefined)
```

Since troll is coerced to a boolean type, having the troll variable
holding an object value will evaluate to *truthy* and having it holding
null or undefined will be *falsey*. In either case the if statement will
fulfill its purpose while being much nicer to read.

OR and AND

OR (||) and AND (&&) operations also behave in an interesting way.
The *OR* operation will return the first truthy expression or the last
falsey expression (if all expressions are falsey):

```
1   // 0 falsey
2   // 'cucumber' truthy
3   // 42 truthy
4   > 0 || 'cucumber' || 42
5   // => 'cucumber'
6   > 0 || false || undefined
7   // => undefined
```

The *AND* operator will return the last truthy expression or the first
falsey expression (if any falsey expression is encountered):

```
1   // 0 falsey
2   // 'cucumber' truthy
3   // 42 truthy
4   > 0 && 'cucumber' && 42
5   // => 0
6   > true && 'cucumber' && 42
7   // => 42
```

Exception Handling

Exception handling works similar as in C#, you have your familiar
try/catch/finally blocks:

```
1   > try { asdf; }
2     catch (e) { console.log(e.message);}
3     finally { console.log('done!');}
4   // => asdf is not defined
5   // => done!
```

And you can throw new exceptions with the throw keyword:

```
1   > throw new Error("We're all gonna die!");
2   // => Uncaught Error: We're all gonna die!
```

Additionally, you can improve your error semantics and create
custom errors by inheriting the Error prototype.

Regular Expressions

JavaScript also supports regular expressions. You can create a
regular expression in two ways, either by wrapping the expression
between slash (/):

```
1  > var matchNumbers = /\d+/;
2  > matchNumbers.test('40 gold coins');
3  // => true
4  > matchNumbers.exec('40 gold coints');
5  // => ["40"]
```

Or by creating a RegExp object:

```
1  > var matchItems = new RegExp('\\D+');
2  > matchItems.test('40 gold coins');
3  // => true
4  > matchItems.exec('40 gold coints');
5  // => [" gold coins"]
```

Strings have built-in support for regular expressions as well with the match and search methods:

```
1  > var bagOfGold = '30 gold coins';
2  > bagOfGold.match(/\d+/);
3  // => ['30']
4  > bagOfGold.search(/\d+/);
5  // => 0 (index where first match is found)
```

But Beware, JavaScript Can Be Weird and Dangerous

So far you've seen the bests parts of JavaScript and nothing too weird or inconsistent. But sometimes you'll experience strange behaviors in some less visited corners of JavaScript like any of the following:

```
1   > x = 10;
2   // => added a variable to the global scope (window.x)
3   > NaN == NaN
4   // => false
5   > null == undefined
6   // => true
7   > typeof(null)
8   // => object
9   > [] + []
10  // => ' '
11  > [] + {}
12  // => {}
13  > {} + []
14  // => 0
15  > {} + {}
16  // => NaN
```

Oftentimes you won't run into these issues when building real web applications and my advice is that you ignore them. Be aware that they exist but just don't use them, or use patterns or conventions to avoid them.

Concluding

And that was a summary of pretty much the whole JavaScript language. I really hope it has sparkled your interest for JavaScript and that you cannot wait to turn the next page and learn more. But first, let's make a quick review of what you've learned in this chapter.

We've seen that JavaScript is a very flexible dynamic language that supports many paradigms of programming and has a lot of great features.

You have learned the many things you can do with strings and ES6 string templates. How functions are very independent entities that can live their own lives completely separate from objects and how they are a fundamental building block of applications in JavaScript.

You also discovered arrow functions that resemble lambdas in C# and let you write super terse and beautiful code.

We took a look at objects, object initializers, prototypical inheritance and ES6 classes. We saw the different data structures supported, the versatility of the array and an overview of the new ES6 Map and Set.

We also examined more general language features like the flow control structures and logical operators. We saw the difference between abstract comparison and strict comparison, highlighted the implicit type conversion inherent to JavaScript, the existence of the concepts of *truthy* and *falsey* and the way the *OR* and *AND* operators work.

Finally we reviewed exception handling and regular expressions, and we saw some of the weird and best-avoided behaviors in JavaScript.

```
/*

The first rays of a new day like dubious trendils of light
start approaching the clearing when Randalf notices that the
stranger is looking weirdly at him...

*/

randalf.says("Yes, I know what you are thinking, " +
            " it is a lot to take in...");
stranger.says('...err... no... Who the hell are you? ' +
            'and whaaaat is a kender?!');
```

The Basics Of JavaScript Functions

functions,
functions everywhere

- Buzz Lightyearvascript
Explorer

The Basics Of Functions

Functions are the most fundamental building blocks of JavaScript applications. They are the safekeepers of the logic within our programs but also the primitives upon which we build programmatic constructs such as classes and modules.

JavaScript provides different ways to declare and use functions, each with their own nuances and limitations. So given the fact that they are such a fundamental part of the language it is important that you are aware of these characteristics when you are writing JavaScript.

Welcome to the first step in your journey to JavaScript mastery! Let's get started!

```
/*

   ...In the previous chapter...
   stranger.says('...err... who the hell are you?' +
                 'and whaaaat is a kender?!');

*/

randalf.says(`Well... I am Randalf. Randalf the Red...
JavaScriptmancer of the First Order... Guardian of the
Sacred Flame... Freedom fighter and Poet...`);

stranger.says('uh?');

randalf.says(`Yes! And you are the Chosen one! The Child of
Prophecy! The one that will bring balance to the force!
Muad'Dib! The Dragon reborn! Brought to this land in the
twelfth moon of the twelfth month of the twelfth year of
the Wyrm to save the world from certain destruction!`);

stranger.says(`I am Mooleen actually...
and this is the weirdest dream I've ever had...`);
let mooleen = stranger;

randalf.says(`There's no time for this child. You need to
learn how to defend yourself, it isn't safe here... It all
```

```
starts with functions, functions are the key...`);
```

Functions are the Key

Experiment JavaScriptmancer!!

You can experiment with all examples in this chapter directly within this jsFiddle[29] or downloading the source code from GitHub[30].

Did you know that there are not one but two ways to write functions in JavaScript? Well, now you do. You can either write them as **function expressions** or **function declarations**. It will be very helpful for you to understand the difference and the implications of writing functions in either of these two styles because they work in a very different manner that will impact the readability of your code and how easy or hard it is to debug.

This is a **function expression**:

```
1   // anonymous function expression
2   var castFireballSpell = function(){
3     // chaos and mayhem
4   };
```

And this is a **function declaration**:

---

[29]http://bit.ly/javascriptmancy-fiddle-basic-functions
[30]https://github.com/vintharas/javascriptmancy-code-samples

```
1   // function declaration
2   function castFireballSpell(){
3     // it's getting hot in here...
4   }
```

As you can appreciate, in their most common incarnations *function expressions* and *function declarations* look very similar. That's why it is especially important to understand that they are actually very different and behave in disparate ways from each other.

Let's examine each of them in greater detail.

Function Expressions

We use the *function expression* style whenever we declare a function like an expression, either by assigning it to a variable:

```
1   // an anonymous function expression
2   var castFireballSpell = function(){
3       console.log('...chaos and mayhem');
4   };
5   castFireballSpell();
6   // => ...chaos and mayhem
```

A property within an object:

```
1   // another anonymous function expression as a property of an object
2   var magician = {
3       castFireballSpell: function() {
4           console.log('muahaha! Eat this fireball!');
5       }
6   };
7   magician.castFireballSpell();
8   // => muahaha! Eat this fireball!
```

Or passing it as an argument to another function (like a lambda - note that I am using the term *lambda* in the sense of *function as value*):

```
1    // yet another anonymous function expression passed as an argument
2    var castCombo = function(spellOne, spellTwo){
3        console.log('Combo Magic!!!!');
4        spellOne();
5        spellTwo();
6    }
7
8    castCombo( function(){
9        console.log('FireBalllllzzz!!');
10   }, function(){
11       console.log('And Spectral Shield!!');
12   });
13
14   // => Combo Magic!!!!
15   // => FireBalllllzzz!!
16   // => And Spectral Shield!!
```

There are a couple of important considerations you need to take into account when using *function expressions* like the ones above: they are all **anonymous functions** - they don't have a name - and if stored within a variable they are subjected to the same **hoisting** rules that apply to any other variable in JavaScript. But **what is hoisting? And how a function being anonymous can affect our programs?**.

JavaScript Arcana: Function Scope and Hoisting

One of the things that confuses us the most when we start learning JavaScript is that while JavaScript looks a lot like C#, in many ways it does not behave like it.

These **JavaScript Arcana** bits will help you understand these hairy parts where JavaScript behaves in a completely different way to what you would expect. You'll discover them throughout the book as we venture deeper into the world of JavaScript.

Oftentimes you'll see *JavaScript Arcana* paired with *JavaScript Arcana Resolved* sections that will provide tips and solutions to help you tackle JavaScript strange behaviors.

JavaScript Arcana: Function Scope and Hoisting

An interesting quirk about JavaScript is that, unlike many other languages, **variables in JavaScript have function scope** (as opposed to block scope). That is, it is the functions themselves that create scopes for variables and not the blocks. This can be better illustrated by an example:

```javascript
function openPandoraBox(){

    if (true){
        var treasure = 'mouse';
    }
    console.log('the pandora box holds a: **' + treasure + '**');
}
openPandoraBox();
// => the pandora box holds a: **mouse**
// WAT!? x is declared inside an if block.
// How can it be picked up by the console.log??
// one word: function-scope
```

What happens in this piece of code above is that the JavaScript runtime hoists[31] (*moves up*) all variables within a function definition to
the beginning of the function body. And does it even with variables
declared within blocks of code such as if statements. This means
that the function that you see above is equivalent to this one:

```
1  function openPandoraBox(){
2      // The variable definition is hoisted up here
3      var treasure = undefined;
4      if (true){
5          treasure = 'mouse';
6      }
7      console.log('the pandora box holds a: **' + treasure + '**');
8      // => the pandora box holds a: **mouse**
9  }
```

Where the scope of the treasure variable isn't only the if statement but the whole function. In yet another example of *hoisting*
the variable i that we declare inside the for loop is actually part of
the entire function (*Shocker!!*):

```
1  function aMagicFunctionToIllustrateHoisting(){
2      // in reality
3      // var i = undefined
4
5      console.log('before i =' + i);
6      // => before i = undefined
7
8      for(var i = 0; i < 10; i++){
9          // jara jara
10     }
11
12     console.log('after i = ' + i);
13     // => after i = 10
14 }
```

This is the reason why JavaScript developers - seasoned JavaScript-
mancers - usually write all variable declarations at the beginning

---
[31]http://bit.ly/hoisting-mdn

of a function. They do it in order to be more explicit about what is really happening when a function is evaluated and to avoid unnecessary bugs.

If you take a look at jQuery[32] for instance, a popular JavaScript open source library, you'll be able to appreciate this technique everywhere:

```
1   /**
2    * Load a url into a page
3    */
4   jQuery.fn.load = function( url, params, callback ) {
5       var selector, type, response,
6           self = this,
7           off = url.indexOf(" ");
8
9       //... more codes here
10  }
```

Functions being the stewards of scope of an application is pretty interesting because, all of the sudden, a function is not only used for encapsulating and abstracting a piece of logic but also for structural reasons. That is, a way to organize and distribute bits and pieces of functionality and code. For instance, you'll often see functions being declared inside other functions:

```
1   // declaring a function inside a function?
2   // Ain't that weird????
3   function blessMany(many){
4     many.forEach(bless);
5
6     function bless(target){
7       console.log('You bless ' + target + '. (+5 WillPower) ');
8     }
9   }
10
11  blessMany(['john snow', 'sansa stark']);
```

---

[32]http://bit.ly/jquery-loadjs

```
12   // => You bless John Snow (+5 Willpower)
13   // => You bless Sansa Stark (+5 Willpower)
```

This probably looks very weird if you are coming from C#. But up until the recent advent of ES6 modules this was the only way we had to group pieces of loosely related functionality.

JavaScript Arcana Resolved: Variables with Block Scope With ES6 let and const

Happily for you and happily for me ES6 comes with not one, but two ways to declare variables with block scope: the new let and const keywords. From this point forward I invite to start using let and achieve a more C#-like style of writing code where you declare variables closer to where you use them.

And so, if we rewrite the example we used to illustrate function scope with let, we'll obtain a very different yet more familiar result:

```
1    function openPandoraBoxWithBlockScope(){ // new scope for function b\
2    lock
3
4        if (true){ // new scope for if block
5            let treasure = 'mouse';
6        }
7        console.log('the pandora box holds a: **' + treasure + '**');
8    }
9    openPandoraBoxWithBlockScope();
10   // ReferenceError: treasure is not defined
11   // fiuuuu now everything makes sense again
```

Now the treasure variable only exists within the if statement block.

Alternatively, you can use the const keyword to declare constant variables with block scope.

```
1   function shallIPass(){ // new scope for youShallNotPass block
2       let youShallPass = 'you Shall Pass!',
3           youShallNotPass = 'You Shall Not Pass!';
4       // console.log(canIPass); // => ReferenceError
5
6       if (true){ // new scope for if block
7           const canIPass = youShallNotPass;
8           console.log(canIPass); // => 'You Shall Not Pass!'
9           canIPass = youShallPass;
10          // => TypeError: Assignment to a constant variable
11      }
12
13      console.log(canIPass); // => undefined
14      // ReferenceError: x is not defined
15  }
16  shallIPass();
17  // => you Shall not Pass!
18  // => TypeError: Assignment to a constant variable
```

Variables declared with the const keyword behave in a very similar way to C#. Attempting to make the constant refer to a different value will cause an exception.

However, it is important to understand that if the constant refers to an object, you can still modify its properties:

```
1   const fourHorsemen = ['conquest', 'war', 'famine', 'death'];
2   fourHorsemen.push('jaime');
3   console.log(`${fourHorsemen} waaat`);
4   // => ['conquest', 'wat', 'famine', 'death', 'jaime'] waaat
```

This means that const only affects the act of binding a value to a variable, and not the act of modifying that value itself. In order to make an object immutable you need to use Object.freeze but that's knowledge best kept for another chapter about the beauty of objects. We'll stick to functions for a little bit longer.

Another aspect of let and const that is interesting is that **they do not hoist variables to the top of a block.** Instead, if you attempt to use a variable before it has been defined you'll get an exception (cheers for some sane behavior):

```
1   function openPandoraBoxWithBlockScopeAndHoisting(){
2       // new scope for function block
3
4       if (true){
5           // new scope for if block
6           console.log('the pandora box holds a: **' + treasure + '**');
7           // => ReferenceError: treasure is not defined;
8           let treasure = 'mouse';
9       }
10  }
11  openPandoraBoxWithBlockScopeAndHoisting();
12  // => ReferenceError: treasure is not defined;
```

Use ES6 Let and Const For Block Scoped Variables and To Avoid Hoisting

Use ES6 let and const to declare block-scoped variables closer to where you use them and thus improve readability. Moreover, let and const do not hoist variables to the top of their respective block, and therefore fix any problem that may be caused by hoisting.

Now that you've learnt some of the main characteristics of function expressions let's take a look at the two types of *function expressions* that are available to you in JavaScript: *anonymous function expressions* and *named function expressions*.

Anonymous Function Expressions

Anonymous function expressions are particularly interesting because even though you read the following:

```
1   var castFireballSpell = function(){
2       console.log('...chaos and mayhem');
3   };
```

And you may be tempted to think that the name of the function is castFireballSpell, **it is not!?!** castFireballSpell is just a variable we use to store an *anonymous function*. You can appreciate this anonymity by inspecting the name property of the function itself:

```
1   var castFireballSpell = function(){
2       console.log('...chaos and mayhem');
3   };
4   console.log(castFireballSpell.name);
5   // => ""
6   // no name!
```

Luckily for us, as long as an anonymous function is bound to a variable, the developer tools in modern browsers will use that variable when displaying errors in call stacks (**which is a savior when debugging**):

```
1   // inspecting a call stack for an anonymous function bound
2   // to a variable
3   var castFireballSpellWithError = function(){
4       console.log('...chaos and mayhem');
5       try {
6           throw new Error();
7       } catch (e) {
8           console.log('stack: ', e.stack);
9       }
10  };
11  castFireballSpellWithError();
12  //=> stack:  Error
13  // at castFireballSpellWithError (somefile:53:15)
14  // at window.onload (somefile:58:1)
```

Even if we use this function as a argument:

```
 1  // If you use this function as a lambda the name is
 2  // still shown in the call stack:
 3  var spellLauncher = function(f){ f(); }
 4  spellLauncher(castFireballSpellWithError);
 5  // => stack: Error
 6  // at castFireballSpellWithError (somefile:56:15)
 7  // at spellLauncher (somefile:68:35)
 8  // at window.onload (somefile:69:1)
```

However, **an unbound anonymous function will show as completely anonymous within the call stack making it harder to debug when errors occur** (I will refer to these functions as *strict anonymous function* from now on):

```
 1  // strict anonymous function don't appear in the call stack
 2  spellLauncher(function(){
 3      console.log('...chaos and mayhem');
 4      try {
 5          throw new Error();
 6      } catch (e) {
 7          console.log('stack: ', e.stack);
 8      }
 9  });
10  //=> stack: Error
11  // at somefile:76:15
12  // at spellLauncher (somefile:68:35)
13  // at window.onload (somefile:73:1)
```

This lack of name will also affect the ability to use **recursion** because a function that doesn't have a name cannot call itself from inside its body. In spite of that and just like in the previous examples, if we have the *anonymous function* bound to a variable we take a free pass and can take advantage of *JavaScript lexical scope* to access the function through that variable:

 Lexical Scope

Lexical Scope is the scoping scheme used in JavaScript where every inner scope has access to the outer scopes. C# also enjoys this type of scoping.

Closures

Even though closures exist in C# they are more common in JavaScript. A closure is a function that encloses or captures variables from its surrounding environment.

We dive deeper into closures in the tome devoted to functional programming.

```
1   // you can use recursion when an anonymous function is bound to a va\
2   riable
3   var castManyFireballsSpell = function(n){
4       // this function encloses the castManyFireballsSpell variable
5       // and thus becomes a closure
6       console.log('... SHOOOOOOOOOSH ....');
7       if (n > 0)
8           castManyFireballsSpell(n-1);
9   };
10  castManyFireballsSpell(3);
11  // => ... SHOOOOOOOOOSH ....
12  //      ... SHOOOOOOOOOSH ....
13  //      ... SHOOOOOOOOOSH ....
14  //      ... SHOOOOOOOOOSH ....
```

Notice that this is a pretty brittle way to use of recursion. In this example we are using the variable castManyFireballsSpell to access the anonymous function from within itself. If, at some later point in time, you happen to set the variable to another function you'll get into a pickle. A tricky situation with a very subtle bug where the original function will call this new function instead of itself (*so no more recursion and weird unexpected stuff happening*).

A *strict anonymous function*, on the other hand, has no way to refer to itself and thus you lose the ability to use recursion. For instance, this is the case when we define an *anonymous function expression* and we invoke it right away:

```
1   // but there's no way for an anonymous function
2   // to call itself in any other way
3   (function(n){
4       console.log('... SHOOOOOOOOOSH ....');
5       if (n > 0) {
6           // I cannot call myself... :(
7       }
8   }(5));
9   // => ... SHOOOOOOOOOSH ....
```

In summary, **the fact that common function expressions are anonymous makes them harder to debug and complicates the use of recursion**. And the fact that they are hoisted as variables, a trait common to all function expressions, **also makes them less readable** as we'll see in a bit with a larger program as example.

 ## Avoid Anonymous Function Expressions

Anonymous function expressions are less readable, harder to debug and harder to use in recursion.

Let's see some ways to ameliorate or lessen these issues.

Named Function expressions

You can solve the problem of anonymity that we've seen thus far by using **named function expressions**. You can declare *named function expressions* by adding a name after the function keyword:

```
1    // named function expression
2    var castFireballSpell = function castFireballSpell(){
3      // mayhem and chaos
4    };
5    console.log("this function's name is: ", castFireballSpell.name);
6    // => this function's name is castFireballSpell
```

The example above shows a variable and a *function expression* both named castFireballSpell. A *named function expression* always appears correctly represented in the call stacks even when used as an argument (and not bound to a variable):

```
1    // A named function expression always appears in the call stack
2    spellLauncher(function spreadChaosAndMayhem(){
3      console.log('...chaos and mayhem');
4      try {
5        throw new Error();
6      } catch (e) {
7        console.log('stack: ', e.stack);
8      }
9    });
10   // stack:  Error
11   // at spreadChaosAndMayhem (somefile:134:15)
12   // at spellLauncher (somefile:68:35)
13   // at window.onload (somefile:131:1)
```

This helps while debugging and makes your code more readable since **you can read the name of the function and understand what it's meant to do without looking at its implementation.**

An interesting fact about *named function expressions* is that you cannot call them by their name from the outside:

```
1   var castFireballSpell = function cucumber(){
2       // cucumber?
3   };
4   cucumber();
5   // => ReferenceError: cucumber is not defined
```

The name of a *function expression* is more of an internal identifier that can be used from inside the function body. This is very useful when working with recursion. For instance, if we declare a recursive *named function expression* and invoke it right away it just works:

```
1   // but you can call it from the function body
2   // which is helpful for recursion
3   (function fireballSpellWithRecursion(n){
4     console.log('... SHOOOOOOOOOSH ....');
5     if (n > 0) {
6       fireballSpellWithRecursion(n-1);
7     }
8   }(5));
9   // =>  ... SHOOOOOOOOOSH ....
10  //     ... SHOOOOOOOOOSH ....
11  //     ... SHOOOOOOOOOSH ....
12  //     ... SHOOOOOOOOOSH ..... etc..
```

In summary, **named function expressions improve on anonymous function expressions by increasing readability, improving the debugging process and allowing for a function to call itself.**

Use Named Function Expressions

Use named function expressions over anonymous ones, they are more readable, easier to debug and can call themselves in recursion.

Function Expressions are Hoisted as Variables

Function expressions are still problematic because they are **hoisted like variables**. But what does this mean exactly? It means that

you can only use a function expression after you have declared it and therefore it forces you to write your code starting from the implementation details and continuing into higher levels of abstraction.

This is the opposite of what you want. Think about it. When you write a class as a C# developer, you start with the public API at the top of the class definition. Then you write the implementation of each method from top to bottom, from higher to lower levels of abstraction so that reading becomes natural. You open a file at the top, understand what it does at a glance by reading the intentional names that compose its public API and then you traverse the file down looking at the implementation details only when you need or want to.

Being forced to start from the opposite direction will have a negative impact in the readability of your code:

```
1   (function (magic){
2     // this function represents a module 'magic'
3     // it's just a way to group like-minded pieces of code
4
5     var oven = {
6       open: function(){},
7       placeBaking: function(){},
8       increaseTemperature: function(){},
9       claimVictory: function(){ return 'awesome cake';}
10    };
11
12    var mix = function mix(ingredients){
13      console.log('mixin ingredients:', ingredients.join(''));
14      return 'un-appetizing mixture';
15    }
16
17    var work = function work(mixture){
18      console.log('working ' + mixture);
19      return 'yet more un-appetizing dough';
20    };
21
22    var bake = function bake(dough){
```

```
23      oven.open();
24      oven.placeBaking(dough);
25      oven.increaseTemperature(200);
26      // insta-oven!
27      return oven.claimVictory();
28    };
29
30    var enchant = function enchant(ingredients){
31      var mixture = mix(ingredients),
32        dough = work(mixture),
33        cake = bake(dough);
34      return cake;
35    };
36
37    // This is the public API of this module
38    // and it's almost hidden down here
39    magic.enchant = enchant;
40
41  }(window.magic || (window.magic = {})));
42
43  var cake = magic.enchant(['flour', 'mandragora', 'dragon', 'chicken \
44  foot']);
45  // => mixin ingredients:  flour mandragora dragon chicken foot
46  // => working un-appetizing mixture
47  console.log(cake);
48  // => awesome cake
```

If you try to reorder the different functions within the module so that they start from the public API and continue from top to bottom, from higher to lower levels of abstraction you'll encounter many issues:

```
1   (function (magic){
2     // this function represents a module 'magic'
3     // it's just a way to group like-minded pieces of code
4
5     // exposing enchant as the API for the 'magic' module
6     magic.enchant = enchant;
7     // => hoisting issue, enchant is undefined at this point
8     // so we are just exposing an undefined variable thinking it is a \
9   function
10
11    // if uncommented this would cause an exception
12    // enchant();
13    // => TypeError: enchant is not a function
14    // => hoisting issue, enchant is undefined at this point
15
16    var enchant = function enchant(ingredients){
17      var mixture = mix(ingredients),
18        dough = work(mixture),
19        cake = bake(dough);
20      return cake;
21    };
22
23    // if uncommented this would cause an exception
24    // enchant();
25    // => TypeError: mix is not a function (it's undefined at this poi \
26  nt)
27    // hoisting issue, mix is undefined at this point
28
29    /* rest of the code...
30    var mix = function mix(ingredients){}
31    var work = function work(mixture){};
32    var bake = function bake(dough){};
33    var oven = {};
34    */
35
36  }(window.magic || (window.magic = {})));
37
38  try {
39    var cake = magic.enchant(['flour', 'mandragora', 'dragon', 'chicke\
40  n foot']);
41    console.log(cake);
42  } catch (e) {
43    console.warn('ups!!!!!!', e);
```

```
44    // => ups!!!!!! TypeError: magic.enchant is not a function
45  }
```

In this example we use *function expressions* to define every function. Because they are **hoisted like variables** when we try to assign the enchant function to our magic.enchant object its value is undefined. This results in us exposing an undefined value to the outside world instead of a helpful function to enchant delicious cakes. In a similar way, when we attempt to call the enchant function before either enchant or mix have been initialized we get a TypeError exception.

In summary, both named and anonymous function expressions are hoisted as variables. **This affects their readability and can cause bugs when we try to run a function or expose it as part of the public API of a module before it has been defined.** Although you could use let and const to prevent *hoisting*, there's a better way you can declare your functions: **Function declarations.**

Function Declarations

Function declarations have some advantages over function expressions:

- **They are named**, and you can use that name from outside and from within the function.
- **They are not hoisted as variables but as a whole, which makes them impervious to hoisting problems.**

This is how you write a *function declaration*:

```
1  // function declaration
2  function castFireballSpell(){
3    // it's getting hot in here...
4  }
```

As you learned just a moment ago, *function declarations* are hoisted in a very special way. When the JavaScript runtime processes this piece of code:

```
1  var message = "hello";
2
3  // some more code here...
4
5  // function expression
6  var sayHi = function(){console.log('hi!')};
7
8  // some more code here...
9
10 // function declaration
11 function sayHello(){
12   console.log(msg);
13 }
```

It's going to rearrange it by hoisting the whole sayHello function and only the declaration of the variables message and sayHi:

```
1  // hoisted as variables
2  var message, sayHi;
3
4  // hoisted as a whole
5  function sayHello(){
6  console.log(msg);
7  }
8
9  message = "hello";
10 // some more code here...
11 sayHi = function(){console.log('hi!')};
12 // some more code here...
```

Because of this special *hoisting* behavior, *function declarations* will enable you to write your JavaScript modules from higher to lower levels of abstraction just like we discussed earlier and as you can see in this example below:

```javascript
// with function declarations you can write functions like this
// and don't worry about hoisting issues at all
(function(magic){

  // public API of the magic module
  magic.enchant = enchant;

  // functions from higher to lower level of abstraction
  function enchant(ingredients){
    var mixture = mix(ingredients),
      dough = work(mixture),
      cake = bake(dough);
    return cake;
  }

  // these are private functions to this module
  function mix(ingredients){
    console.log('mixin ingredients:', ingredients.join(''));
    return 'un-appetizing mixture';
  }

  function work(mixture){
    console.log('working ' + mixture);
    return 'yet more un-appetizing dough';
  }

  function bake(dough){
    oven.open();
    oven.placeBaking(dough);
    oven.increaseTemperature(200);
    // insta-oven!
    return oven.claimVictory();
  }

  var oven = {
    open: function(){},
    placeBaking: function(){},
```

```
38        increaseTemperature: function(){},
39        claimVictory: function(){ return 'awesome cake';}
40      };
41
42    }(window.magic || (window.magic = {})));
43
44    var cake = magic.enchant(['flour', 'mandragora', 'dragon', 'chicken \
45    foot']);
46    // => mixin ingredients:  flour mandragora dragon chicken foot
47    // => working un-appetizing mixture
48    console.log(cake);
49    // => awesome cake
```

And, just like *function expressions*, you can also use *function declarations* as values (and arguments). Notice the disintegrate function below:

```
1    var orc = {toString: function(){return 'a mighty evil orc';}};
2    var warg = {toString: function(){return 'a terrible warg';}};
3    var things = [1, orc, warg, false];
4
5    // using the disintegrate function declaration as an argument
6    // nice and readable
7    things.forEach(disintegrate);
8
9    function disintegrate(thing){
10     console.log(thing + ' suddenly disappears into nothingness...');
11   }
12
13   // => 1 suddenly disappears into nothingness...
14   // a mighty evil orc suddenly disappears into nothingness...
15   // a terrible warg suddenly disappears into nothingness...
16   // false suddenly disappears into nothingness...
```

There's something interesting happening in this example above that is worthy of note: *type coercion*. When the body of the disintegrate function is evaluated, the expression below:

```
1   thing + ' suddenly disappears into nothingness...'
```

Coerces the `thing` variable to a `string` type. In the case of the `orc` and `warg` which are objects that means calling the `toString` method and obtaining a `string` representation of either of these objects.

Concluding: Prefer Function Declarations and Named Function Expressions

Function expressions have some limitations:

1. They are **anonymous**, which can make them less readable, harder to debug and use in recursion
2. They are **hoisted as variables** which can lead to bugs and forces you to declare them before you can use them

Named function expressions solve the problem of anonymity. They make your vanilla *function expressions* more readable, easier to debug and enable recursion.

Function declarations solve both problems of anonymity and hoisting (they are hoisted as a whole), and even allow you to write code from higher to lower levels of abstraction.

You can use the `let` and `const` keywords to solve the problems with *hoisting* related to *function expressions* but you don't get the nice top to bottom narrative that you get with *function declarations*. That is, with `let` and `const` you cannot use a function before you have declared it, if you attempt to do so you'll get an exception.

In summary, and based on the characteristics of functions in JavaScript, **prefer named function expressions and function declarations over anonymous function expressions.**

Hope you have enjoyed this chapter about the different ways you can write functions in JavaScript. Up next, We will discuss the most common patterns to achieve default values, multiple arguments and function overloading when writing functions in JavaScript and we'll see how some of the new features in ES6 provide native support for some of these.

```
/*

<Grrrrrr...>

*/

randalf.says('Are you hungry?');

mooleen.says('What? That was you!!?!');

randalf.says('All right... all right...' +
             ' no need to start pointing fingers...');
randalf.says('We'll need to make some time for break...');

/*

A huge fire explosion suddenly obliterates part of the forest
right beside you, It rapidly extinguishes in a very unnatural
way and a figure emerges from the smoke and cinders.

*/

randalf.says('oh great...');
great.says(`Do you really think you could hide your schemes
    and machinations from the great-est javascriptmancer!?`)
great.says('It's time to burn...');

/*

Great (really?) lifts his arm and an igneous ball of fire
starts forming on his hand...

*/
```

Exercises

Experiment JavaScriptmancer!

You can experiment with these exercises and some possible solutions in this jsFiddle[33] or downloading the source code from GitHub[34].

```
1   randalf.says('Oh no... we are going to die.');
2   mooleen.says('Wait? What? This is just a dream...');
3
4   randalf.says('Does the unbearable heat of that torrent of flames ' +
5               'feel dreamy to you?');
6   mooleen.says('Damn...');
7   mooleen.says(`Well... JavaScriptmancer of the First Order,
8     guardian of the secret flame, can you do something!?`);
9
10  randalf.says('Sacred Flame...')
11  randalf.says('hmm I kind of ...ehem.. have lost my power');
12  mooleen.says('Shit');
```

Oh No! You Are About To Be Incinerated!?

Write a **function expression** to cast a magic shield around you and protect you from sure death. The function should at least satisfy the following example:

```
1   castMagicShield("Mooleen");
2   // -> The air shimers around Mooleen as Mooleen is surrounded
3   //    by a magic shield
4   castMagicShield("cat");
5   // => The air shimers around cat as cat is surrounded by a
6   //    magic shield
```

---

[33]http://bit.ly/javascriptmancy-basic-functions-exercises
[34]https://github.com/vintharas/javascriptmancy-code-samples

Solution

```
1   var castMagicShield = function(target){
2     console.log('The air shimmers around ' + target + ' as ' +
3     target + ' is surrounded by a magic shield');
4     target.defense = 1000000;
5   }
6
7   mooleen.weaves('castMagicShield(mooleen)');
8   // => The air shimmers around Mooleen as Mooleen is surrounded
9   //    by a magic shield
10  mooleen.weaves('castMagicShield(randalf)');
11  // => The air shimmers around Randalf, the Red as Randalf,
12  //    the Red is surrounded by a magic shield
13
14  great.weaves('fireball(mooleen, randalf)');
15  // => A giant fireball blasts Mooleen and Randalf, the Red
16
17  /*
18
19  While all the surrounding vegetation springs into flames
20  the space surrouding Mooleen and Randalf remains eerily
21  intact.
22
23  */
24
25  great.says(`What!? How are you alive?! It can't be!
26  You old fool lost the ability to weave long ago`);
27
28  great.says(`It doesn't matter, If I cannot burn you,
29          I'll bury you both`);
30
31  /*
32
33  The earth starts rumbling under your feet as Great
34  concentrates...
35
36  */
```

Tap Into the Source and Fight Back!

Hoisting can be problematic. Fix the bug in this spell
and release destruction upon your enemies!

```
1   (function(source){
2
3     source.supercharge = supercharge;
4
5     var supercharge = function(spell){
6       console.log('you tap into the One True Source an are ' +
7                   'inundated by power');
8       console.log('you concentrate all your power in ' + spell.name);
9       spell.mana = 1000000;
10    }
11
12  }(window.source = {}));
```

Solution

```
1   (function(source){
2
3   // the bug was here
4   // at this point supercharge is undefined
5   // it is the equivalent to:
6   // var supercharge;
7   //source.supercharge = supercharge;
8
9   var supercharge = function(spell){
10    console.log('you tap into the One True Source an are ' +
11                'inundated by power');
12    console.log('you concentrate all your power in ' + spell.name);
13    spell.mana = 1000000;
14  }
15
16  source.supercharge = supercharge;
17
18  }(window.source = {}));
19
20  function fireball(...targets){
21    if (!fireball.mana || fireball.mana < 1000000)
22      world.spell(`A giant fireball blasts ${targets.join(' & ')}`);
```

```
23    else
24      world.spell(`An immense and unending torrent of molten lava
25          surges from your fingers and impacts ${targets.join(' & ')}`);
26    }
27
28  mooleen.weaves('source.supercharge(fireball)');
29  // => you tap into the One True Source and are inundated by Power
30  // => you concentrate all your power in fireball
31  mooleen.weaves('fireball(great)');
32  // => An inmense and unending torrent of molten lava
33  //    surges from your fingers and impacts Great
34
35  mooleen.weaves('source.supercharge(fireball)');
36  // => you tap into the One True Source and are inundated by Power
37  // => you concentrate all your power in fireball
38  mooleen.weaves('fireball(great)');
39  // => An inmense and unending torrent of molten lava
40  //    surges from your fingers and impacts Great
41
42  great.says('Glurrrp');
43  randalf.says("Omg! You are awesome! Now, let's flee!");
```

Escape with a Function Declaration

Write a teleportation spell using a function declaration while Great recovers. The function should at least satisfy the following example:

```
1  teleport("out of the forest", "Mooleen");
2  // => Mooleen teleports out of the forest
3  teleport("to Fiji", "Mooleen");
4  // => Mooleen teleports to Fiji
```

Solution

```
1  function teleport(where, ...who){
```

```
2              console.log(`${who.join(' and ')} teleport ${where}`);
3    }
4
5    mooleen.weaves('teleport("out of the forest", mooleen, randalf)');
6    // => Mooleen and Randalf, the Red teleport out of the forest
7    mooleen.says('I feel so tired...');
8
9    /*
10   Mooleen collapses into the ground...
11   */
```

Useful Function Patterns: Default Arguments

Put yourself in the place of the listener,
of the eater,
of the reader,
of the user of your carefully crafted spells.

Think from the outside in,
and you'll be rewarded manyfold.

Think developer experience!!

> - Llroc
> Warrior Poet

```
/*

A distant sound....

A booming sound...

Or a... the flapping of the wings of some giant bird

Salt in your mouth...

clap! clap! clap!

*/

randalf.says('Well that was close... but I am impressed!');

moolean.wakesUp(['slowly', 'groggily']);
mooleen.laughsWeakly();

/*

Mooleen awakes to an infinite sea, a vast ocean, and dunes
as far as the eye can see.

*/

mooleen.says('I am a fast learner...')
mooleen.says('And now I want to learn what' +
    ' the heck is going on?');

randalf.says('There will be time for that soon. ' +
    'Now you need to recover.');

mooleen.says('but...');

randalf.says('You know... I think you can add some improvements ' +
'to those spells... I know a couple of tricks... ' +
'have you heard of defaults?');
```

Have You Heard Of Defaults?

I don't know you but I'm always trying to write less code and build beautiful APIs for myself and other developers. One small way to achieve that is by using default arguments. Defaults let you add more intention behind your APIs and provide a shortcut to the most common functionality or task carried out by a function.

In this and the next few chapters we'll discuss several patterns that you can use to improve the usability of the functions you write in JavaScript: defaults, multiple arguments and function overloading. Let's get started with defaults in ES5 and ES6.

Using Default Arguments in JavaScript Today

Experiment JavaScriptmancer!!

You can experiment with all examples in this chapter via this jsFiddle[35] or downloading the source code from GitHub[36].

If you have had the chance to take a look at some Javascript code, you may have encountered the following statement and wondered what (the heck) it meant:

```
1  var type = type || "GET";
```

Hold on tight because we are about to unveil the mystery. That statement right there has been the prevalent approach to writing defaults in JavaScript for ages. If you do a little of a mental exercise

[35]http://bit.ly/javascriptmancy-fiddle-function-defaults
[36]https://github.com/vintharas/javascriptmancy

and try to remember what you read about the || (OR) operator in the introduction you'll recall that this operator behaves in quite a special way: It returns the first truthy expression of those being evaluated or the last expression if none is truthy. As usual, this behavior is better illustrated through an example:

```
1   > false || 42 || false
2   // => 42
3
4   > "" || false
5   // => false
6
7   > "" || {}
8   // => Object {}
9
10  > var numberOfPotatos = undefined
11  > numberOfPotatos || 3
12  // => 3
13
14  > numberOfPotatos = 5
15  > numberOfPotatos || 3
16  // => 5
```

Since up until ES6 there was no native support for defaults and using the || operator was the most compact way to achieve it, this pattern soon became the *de facto* standard for defaults throughout the community and is often used in JavaScript applications. You just need to take a sneak peak in any popular open source library to find it used in innumerable situations:

```
1   // from jquery loads.js
2   // (https://github.com/jquery/jquery/blob/master/src/ajax/load.js)
3   type: type || "GET",
4
5   // or from yeoman router.js
6   // (https://github.com/yeoman/yo/blob/master/lib/router.js)
7   this.conf = conf || new Configstore(pkg.name, {
8       generatorRunCount: {}
9     });
```

One of the most common use of defaults happens when evaluating the arguments of a function like in this castIceCone spell:

```
1   function castIceCone(mana, options){
2     // we take advantage of the || operator to define defaults
3     var mana = mana || 5,
4       options = options || {direction: 'forward', damageX: 10},
5       direction = options.direction || 'forward',
6       damageX = options.damage || 10,
7       damage = 2*mana + damageX;
8
9     console.log("You spend " + mana +
10                " mana and cast a frozen ice cone " + direction +
11                " (" + damage + " DMG).");
12  }
```

The castIceCone function has two arguments: a mana argument that represents the amount of mana a powerful wizard is going to spend in casting the ice cone and an additional options object with finer details.

The function makes extensive use of the || operator to provide defaults for all possible cases. In the simplest and most convenient of scenarios the user of this function would just call it directly, and when more finesse is needed she or he could populate the richer options argument:

```
1   castIceCone();
2   // => You spend 5 mana and cast a frozen ice cone forward (20 DMG)
3   castIceCone(10);
4   // => You spend 5 mana and cast a frozen ice cone forward (20 DMG)
5   castIceCone(10, { damage: 200});
6   // => You spend 5 mana and cast a frozen ice cone forward (220 DMG)
7   castIceCone(10, { direction: 'to Mordor'})
8   // => You spend 10 mana and cast a frozen ice cone to Mordor (30 DMG)
9   castIceCone(10, { direction: 'to Mordor', damage: 200})
10  // => You spend 10 mana and cast a frozen ice cone to Mordor (220 DM\
11  G)
```

An alternative way to do defaults is to wrap them within an object.

Defaults with Objects

In addition to relying on the || operator, you can use an object
to gather your default values. Whenever the function is called you
merge the arguments provided by the user with the object that
represents the defaults. The default values will only be applied when
the actual arguments are missing.

You can define a mergeDefaults function to perform the merge
operation:

```
1   function mergeDefaults(args, defaults){
2     if (!args) args = {};
3     for (var prop in defaults) {
4       if (defaults.hasOwnProperty(prop) && !args[prop]) {
5         args[prop] = defaults[prop];
6       }
7     }
8     return args;
9   }
```

And then apply it to the arguments passed to the function like in
this castLightningBolt spell:

```
1   function castLightningBolt(details){
2     // we define the defaults as an object
3     var defaults = {
4           mana: 5,
5       direction: 'forward'
6     };
7     // merge details and defaults
8     // properties are overwritten from right to left
9     details = mergeDefaults(details, defaults);
10
11    console.log('You spend ' + details.mana +
12        ' and cast a powerful lightning bolt ' +
13        details.direction + '!!!');
14  }
```

Which provides a similar defaults developer experience to that of
the first example:

```
1   castLightningBolt();
2   // => You spend 5 and cast a powerful lightning bolt forward!!!
3   castLightningBolt({mana: 100});
4   // => You spend 100 and cast a powerful lightning bolt forward!!!
5   castLightningBolt({direction: 'to the right'});
6   // => You spend 5 and cast a powerful lightning bolt to the right!!!
7   castLightningBolt({mana: 10, direction: 'to Mordor'});
8   // => You spend 10 and cast a powerful lightning bolt to Mordor!!!
```

More often though you will probably rely on a popular open source
library. Libraries like *jQuery*, *underscore* or *lodash* usually come
with a lot of utility functions that you can use for this and many
other purposes. For instance, *jQuery* comes with the $.extend
function and *underscore* comes with both the _.defaults and
_.extend functions that could help you in this scenario.

Let's update the previous example with code from these two libraries:

```
1   function castLightningBoltOSS(details){
2     // we define the defaults as an object
3     var defaults = {
4             mana: 5,
5         direction: 'in front of you'
6     };
7     // extend details with defaults
8     // properties are overwritten from right to left
9     // jQuery:
10    details = $.extend({}, defaults, details);
11    // underscore:
12    //details = _.extend({}, defaults, details);
13
14    // to use defaults switch argument places
15    // properties are only overwritten if they are undefined
16    // underscore:
17    //details = _.defaults({},details, defaults);
18
19    console.log('You spend ' + details.mana +
20        ' and cast a powerful lightning bolt ' +
21        details.direction + '!!!!');
22  }
```

If you have kept an eye on ES6 you may know that it comes with a native version of the jQuery $.extend method called Object.assign. Indeed, you can update the previous example as follows and achieve the same result:

```
1   //details = $.extend({}, defaults, details);
2   details = Object.assign({}, defaults, details);
```

However, if you are planning to use ES6, there's an even better way to use defaults.

Native Default Arguments with ECMAScript 6

ES6 makes it dead easy to declare default arguments. Just like in C# you use the equal sign "=" and assign a default value beside the argument itself:

```
1  function castIceCone(mana=5){
2    console.log(`You spend ${mana} mana and casts a terrible ice cone`\
3    );
4  }
5
6  castIceCone();
7  // => You spend 5 mana and casts a terrible ice cone
8  castIceCone(10);
9  // => You spend 10 mana and casts a terrible ice cone
```

JavaScript takes defaults even further because they are not limited to *constant* expressions like C# *optional arguments*[37]. In JavaScript, any expression is a valid default argument.

For instance, you can use entire objects as defaults:

```
1  function castIceCone(mana=5, options={direction:'forward'}){
2    console.log(`You spend ${mana} mana and casts a ` +
3      `terrible ice cone ${options.direction}`);
4  }
5
6  castIceCone();
7  // => You spend 5 mana and casts a terrible ice cone forward
8  castIceCone(10);
9  // => You spend 10 mana and casts a terrible ice cone forward
10 castIceCone(10, {direction: 'to Mordor'});
11 // => You spend 10 mana and casts a terrible ice cone to Mordor
12 castIceCone(10, {duck: 'cuack'});
13 // => You spend 10 mana and casts a terrible ice cone undefined
```

If you take a closer look at the end of the example above, you'll realize that we have a small bug in our function. We are setting a default for the entire options object but not for parts of it. So if the developer provides an object with the direction property missing, we will get a strange result (writing undefined to the console).

---

[37] https://msdn.microsoft.com/en-us/library/dd264739.aspx

We can solve this problem by taking advantage of the new **destructuring syntax** which allows you to assign argument properties directly to variables within a function, and at the same time provide defaults to parts of an object:

```
function castIceConeWithDestructuring(mana=5,
          {direction='forward'}={direction:'forward'}){

  console.log(`You spend ${mana} mana and casts a ` +
    `terrible ice cone ${direction}`);
}
castIceConeWithDestructuring();
// => You spend 5 mana and casts a terrible ice cone forward
castIceCone(10, {direction: 'to Mordor'});
// => You spend 10 mana and casts a terrible ice cone to Mordor
castIceConeWithDestructuring(10, {duck: 'cuack'});
// => You spend 10 mana and casts a terrible ice cone forward
```

In this example we use argument destructuring `{direction='forward'}` to:

- **Extract the property `direction` from the argument provided to the function at once.** This allows us to write `direction` instead of the more verbose `options.direction` that we used in previous examples.
- **Provide a default value for the `direction` property** in the case that the function is called with a *options* object that misses that property. It therefore solves the problem with the `{duck: 'cuack'}` example.

Finally, taking the freedom of defaults to the extreme, you are not limited to arbitrary objects either, you can even use a function expression as a default (*I expect your mind has just been blown by this, this... very... second*):

```
1  function castSpell(spell=function(){console.log('holy shit a callbac\
2  k!');}){
3    spell();
4  }
5
6  castSpell();
7  // => holy s* a callback!
8  castSpell(function(){
9    console.log("balefire!!!! You've been wiped out of existence");
10 });
11 // => balefire!!!! You've been wiped out of existence
```

Concluding

Yey! In this chapter you've learned several ways in which you can use defaults in JavaScript whether you are using ES5 or ES6 and beyond. Taking advantage of defaults will let you write less code and provide a slightly better user experience to the consumers of the functions that you write.

Up next, more function patterns with multiple arguments and the rest operator!

```
randalf.says('See? By using defaults you can make ' +
             'your spellcasting more effective');

mooleen.says('hmm... indeed... indeed...');
mooleen.says('Do I get to know why I am here? And what here is?');

randalf.says('Sure! Just start practicing while I go get us lunch');
```

Exercises

Experiment JavaScriptmancer!

You can experiment with these exercises and some possible solutions in this jsFiddle[38] or downloading the source code from GitHub[39].

Time to light a Fire!

Improve this fire function using defaults in ES5. The default amount of mana should ensure a strong fire and the default target should be something that lights easily like dry wood.

```
1   function fire(mana, target){
2     if (mana > 10)
3       console.log('An enormous fire springs to life on ' + target);
4     else if (mana > 4)
5       console.log('You light a strong fire on ' + target);
6     else if (mana > 2)
7       console.log('You light a small fire on' + target);
8     else if (mana > 0)
9       console.log('You try to light a fire but ' +
10        'only achieve in creating teeny tiny sparks. ' +
11        'Beautiful but useless.');
12  }
```

Solution

```
1   mooleen.says('damn old man...');
2   mooleen.says('let me modify this spell for the most' +
3                ' cost-effective use case');
```

---

[38]http://bit.ly/javascriptmancy-basic-functions-defaults-exercises
[39]https://github.com/vintharas/javascriptmancy-code-samples

```
4
5   function fireImproved(mana, target){
6     mana = mana || 3;
7     target = target || 'dry wood';
8     if (mana > 10)
9       console.log('An enormous fire springs to life on ' + target);
10    else if (mana > 4)
11      console.log('You light a strong fire on ' + target);
12    else if (mana > 2)
13      console.log('You light a small fire on ' + target);
14    else if (mana > 0)
15      console.log('You try to light a fire but ' +
16                    'only achieve in creating teeny tiny sparks.' +
17                    ' Beautiful but useless.');
18  }
19
20  mooleen.weaves('fireImproved()');
21  // => You light a small fire on dry wood;
22  mooleen.says('aha!');
```

And now try ES6 Defaults

Improve the `fire` function using ES6 defaults. Use the same default values as you did in the previous exercise.

Solution

```
1   function fireImprovedES6(mana=3, target='dry wood'){
2     if (mana > 10)
3       console.log('An enormous fire springs to life on ' + target);
4     else if (mana > 4)
5       console.log('You light a strong fire on ' + target);
6     else if (mana > 2)
7       console.log('You light a small fire on ' + target);
8     else if (mana > 0)
9       console.log('You try to light a fire but ' +
10        'only achieve in creating teeny tiny sparks.' +
```

```
11          'Beautiful but useless.');
12    }
13
14    mooleen.weaves('fireImprovedES6()');
15    // => You light a small fire on dry wood
16
17    randalf.says('Excellent! Nothing like a bonfire for telling a good s\
18    tory!');
```

More Useful Function Patterns: Arbitrary Arguments

What works for one,
may work for many...

> - Eccason,
>   Maester of the Aethis

```
/*
An endless beach, the rumor of the sea, fire crackling nearby...
*/


randalf.says('It was a long time ago...');
randalf.says('Damn! Just thinking about it makes me feel ancient.');

randalf.says('The birth of JavaScript-mancy.');
randalf.says('I remember it clearly...');
randalf.says('I was there the very second it happened');


/*
Branden was special. He looked at the world in a different light.
He would often wander and ponder about the workings of the world
and how to make it better for everyone. He would build wondrous
inventions, some of them useless I'll grant, some of them even
dangerous. He studied and pursuited his goals with a near mad
passion and intent, and one day he found it.

He found what would change the world for ever: JavaScript-mancy and
the sacred REPL.
*/


mooleen.says('wait, wait... ' +
             'Do you mean the Read-Evaluate-Print-Loop??');
randalf.says('What? No child, the REPL is just... well, the REPL');


/*
Anyhow, historians always claim he was working on a great wonder
when he found it. You know what? He wasn't!

He was boiling eggs!! He had made this useless machine to boil
an egg and was racking his brain to boil an arbitrary number
of eggs...
*/
```

An Arbitrary Number of Arguments

Sometimes you write a function that performs some sort of action based on a single argument. Some time later you realize that it would be nice if you could use that same function, but this time, with an arbitrary number of arguments. You may be tempted to change the interface of the original function to take an array instead of a single item. In doing so, however, you break the code that is using the function and force any future developers to wrap the arguments being sent inside an array, even when there's only a single argument.

In this specific scenario, you may want to do something different. You may want to keep the function interface as it is and elegantly extend it to support multiple arguments without affecting any existing code. That's what we do in C# with the params keyword, and what you can achieve in JavaScript via the arguments object or ES6 *rest parameter syntax.*

This is what you'll learn in this chapter. But first, did you know that JavaScript functions are pretty peculiar about their arguments?

The Craziness Of Function Arguments in JavaScript

 Experiment JavaScriptmancer!!

You can experiment with all examples in this chapter within this jsFiddle[40] or downloading the source code from GitHub[41].

JavaScript gives you a lot of freedom when it comes to handling function parameters and arguments. For instance, you can declare a function with a specific number of parameters and, if you wish, call it without any arguments at all.

Imagine a function heal that casts a healing spell on a person:

---
[40]http://bit.ly/javascriptmancy-functions-multiple-arguments
[41]https://github.com/vintharas/javascriptmancy

```
1   function heal(person, inchantation, modifier){
2     var healedHp;
3     modifier = modifier || 1;
4     healedHp = modifier * 100;
5
6     console.log('you heal ' + person + ' with ' + inchantation +
7                 ' spell (+' + healedHp + 'hp)' );
8     person.hp += healedHp;
9   }
```

This function has an **arity** of 3, that is, it expects 3 arguments. You can verify this accessing its length property. (A popular interview question by the way):

```
1   console.log(heal.length);
2   // => 3
```

Thanks to the magic of JavaScript's infinite freedom you can call it without any arguments at all. Although this doesn't mean that it will work:

```
1   try {
2     heal();
3   } catch (e) {
4     console.log(e)
5   }
6   // => you heal undefined with undefined spell (+100hp)
7   // => TypeError: cannot read property hp of undefined
```

You can also call it with as many of those 3 arguments as you want:

```
1    var JonSnow = {name: 'Jon Snow', hp: 5,
2                      toString: function(){return this.name;}};
3
4    heal(JonSnow);
5    // => you heal Jon Snow with undefined spell (+100hp)
6
7    heal(JonSnow, 'cure');
8    // => you heal Jon Snow with cure spell (+100hp)
9
10   heal(JonSnow, 'super heal', /* modifier */ 2);
11   // => you heal Jon Snow with super heal spell (+200hp)
```

Or even with more arguments than the parameters defined in the function itself:

```
1    heal(JonSnow, 'heal', 1, 3, 2, 3, 'cucumber',
2        {a: 1, b:2}, 'many arguments');
3    // => you heal Jon Snow with heal spell (+100hp)
```

It is up to you to implement the body of a function and handle each case as you see fit. But **what happens when you want to write a function that takes an arbitrary number of arguments?**

Functions with Arbitrary Arguments Right Now!

In C#, whenever we want to write such a function we use the params keyword[42]. In JavaScript (up to ES5), on the other hand, there's no keyword nor operator that allows us to do that.

The only possible approach is to use the arguments object. arguments, like this, is a special kind of object present within every function in JavaScript. Its whole purpose is to give access to the arguments used to call a function from inside the function itself.

Think about an obliterate spell that you could use to completely wipe out an enemy:

---

[42]https://msdn.microsoft.com/en-us/library/w5zay9db.aspx

```
1    function obliterate(enemy){
2      console.log(enemy + " wiped out of the face of the earth");
3    }
4
5    obliterate('batman');
6    // => batman wiped out of the face of the earth
```

But why stop at one? With arguments you can make an obliterate
spell to wipe out all your enemies at once!

```
1    function obliterate(){
2      // Unfortunately arguments is not an array :O
3      // so we need to convert it ourselves
4      var victims = Array.prototype.slice.call(arguments, /* start */ 0);
5
6      victims.forEach(function(victim){
7        console.log(victim + " wiped off of the face of the earth");
8      });
9      console.log('*Everything* has been obliterated, ' +
10               'oh great master of evil and deceit!');
11   }
```

Indeed, we can use our obliterate function with one or as many
arguments as we want. We have extended our function API without
breaking it:

```
1    obliterate('batman');
2    // => batman wiped out of the face of the earth
3    // *Everything* has been obliterated, oh great master
4    // of evil and deceit!
5
6    obliterate("John Doe", getPuppy(), 1, new Minion('Willy', 'troll'));
7    /*
8    John Doe wiped off of the face of the earth
9    cute puppy wiped off of the face of the earth
10   1 wiped off of the face of the earth
11   Willy the troll wiped off of the face of the earth
12   *Everything* has been obliterated, oh great master
13   of evil and deceit!
```

```
14    */
15
16    function getPuppy(){
17      return {
18        cuteWoof: function(){console.log('wiii');},
19        toString: function(){return 'cute puppy';}
20      };
21    };
22
23    function Minion(name, type){
24      this.name = name;
25      this.type = type;
26      this.toString = function(){ return name + " the " + type;};
27    }
```

As it goes, there are a couple of interesting things to point out in this example.

The first one is the fact that we are sending arguments of different types to the function and they are all treated seamlessly. That's an example of duck typing[43] in action where **an object is defined by what it can do and not by its type**. As long as the values that we pass as arguments support the interface the function expects - in this case the toString method - everything will work just fine.

Duck Typing

A concept common to the JavaScript community and to the dynamic programming language community at large is the idea of duck typing often illustrated by this sentence:

"If it walks like a duck and quacks like a duck, then it is a duck"

This summarizes JavaScript polymorphism story by alluding to the fact that in JavaScript we care about what objects can do, they're runtime interface and not their type. It doesn't

---

[43]http://bit.ly/duck-typing-js

> matter if *something* is not a duck, as long as it has the same
> interface walk and quack.

The second thing to point out is the use of the Array.prototype.slice function. We use it to convert the arguments variable into a real array victims. While you would expect the arguments variable to be an array, it is not, it is an **array-like** object[44] (and this, my friend, is another of JavaScript quirks right here).

 ## JavaScript Arcana: Array-Like Objects

Because simple things are not as fun, JavaScript has the concept of **Array-like** objects. They look like arrays, smell like arrays but they are not arrays. You can index them, enumerate them and access their length property but the similarity ends there as they don't inherit from 'Array.prototype'.

It's just like if you yourself would create an object with indexed properties and added a length property to it.

Notable examples of array-like culprits are the arguments object and the HTML node sets returned by document.querySelectorAll, document.getElementsByTagName and document.forms (functions of the DOM API in the browser).

---

[44]http://bit.ly/mdn-arguments-object

Array-Like Objects

Here are the things you can do with an array-like object:

```javascript
function inspectArguments(){

  // you can index it:
  console.log("the first argument is ", arguments[0]);
  console.log("the second argument is ", arguments[1]);

  // you an enumerate it:
  // as in the arguments are enumerable like
  // any common array or object, and thus you can use
  // the for/in loop
  for (var idx in arguments) {
    console.log("item at position " + idx +
                " is " + arguments[idx]);
  }

  // it has a length property
  console.log("there are " + arguments.length + " arguments");
}

inspectArguments("cucumber", "dried meat", "dagger", "rock");
// => the first argument is cucumber
// => the second argument is dried meat
// => item at position 1 is cucumber
// => etc...
// => there are 4 arguments
```

Because it is not an array it does not have any of the array functions that you would expect:

```
1   function inspectArgumentsFunctions(){
2     console.log("arguments.foreach is ", arguments.foreach);
3     console.log("arguments.map is ", arguments.map);
4     console.log("arguments.some is", arguments.some);
5   }
6
7   inspectArgumentsFunctions();
8   // => arguments.foreach is undefined
9   // => arguments.map is undefined
10  // => arguments.some is undefined
```

Using the slice function of Array.prototype allows you to convert arguments to an array and take advantage of all the nice array functions. This is what we did with the obliterate function:

```
1   function obliterate(){
2     //...
3     var victims = Array.prototype.slice.call(arguments, /* start */ 0);
4     victims.forEach(function(victim){
5         console.log(victim + " wiped out of the face of the earth");
6     });
7     //...
8   }
```

Alternatively, you can use the ES6 Array.from method for a more natural conversion of an array-like object into an array:

```
1   function obliterate(){
2     //...
3     var victims = Array.from(arguments);
4     victims.forEach(function(victim){
5         console.log(victim + " wiped out of the face of the earth");
6     });
7     //...
8   }
```

In the specific case of the arguments object **ES6 rest syntax** offers a much better alternative[45] as you'll find out soon.

Native Arbitrary Arguments with ES6 Rest Parameters

ES6 comes with a native way to handle arbitrary arguments: rest parameters[46].

All the complexity of using the `arguments` object in the previous examples can be substitued by rest parameters and handled seamlessly:

```
function obliterate(...victims){
  victims.forEach(function(victim){
    console.log(victim + " wiped out of the face of the earth");
  });
  console.log('*Everything* has been obliterated, ' +
              'oh great master of evil and deceit!');
}
```

When using rest parameters, `victims` becomes an array automatically so there's no need to perform additional conversions. Indeed, if we use the new `obliterate` function as we did before it works perfectly:

---

[45]An interesting thing to think about is that Array.from can be easily polyfilled while the rest syntax requires transpilation. If you, for some reason, cannot or don't want to add the transpilation step to your project then you can still use Array.from by adding a polyfill or a shim. Which is a very painless alternative.

[46]http://bit.ly/mdn-rest-parameters

```
1   obliterate('batman');
2   // => batman wiped out of the face of the earth
3   // *Everything* has been obliterated, oh great master
4   // of evil and deceit!
5
6   obliterate("John Doe", getPuppy(), 1, new Minion('Willy', 'troll'));
7   /*
8   John Doe wiped off of the face of the earth
9   cute puppy wiped off of the face of the earth
10  1 wiped off of the face of the earth
11  Willy the troll wiped off of the face of the earth
12  *Everything* has been obliterated, oh great master of evil and decei\
13  t!
14  */
```

Rest paratemers can also be used in combination with normal parameters. For instance, imagine that the obliterate spell had an extra effect on the first enemy it encountered. We could rewrite it like this:

```
1   function obliterate(unfortunateVictim, ...victims){
2     console.log(unfortunateVictim +
3                 " wiped out of the face of EXISTENCE " +
4                 "as if it had never existed.... Woooo");
5     victims.forEach(function(victim){
6       console.log(victim + " wiped out of the face of the earth");
7     });
8     console.log('*Everything* has been obliterated, ' +
9                 'oh great master of evil and deceit!');
10  }
```

Upon using this malignant spell the first enemy would be removed from existence completely and utterly:

```
1   obliterate("John Doe", getPuppy(), 1, new Minion('Willy', 'troll'));
2   /*
3   John Doe wiped out of the face of EXISTENCE as if it had
4   never existed.... Woooo
5   cute puppy wiped off of the face of the earth
6   etc...
7   */
```

Note how easily the rest parameters capture all the remaining arguments after unfortunateVictim. Beautiful!

You now know different ways to implement a function that takes an arbitrary number of arguments. A function that provides the same API regardless of being called with one or many arguments. But what if you just happen to have an array? What happens if the output of another function is an array of enemies that need to be obliterated? Well, that's when the **ES6 spread operator** comes in handy.

The **ES6 spread operator**, among other things that you'll learn later in this book, lets you seamlessly call these type of functions using an array as argument:

```
1    let mortalEnemies = ["John Doe", getPuppy(), 1,
2                         new Minion('Willy', 'troll')];
3
4    obliterate(...mortalEnemies);
5    /*
6    John Doe wiped out of the face of EXISTENCE as if
7    it had never existed.... Woooo
8    cute puppy wiped off of the face of the earth
9    etc...
10   */
```

Note how the *spread operator* ...mortalEnemies is super similar to *rest parameters syntax* but performs the opposite operation, instead of gathering arguments into an array, it spreads an array into arguments.

Concluding

Congratulations! You have cleared another obstacle in the path to writing functions with beautiful and thoughtful APIs.

Function parameters and arguments are yet another example of the flexibility and freedom that JavaScript offers. In JavaScript you can call a function with as many argument as you want regardless of the signature of the function itself.

In some ocassions you'll need to design a function that takes an arbitrary number of arguments. If you are using ES5, you can take advantage of the arguments object. The arguments object is present in every function and gives you access to the arguments with which a function was called. Unfortunately, it is an *array-like* object and you may need to convert it to an array before you can use it. If you are using ES6 or above, *rest parameters* offer a great developer experience similar to C# params. You can combine *rest parameters* with normal parameters and even call one of these special functions with an array using the *spread operator.*

In the next chapter you'll find out how to override functions (and methods) in JavaScript.

```
randalf.says('He did it. He gained access to the REPL');
randalf.says('He understood its secret language and ' +
            'everything changed');

/*
All of the sudden he gained the power to command the world
around him. No longer did he need to use his bare hands he
could just create things out of nothingness.

Disturbing but amazing to witness.

And then he started teaching it, and a golden age of
civilization began.
*/
```

```
randalf.says('and it all started with eggs...');
randalf.stomach.says('brrrrrrr....');
randalf.says('hmm... care for some eggs??');
```

Exercises

Experiment JavaScriptmancer!

You can experiment with these exercises and some possible solutions in this jsFiddle[47] or downloading the source code from GitHub[48].

Boil Some Eggs!

Transform this function to enable boiling an arbitrary number of eggs using ES5 and the arguments object.

```
1   function boil(item){
2       console.log('You summon a bubble of boiling water ' +
3                   'that boils the ' + item);
4   }
5
6   mooleen.weaves("boil('egg')");
7   // => You summon a bubble of boiling water that boils the egg
8
9   // now boil all of these!
10  var dragonEgg = 'dragon egg',
11      egg = 'unasumming egg',
12      goldenEgg = 'golden egg';
```

---

[47]http://bit.ly/javascriptmancy-basic-functions-multiple-arguments-exercises
[48]https://github.com/vintharas/javascriptmancy-code-samples

Solution

```
1   mooleen.says('I think I am getting the hang of it...');
2
3   function boilMany(){
4     var items = Array.prototype.slice.apply(arguments);
5     items.forEach(function(item) {
6       boil(item);
7     });
8   }
9
10  mooleen.weaves('boilMany(dragonEgg, egg, goldenEgg)');
11  // => You summon a bubble of boiling water that boils the dragon egg
12  // You summon a bubble of boiling water that boils the unsumming egg
13  // You summon a bubble of boiling water that boils the golden egg
```

Now Improve it with ES6

Use ES6 rest parameters to improve boilMany.

Solution

```
1   mooleen.says('All right! I reckon that if I... ');
2
3   function boilManyES6(...items){
4     items.forEach(function(item) {
5       boil(item);
6     });
7   }
8
9   mooleen.weaves('boilManyES6(dragonEgg, egg, goldenEgg)');
10  // => You summon a bubble of boiling water that boils the dragon egg
11  // You summon a bubble of boiling water that boils the unsumming egg
12  // You summon a bubble of boiling water that boils the golden egg
13
```

```
14  mooleen.says('Booom!');
```

 ## Wait! Can You Boil This Array of Veggies?

Randalf found these veggies in one of his many pockets:

```
1  let veggies = ['cucumber', 'iceberg salad', 'onion', 'zucchini', 'to\
2  mato'];
```

Could you boil them without changing the body of the previous function?

Solution

```
1   mooleen.says("didn't you say something about a spread operator?");
2
3   mooleen.weaves('boilManyES6(...veggies)');
4   // => You summon a bubble of boiling water that boils the cucumber
5   // You summon a bubble of boiling water that boils the iceberg salad
6   // etc...
7
8   mooleen.says("Ok! Ready, will you now tell me what am I doing here?"\
9   );
10  randalf.says("I'm getting there");
11  randalf.says("...golden age of civilization... yeah!");
12  randalf.says("Well, that didn't last long");
```

More Useful Function Patterns: Function Overloading

One same API,
to provide similar function,
that's a smart thing,
memorable, familiar, consistent

> \- Siwelluap
> Chieftain of the twisted fangs

```
randalf.sighs();
randalf.says("it didn't last long at all");
randalf.says("You know? Not everyone could tap into the power " +
"of the REPL...")

/*

Only a few could harness it. And some of them, some of them
were crooked, either that or they just couldn't handle
the power.

Before Branden could do anything about it, they shattered
the world, enslaved the normals, herded and annihilated
those of us who opposed them and that's the state of things.

We are governed by a bunch of egocentric megalomaniac mad
men and women.

*/

mooleen.says("How is it that you're still here then?");
randalf.says("Well they did something worse to me. They took it");

mooleen.says("You cannot cast spells any more?");
randalf.says("I cannot. But I do remember everything");
randalf.says("Talking about knowledge. " +
             "Have you heard about the marvels of overloading?");
```

Have you Heard About The Marvels Of Overloading?

In the last couple of chapters we learned some useful patterns with functions in JavaScript that helped us achieve defaults and handling arbitrary arguments. We also saw a common thread: The fact that ES6 comes with a lot of new features that make up for past limitations of the language. Features like *native defaults* and *rest parameters* that let you solve these old problems in a more concise style.

This chapter will close this section - useful function patterns - with some tips on how you can achieve function overloading in JavaScript.

Function overloading helps you reuse a piece of functionality and provide a unified API in those situations when you have slightly different arguments yet you want to achieve the same thing. Unfortunately, there's a problem with function overloading in JavaScript.

The Problem with Function Overloading in JavaScript

 Experiment JavaScriptmancer!!

You can experiment with all examples in this chapter directly within this jsFiddle[49] or downloading the source code from GitHub[50].

There's a slight issue when you attempt to do function overloading in JavaScript like you would in C#. **You can't do it**.

Indeed, one does not simply overload functions in JavaScript willy nilly. Imagine a spell to raise a skeleton army:

```
1  function raiseSkeleton(){
2    console.log('You raise a skeleton!!!');
3  }
```

And now imagine that you want to overload it to accept an argument mana that will affect how many skeletons can be raised from the dead at once:

---

[49]http://bit.ly/javascriptmancy-function-overloading
[50]https://github.com/vintharas/javascriptmancy

```
1  function raiseSkeleton(mana){
2    console.log('You raise ' + mana + ' skeletons!!!');
3  }
```

If you now try to execute the raiseSkeleton function with no arguments you would probably expect the first version of the function to be called (just like it would happen in C#). However, what you'll discover, to your dismay, is that raiseSkeleton has been completely overwritten:

```
1  raiseSkeleton();
2  // => You raise undefined skeletons!!!
```

In JavaScript, you cannot override a function by defining a new one with the same name and a different signature. If you try to do so, you'll just succeed in overwriting your original function with a new implementation.

How Do We Do Function Overloading Then?

Well, as with many things in JavaScript, you'll need to take advantage of the flexibility and freedom the language gives you to emulate function overloading yourself. In the upcoming sections you'll learn four different ways in which you can achieve it, each with their own strengths and caveats:

1. Inspecting arguments
2. Using an *options* object
3. Relying on ES6 defaults
4. Taking advantage of polymorphic functions

Function Overloading by Inspecting Arguments

One common pattern for achieving function overloading is to use the arguments object to **inspect the arguments** that are passed into a function:

```
1   function raiseSkeletonWithArgumentInspecting(){
2     if (typeof arguments[0] === "number"){
3       raiseSkeletonsInNumber(arguments[0]);
4     } else if (typeof arguments[0] === "string") {
5       raiseSkeletonCreature(arguments[0]);
6     } else {
7       console.log('raise a skeleton');
8     }
9
10    function raiseSkeletonsInNumber(n){
11      console.log('raise ' + n + ' skeletons');
12    }
13    function raiseSkeletonCreature(creature){
14      console.log('raise a skeleton ' + creature);
15    };
16  }
```

Following this pattern you inspect each argument being passed to the overloaded function(or even the number of arguments) and determine which internal implementation to execute:

```
1   raiseSkeletonWithArgumentInspecting();
2   // => raise a skeleton
3   raiseSkeletonWithArgumentInspecting(4);
4   // => raise 4 skeletons
5   raiseSkeletonWithArgumentInspecting('king');
6   // => raise skeleton king
```

This approach can become unwieldy very quickly. As the over-loaded functions and their parameters increase in number, the function becomes harder and harder to read, maintain and extend.

At this point you may be thinking: *"...checking the type of the arguments being passed? seriously?!"* and I agree with you, that's why I like to use this next approach instead.

Using an Options Object

A better way to achieve function overloading is to use an *options* object. This object acts as a container for the different parameters a function can consume:

```
1  function raiseSkeletonWithOptions(spellOptions){
2    spellOptions = spellOptions || {};
3    var armySize = spellOptions.armySize || 1,
4      creatureType = spellOptions.creatureType || '';
5
6    if (creatureType){
7      console.log('raise a skeleton ' + creatureType);
8    } else {
9      console.log('raise ' + armySize + ' skeletons ' + creatureType);
10   }
11 }
```

This allows you to call a function with different arguments:

```
1  raiseSkeletonWithOptions();
2  // => raise a skeleton
3  raiseSkeletonWithOptions({armySize: 4});
4  // => raise 4 skeletons
5  raiseSkeletonWithOptions({creatureType:'king'});
6  // => raise skeleton king
```

It is not strictly function overloading but it provides the same benefits: It gives you different possibilities in the form of a unified API, and additionally, named arguments and easy extensibility. That is, you can add new options without breaking any existing clients of the function.

Here is an example of both *argument inspecting* and the *options* object patterns in the wild, the jQuery ajax function[51]:

```
 1  ajax: function( url, options ) {
 2    // If url is an object, simulate pre-1.5 signature
 3    if ( typeof url === "object" ) {
 4      options = url;
 5      url = undefined;
 6    }
 7
 8    // Force options to be an object
 9    options = options || {};
10
11    var transport,
12      // URL without anti-cache param
13      cacheURL,
14      // Response headers
15      responseHeadersString,
16      responseHeaders,
17      // timeout handle
18      timeoutTimer,
19      // etc...
20  }
```

Relying on ES6 Defaults

Although ES6 doesn't come with classic function overloading, it brings us default arguments which give you better support for function overloading than what we've had so far.

If you reflect about it, default arguments are a specialized version of function overloading. A subset of it, if you will, for those cases in which you can use an increasing number of predefined arguments:

---

[51]http://bit.ly/jquery-ajax-js

```
1   function castIceCone(mana=5, {direction='in front of you'}={}){
2     console.log(`You spend ${mana} mana and casts a ` +
3       `terrible ice cone ${direction}`);
4   }
5   castIceCone();
6   // => You spend 5 mana and casts a terrible ice cone in front of you
7   castIceCone(10, {direction: 'towards Mordor'});
8   // => You spend 10 mana and casts a terrible ice cone towards Mordor
```

Taking Advantage of Polymorphic Functions

Yet another interesting pattern for achieving function overloading is to rely on JavaScript great support for functional programming. In the world of functional programming there is the concept of **polymorphic functions**, that is, functions which exhibit different behaviors based on their arguments.

Let's illustrate them with an example. Our starting point will be this function that we saw in the *inspecting arguments* section:

```
1    function raiseSkeletonWithArgumentInspecting(){
2      if (typeof arguments[0] === "number"){
3        raiseSkeletonsInNumber(arguments[0]);
4      } else if (typeof arguments[0] === "string") {
5        raiseSkeletonCreature(arguments[0]);
6      } else {
7        console.log('raise a skeleton');
8      }
9
10     function raiseSkeletonsInNumber(n){
11       console.log('raise ' + n + ' skeletons');
12     }
13     function raiseSkeletonCreature(creature){
14       console.log('raise a skeleton ' + creature);
15     };
16   }
```

We will take it and decompose it into smaller functions:

```
1   function raiseSkeletons(number){
2     if (Number.isInteger(number)){ return `raise ${number} skeletons`;}
3   }
4
5   function raiseSkeletonCreature(creature){
6     if (creature) {return `raise a skeleton ${creature}`;}
7   }
8
9   function raiseSingleSkeleton(){
10    return 'raise a skeleton';
11  }
```

And now we create an abstraction (functional programming likes abstraction) for a function that executes several other functions in sequence until one returns a valid result. Where a valid result will be any value different from undefined:

```
1   // This is a higher-order function that returns a new function.
2   // Something like a function factory.
3   // We could reuse it to our heart's content.
4   function dispatch(...fns){
5
6     return function(...args){
7       for(let f of fns){
8         let result = f.apply(null, args);
9         if (exists(result)) return result;
10      }
11    };
12  }
13
14  function exists(value){
15    return value !== undefined
16  }
```

dispatch lets us create a new function that is a combination of all the previous ones: raiseSkeletons, raiseSkeletonCreature and raiseSingleSkeleton:

```
1  let raiseSkeletonFunctionally = dispatch(
2              raiseSkeletons,
3              raiseSkeletonCreature,
4              raiseSingleSkeleton);
```

This new function will behave in different ways based on the arguments it takes. It will delegate any call to each specific raise skeleton function until a suitable result is obtained.

```
1  console.log(raiseSkeletonFunctionally());
2  // => raise a skeleton
3  console.log(raiseSkeletonFunctionally(4));
4  // => raise 4 skeletons
5  console.log(raiseSkeletonFunctionally('king'));
6  // => raise skeleton king
```

Note how the last `raiseSingleSkeleton` is a catch-all function. It will always return a valid result regardless of the arguments being sent to the function. This will ensure that however you call `raiseSkeletonFunctionally` you'll always have a default implementation or valid result.

A super duper mega cool thing that you may or may not have noticed is the **awesome degree of composability** of this approach. If we want to extend this function later on, we can do it without modifying the original function. Take a look at this:

```
1  function raiseOnSteroids({number=0, type='skeleton'}={}){
2    if(number) {
3      return `raise ${number} ${type}s`;
4    }
5  }
6
7  let raiseAdvanced = dispatch(raiseOnSteroids,
8                              raiseSkeletonFunctionally);
```

We now have a `raiseAdvanced` function that augments `raiseSkeletonFunctionally` with the new desired functionality represented by `raiseOnSteroids`:

```
1    console.log(raiseAdvanced());
2    // => raise a skeleton
3    console.log(raiseAdvanced(4));
4    // => raise 4 skeletons
5    console.log(raiseAdvanced('king'));
6    // => raise skeleton king
7    console.log(raiseAdvanced({number: 10, type: 'ghoul'}))
8    // => raise 10 ghouls
```

This is the OCP (Open-Closed Principle)[52] in all its glory like you've never seen it before. Functional programming is pretty awesome right? We will take a deeper dive into functional programming within the sacred tome of FP later in the series and you'll get the chance to experiment a lot more with both higher-order functions and function composition alike.

Concluding

Although JavaScript doesn't support function overloading you can achieve the same behavior by using different patterns: inspecting arguments, using an options object, relying on ES6 defaults or taking advantage of polymorphic functions.

You can use the `arguments` object and **inspect the arguments** that are being passed to a function at runtime. You should only use this solution with the simplest of implementations as it becomes unwieldly and hard to maintain as parameters and overloads are added to a function.

Or you can use an **options object** as a wrapper for parameters. This is both more readable and maintanaible than inspecting arguments, and provides two additional benefits: named arguments and a lot of flexibility to extend the function with new parameters.

ES6 brings improved support for function overloading in some situations with native default arguments.

---

[52]Open for extension and closed for modification. http://bit.ly/ocp-wikipedia

Finally, you can take advantage of functional programming, compose your functions from smaller ones and use a dispatching mechanism to select which function is used based on the arguments.

```
randalf.says("haha! And that's what you need to known " +
            "about overloading!");
mooleen.says("What am I doing here?");

randalf.says("Oh yeah that...");
randalf.says("You are the Chosen one!");

mooleen.says("Yes, yes, the chosen for what?");

randalf.says("You are going to fix everything! " +
            "Bring balance to the force and all that");

randalf.says("But first you need to learn!");
randalf.says("Right now you wouldn't stand a chance");

mooleen.says("Well I reckon that 'Great' wouldn't agree " +
            "on that note.");

randalf.says("Oh child, that was just an avatar");
randalf.says("Do you think that this paranoid psychotic " +
            "megalomaniac would come to you in the flesh??");
```

Exercises

 ### Experiment JavaScriptmancer!

You can experiment with these exercises and some possible solutions in this jsFiddle[53] or downloading the source code from GitHub[54].

---

[53]http://bit.ly/javascriptmancy-function-overloading-exercises
[54]https://github.com/vintharas/javascriptmancy-code-samples

Create Your Own Avatar

Write a function createAvatar using function overloading by inspecting arguments. It should satisfy the following snippet:

```
1    createAvatar(/* description */ 'a blue wisp hovering around');
2    // => you create an avatar in the form of a blue wisp hovering around
3
4    createAvatar({ appearance: 'a blue wisp',
5                    stance: 'hovering around'});
6    // => you create an avatar in the form of a blue wisp hovering around
```

Solution

```
1    mooleen.says('An avatar...');
2    mooleen.says('Let me see if I can do it myself...');
3
4    function createAvatar(){
5      if (typeof arguments[0] === "string"){
6        var description = arguments[0];
7        console.log('you create an avatar in the form of ' +
8                    description);
9      } else {
10       var attributes = arguments[0],
11         appearance = attributes.appearance,
12         stance = attributes.stance;
13       console.log('you create an avatar in the form of '
14                   + appearance + " " + stance);
15     }
16   }
17
18   mooleen.weaves("createAvatar('a blue wisp hovering around')");
19   // => you create an avatar in the form of a blue wisp hovering around
20   mooleen.weaves("createAvatar(" +
21          "{ appearance: 'a blue wisp', stance: 'hovering around'})");
22   // => you create an avatar in the form of a blue wisp hovering around
```

Options

Update the createAvatar function to use an options object that satisfies the following:

```
1   createAvatar({ description: 'a blue wisp hovering around'});
2   // => you create an avatar in the form of a blue wisp hovering around
3
4   createAvatar({ appearance: 'a blue wisp',
5                  stance: 'hovering around'});
6   // => you create an avatar in the form of a blue wisp hovering around
```

Solution

```
1   function createAvatarOptions(options){
2     var appearance = options.appearance || 'no form',
3         stance = options.stance || 'standing',
4         description = options.description || appearance + " " + stance;
5     console.log('you create an avatar in the form of ' + description);
6   }
7
8   mooleen.weaves("createAvatarOptions("+
9                  "{ description: 'a blue wisp hovering around'})");
10  // => you create an avatar in the form of a blue wisp hovering around
11
12  mooleen.weaves("createAvatarOptions("+
13     { appearance: 'a blue wisp', stance: 'hovering around'})");
14  // => you create an avatar in the form of a blue wisp hovering around
```

And Now Create an Avatar Like Mooleen

Write a createAvatar function that is a polymorphic function. It should satisfy the following snippet:

```
1   createAvatar('a beautiful freckled young woman standing defiantly');
2   // => you create an avatar in the form of a beautiful freckled
3          young woman standing defiantly
4
5   createAvatar({ appearance: 'a beautiful young woman',
6                  stance: 'standing defiantly'});
7   // => you create an avatar in the form of a beautiful freckled
8          young woman standing defiantly
9
10  createAvatar();
11  // you create an avatar in shapeless form
```

Solution

```
1   function dispatch(...fns){
2       return function(...args){
3           for(let f of fns){
4               let result = f.apply(null, args);
5               if (exists(result)) return result;
6           }
7       };
8   }
9
10  function exists(value){
11      return value !== undefined
12  }
13
14  function createByDescription(description){
15    if (typeof description === "string"){
16      return 'you create an avatar in the form of ' + description;
17    }
18  }
19
20  function createByAttributes(attributes){
21    if (typeof attributes === 'object'){
```

```
22        var attributes = arguments[0],
23            appearance = attributes.appearance,
24            stance = attributes.stance;
25        return 'you create an avatar in the form of ' + appearance + " "\
26    + stance;
27      }
28    }
29
30    function createDefault(){
31        return 'you create an avatar in a shapeless form';
32    }
33
34    function createAvatarFp(){
35      var createFn = dispatch(
36                      createByDescription,
37                      createByAttributes,
38                      createDefault);
39      console.log(createFn.apply(null, arguments));
40    }
41
42    createAvatarFp('a beautiful freckled young woman standing defiantly'\
43    );
44    // => you create an avatar in the form of a beautiful freckled
45    // young woman standing defiantly
46
47    createAvatarFp({ appearance: 'a beautiful young woman',
48                stance: 'standing defiantly'});
49    // => you create an avatar in the form of a beautiful freckled
50    //     young woman standing defiantly
51
52    createAvatarFp();
53    // => you create an avatar in a shapeless form
54
55    mooleen.says('Damn! That was creepy');
```

On the Art of Summoning Servants and Critters, Or Understanding The Basics of JavaScript Objects

Things are ideas,
ideas are abstractions,
abstractions are objects,
objects are things.

That's the secret of JavaScript-mancy

    - Branden Iech,
    Meditations

```javascript
mooleen.says('So... am I supposed to fix the world?');
randalf.says('Yep, you are our only hope.')
randalf.says('Let me show you something');

/*

Randalf begins walking towards a nearby dune and signals Mooleen
to follow. After 20 minutes of crossing dunes, up and down, and
up and down again, they arrive to the top of higher dune
and Randalf stops.

*/

randalf.says('Tell me Mooleen. What do you see?');
mooleen.looksAround();
mooleen.says('I see sand... and more sand');

randalf.says("Welcome to the White City of Gigia, Gigia the " +
             "magnificent with its high white marble walls, " +
             "its beautiful gardens, its bustling markets and " +
             "its 1337 towers!!");

mooleen.looksAround();
/*

The wind blows and a tumbleweed slowly rolls beside them and
continues rolling until it disappears into the distance.

*/

randalf.says("My point exactly... There's no trace of Gigia, " +
             "of its walls, its gardens, its markets, its towers, " \
+
             "its people.");

mooleen.says("They did this?");

randalf.says("Yes, they did this and worse. " +
             "That's why you'll need an army");
```

An Army of Objects

Hello JavaScriptmancer! It is time to get an introduction to the
basics of objects in JavaScript. In this chapter you'll learn the beauty
of the object initializer and the nice improvements ES6 brings to
objects. If you think that you already know this stuff, think twice!
There is more than one surprise in this chapter and I promise that
you'll learn something new by the end of it.

Let's get started! We'll start by concentrating our efforts in the humble object initializer. This will provide a foundation that we can use
later when we come to the tome of object-oriented programming in
JavaScript and prototypical inheritance.

Objects it is!

Object Initializers (a.k.a. Object Literals)

 ### Experiment JavaScriptmancer!!

You can experiment with all examples in this chapter
directly within this jsBin[55] or downloading the source
code from GitHub[56].

The simplest way to create an object in JavaScript is to use an object
initializer:

```
1   var critter = {}; // {} is an empty object initializer
```

You can add properties and methods inside your object initializer
to your heart's content:

[55]http://bit.ly/javascriptmancy-objects-basics
[56]https://github.com/vintharas/javascriptmancy

```
1   critter = {
2     position: {x: 0, y: 0},
3     movesTo: function (x, y){
4       console.log(this + ' moves to (' + x + ',' + y + ')');
5       this.position.x = x;
6       this.position.y = y;
7     },
8     toString: function(){
9       return 'critter';
10    },
11    hp: 40
12  }
```

And, of course, if you call a method within the critter object it
behaves as you have come to expect from any good self-respecting
method:

```
1   critter.moveTo(10, 10);
2   // => critter moves to (10,10)
```

As you saw in the introduction of the book, you can augment any[57]
object at any time with new properties:

```
1   critter.damage = 1;
2   critter.attacks = function(target) {
3     console.log(this + ' rabidly attacks ' + target +
4                 ' with ' + this.damage + ' damage');
5     target.hp-=this.damage;
6   };
```

And use these new abilities to great devastation:

---

[57]As long as it is not frozen via Object.freeze, which makes an object immutable to all
effects and purposes.

```
1   var rabbit = {hp:10, toString: function(){return 'rabbit';}};
2
3   critter.attacks(rabbit);
4   // => critter rabidly attacks rabbit with 1 damage
```

Alternatively, you can access any property and method within an object by using the *indexing notation* via [ ]:

```
1   critter['attacks'](rabbit);
2   // => critter rabidly attacks rabbit with 1 damage
```

Although a little bit more verbose, this notation lets you use special characters as names of properties and methods:

```
1   critter['sounds used when communicating'] = [
2     'beeeeeh', 'grrrrr', 'tjjiiiiii'
3   ];
4   critter.saysSomething = function(){
5     var numberOfSounds = this['sounds used when communicating'].length,
6         randomPick = Math.floor(Math.random()*numberOfSounds);
7
8     console.log(this['sounds used when communicating'][randomPick]);
9   };
10
11  critter.saysSomething();
12  // => beeeeeh (random pick)
13  critter.saysSomething();
14  // => tjjiiiiii (random pick)
```

As you can see in many of the examples above, you can use the this keyword to reference the object itself and thus access other properties within the same object.

JavaScript Arcana: This in JavaScript

From my experience, this is the biggest source of problems for a C# developer moving to JavaScript. We are so accustomed to work with classes and objects in C#, to be able to blindly rely in the value of this, that when we move to JavaScript, where the behavior of this is so completely undependable, we explode in frustration and anger.

Since this is such a big part of the JavaScript Arcana, I devote the whole next chapter to demystifying it for you. For now, just remember that when calling a method on a object using the dot notation, like in critter.moveTo, the value of this is mostly[58] trustworthy.

Getters and Setters

Getters and setters are an often overlooked feature within object initializers. You'll even find fairly seasoned JavaScript developers that don't know about their existence. They work exactly like C# properties and look like this:

---

[58] I say *mostly* because if you have a this keyword within a method and within a callback function (which I dare say is pretty common) then you are screwed. But worry not! You'll learn everything there is to learn about this in the next chapter.

```
1   var mouse = {
2     strength: 1,
3     dexterity: 1,
4     get damage(){
5       return this.strength*die20() + this.dexterity*die8();
6     },
7     attacks: function(target){
8       console.log(this + ' ravenously attacks ' + target +
9                   ' with ' + this.damage + ' damage!');
10      target.hp-=this.damage;
11    },
12    toString: function() { return 'mouse';}
13  }
```

Notice the strange get damage() function-like thingy? That's a
getter. In this case, it represents the read-only property damage that
is calculated from other two properties strength and dexterity.

```
1   mouse.attacks(rabbit);
2   // => mouse ravenously attacks rabbit with 19 damage!
3   mouse.attacks(rabbit);
4   // => mouse ravenously attacks rabbit with 15 damage!
```

Getters are extremely useful when you need to define computed
properties, that is, properties described in terms of other existing
properties. They save you from needing to keep additional and
unnecessary state that brings the additional burden of keeping it
in sync with the properties it depends on (in this case strength and
dexterity).

We can also use a backing field to perform additional steps or
validation:

```
1    var giantBat = {
2      _hp: 1,
3      get hp(){ return this._hp;},
4      set hp(value){
5        if (value < 0) {
6          console.log(this + ' dies :(')
7          this._hp = 0;
8        } else {
9          this._hp = value;
10       }
11     },
12     toString: function(){
13       if (this.hp > 0){
14         return 'giant bat';
15       } else {
16         return 'a dead giant bat';
17       }
18     }
19   };
```

In this example we ensure that the _hp property of the giant bat
cannot go below 0 (because you can't be deader than dead, unless
you are a necromancer that is):

```
1    mouse.attacks(giantBat);
2    // => "mouse ravenously attacks giant bat with 23 damage!"
3    // => "giant bat dies :("
4    console.log(giantBat.toString());
5    // => a dead giant bat
```

JavaScript Arcana: Getters and Setters Are Not Augmenters

You may have noticed that I have created a couple of new
objects for these two examples instead of augmenting my
beloved critter. Well, there was a reason for that. You cannot
augment objects with getters and setters in the same way that
you add other properties.

> In this special case, you need to rely in the Object.defineProperty or Object.defineProperties both methods also included in ES5. We will take a look at these two low level methods later in the tome of OOP when we examine the mysteries of object internals. Let's go back to object initializers!

Method Overloading

Method overloading within object initializers works just like with functions. As we saw in the previous chapter, if you try to overload a method following the same pattern that you are accustomed to in C#:

```
1   var venomousFrog = {
2     toString: function(){
3       return 'venomous frog';
4     },
5     jumps: function(meters){
6       console.log(this + ' jumps ' + meters + ' meters in the air');
7     },
8     jumps: function(arbitrarily) {
9       console.log( this + ' jumps ' + arbitrarily);
10     }
11   };
```

You'll just succeed in overwriting the former jump method with the latter:

```
1   venomousFrog.jumps(10);
2   // => venomous frog jumps 10
3   // ups we have overwritten a the first jumps method
```

Instead, use any of the patterns that you saw in the previous chapter to achieve method overloading. For instance, you can inspect the arguments being passed to the jump function:

```
1  venomousFrog.jumps = function(arg){
2    if (typeof(arg) === 'number'){
3      console.log(this + ' jumps ' + arg + ' meters in the air');
4    } else {
5      console.log( this + ' jumps ' + arg);
6    }
7  };
```

This provides a naive yet functioning implementation of method
overloading:

```
1  venomousFrog.jumps(10);
2  // => venomous frog jumps 10 meters
3  venomousFrog.jumps('wildly in front of you')
4  // => venomous frong jumps wildly in front of you
```

Creating Objects With Factories

Creating one-off objects through object initializers can be tedious,
particularly whenever you need more than one object of the same
"type". That's why we often use factories[59] to encapsulate object
creation:

```
1   function monster(type, hp){
2     return {
3       type: type,
4       hp: hp || 10,
5       toString: function(){return this.type;},
6       position: {x: 0, y: 0},
7       movesTo: function (x, y){
8         console.log(this + ' moves to (' + x + ',' + y + ')');
9         this.position.x = x;
10        this.position.y = y;
11      }
12    };
13  }
```

---

[59] or the *new operator* that we'll see when we get to glorious tome of OOP

Once defined, we can just use it to instantiate new objects as we
wish:

```
var tinySpider = monster('tiny spider', /* hp */ 1);
tinySpider.movesTo(1,1);
// => tiny spider moves to (1,1)
```

```
var giantSpider = monster('giant spider', /* hp */ 200);
giantSpider.movesTo(10,10);
// => giant spider moves to (10,10);
```

There's a lot of cool things that you can do with factories in
JavaScript. Some of them you'll discover when you get to tome of
OOP where we will see an alternative to classical inheritance in the
shape of object composition via mixins. In the meantime let's take
a look at **how to achieve data privacy.**

Data Privacy in JavaScript

You may have noticed by now that there's no access modifiers in
JavaScript, no `private`, `public` nor `protected` keywords. That's
because **every property is public**, that is, there is no way to declare
a private property by using a mere object initializer. You need to rely
on additional patterns with **closures** to achieve data privacy, and
that's where factories come in handy.

Imagine that we have the previous example of our `monster` but now
we don't want to reveal how we have implemented positioning.
We would prefer to hide that fact from prying eyes and object
consumers. If we decide to change it in the future, for a three
dimensional representation, polar coordinates or who knows what,
it won't break any clients of the object. This is part of what I
call **intentional programming**, every decision that you make, the
interface that you build, the parts that you choose to remain hidden

or public, represent your intentions on how a particular object or API should be used. **Be mindful and intentional when you write code.** Back to the monster:

```
1   function stealthyMonster(type, hp){
2     var position = {x: 0, y: 0};
3
4     return {
5       type: type,
6       hp: hp || 10,
7       toString: function(){return 'stealthy ' + this.type;},
8       movesTo: function (x, y){
9         console.log(this + ' moves stealthily to (' + x + ',' + y + ')\
10  ');
11        // this function closes over (or encloses) the position
12        // variable position is NOT part of the object itself,
13        // it's a free variable that's why you cannot access it
14        // via this.position
15        position.x = x;
16        position.y = y;
17      }
18    };
19  }
```

Let's take a closer look to that example. We have extracted the position property outside of the object initializer and inside a variable within the stealthyMonster scope (remember that functions create scopes in JavaScript). At the same time, we have updated the movesTo function, which creates its own scope, to refer to the position variable within the outer scope effectively creating a closure.

Because position is not part of the object being returned, it is not accessible to clients of the object through the dot notation. Because the movesTo becomes a closure it can access the position variable within the outside scope. In summary, we got ourselves some data privacy:

```
1   var darkSpider = stealthyMonster('dark spider');
2   console.log(darkSpider.position)
3   // now position is completely private
4   // => undefined
5
6   darkSpider.movesTo(10,10);
7   // => stealthy dark spider moves stealthily to (10,10)
```

ES6 Improves Object Initializers

ES6 brings some improvements to object initializers that reduce
the amount of code needed to create a new object. For instance,
with ES6 you can declare methods within objects using shorthand
syntax:

```
1   let sugaryCritter = {
2     position: {x: 0, y: 0},
3     // from movesTo: function(x, y) to...
4     movesTo(x, y){
5       console.log(`${this} moves to (${x},${y})`);
6       this.position.x = x;
7       this.position.y = y;
8     },
9     // from toString: function() to...
10    toString(){
11      return 'sugary ES6 critter';
12    },
13    hp: 40
14  };
15
16  sugaryCritter.movesTo(10, 10);
17  // => sugary ES6 critter moves to (10, 10)
```

As you can appreciate from the movesTo and toString methods
in this example above, using shorthand notation lets you skip
the function keyword and collapse the parameters of a function
directly after its name.

Additionally you can apply shorthand syntax to object properties.
When you write factory functions you'll often follow a pattern
where you initialize object properties based on the arguments
passed to the factory function:

```
1   function simpleMonster(type, hp = 10){
2     return {
3       type: type,
4       hp: hp
5     };
6   }
```

Where you have a little bit of redundant code in type: type and hp:
hp. Property shorthand syntax removes the need to repeat yourself
by letting you write the property/value pair only once. So that the
previous example turns into a much terser factory method:

```
1   function simpleMonster(type, hp = 10){
2     return {
3       // with property shorthand we avoid the need to repeat
4       // the name of the variable twice (type: type)
5       type,
6       hp
7     };
8   }
```

And here you have a complete example where we use both method
and property shorthand to get the ultimate sugary monster:

```
1   function sugaryStealthyMonster(type, hp = 10){
2     let position = {x: 0, y: 0};
3
4     return {
5       // with property shorthand we avoid the need to repeat
6       // the name of the variable twice (type: type)
7       type,
8       hp,
9       toString(){return `stealthy ${this.type}`;},
10      movesTo(x, y){
11        console.log(`${this} moves stealthily to (${x},${y})`);
12        position.x = x;
13        position.y = y;
14      }
15    };
16  }
17
18  let sugaryOoze = sugaryStealthyMonster('sugary Ooze', /*hp*/ 500);
19  sugaryOoze.movesTo(10, 10);
20  // => stealthy sugary Ooze moves stealthily to (10,10)
```

Finally, with the advent of ES6 you can use any expression as the name of an object property. That is, you are no longer limited to normal names or using the square brackets notation that handles special characters. From ES6 onwards you'll be able to use any expression and the JavaScript engine will evaluate it as a string (with the exception of ES6 symbols which we'll see in the next section). Take a look at this:

```
1   let theArrow = () => 'I am an arrow';
2
3   let crazyMonkey = {
4     // ES5 valid
5     name: 'Kong',
6     ['hates!']: ['mario', 'luigi'],
7
8     // ES6 computed property names
9     [(() => 'loves!')()]: ['bananas'],
10    [sugaryOoze.type]: sugaryOoze.type
11    // crazier yet
```

```
12    [theArrow]: `what's going on!?`,
13  }
```

This example let's you appreciate how any expression is valid.
We've used the result of evaluating a function (() => 'loves!')(),
a property from another object sugaryOoze.type and even an arrow
function theArrow as property names. If you inspect the object itself,
you can see how each property has been intrepreted as a string:

```
1   console.log(crazyMonkey);
2   // => [object Object] {
3   //    function theArrow() {
4   //      return 'I am an arrow';
5   //    }: "what's going on!?",
6   //    hates!: ["mario", "luigi"],
7   //    loves!: ["bananas"],
8   //    name: "Kong",
9   //  sugary Ooze: "sugary Ooze"
10  // }
```

And you can retrieve them with the [] (indexing) syntax:

```
1   console.log(crazyMonkey[theArrow]);
2   // => "what's going on!?"
```

Use cases for this particular feature? I can only think of some
pretty far-fetched edge cases for dynamic creation of objects on-
the-fly. That and using symbols as property names wich gracefully
brings us to **ES6 symbols and how to take advantage of them to
simulate data privacy.**

ES6 Symbols and Data Privacy

Symbols are a new type in JavaScript. They were conceived to represent constants and to be used as identifiers for object properties.

The specification even describes them as *the set of all non-string values that may be used as the key of an object property* [60]. They are immutable and can have a description associated to them.

You can create a *symbol* using the Symbol function:

```
let anUndescriptiveSymbol = Symbol();
console.log(anUndescriptiveSymbol);
// => [object Symbol]
console.log(typeof anUndescriptiveSymbol);
// => symbol
console.log(anUndescriptiveSymbol.toString());
// => Symbol()
```

And you can add a description to the *symbol* by passing it as an argument to the same function. This will be helpful for debugging since the toString method will display that description:

```
// you can add a description to the Symbol
// so you can identify a symbol later on
let up = Symbol('up');
console.log(up.toString());
// => Symbol(up)
```

Each symbol is unique and immutable, so even if we create two symbols with the same description, they'll remain two completely different symbols:

```
// each symbol is unique and immutable
console.log(`Symbol('up') === Symbol('up')??
  ${Symbol('up') === Symbol('up')}`);
// => Symbol('up') === Symbol('up')?? false
```

ES6 symbols offer us a new approach to data privacy in addition to closures. Properties that use a symbol as name (or key) can only

---

[60]that's from the one and only JavaScript specification ECMA-262 (http://bit.ly/es6-spec-symbols)

be accessed by a reference to that symbol (the very same symbol
used to identify the property). Because of this special characteristic,
if you don't expose a symbol to the outer world you have provided
yourself with data privacy. Let's see how this works in practice:

```javascript
function flyingMonster(type, hp = 10){
  let position = Symbol('position');

  return {
    [position]: {x: 0, y: 0},
    type,
    hp,
    toString(){return `stealthy ${this.type}`;},
    movesTo(x, y){
      console.log(`${this} flies like the wind from` +
        `(${this[position].x}, ${this[position].y}) to (${x},${y})`);
      this[position].x = x;
      this[position].y = y;
    }
  };
}

let pterodactyl = flyingMonster('pterodactyl');
pterodactyl.movesTo(10,10);
// => stealthy pterodactyl flies like the wind from (0,0) to (10,10)
```

Since outside of the `flyingMoster` function we don't have a reference to the symbol `position` (it is scoped inside the function), we
cannot access the position property:

```javascript
console.log(pterodactyl.position);
// => undefined
```

And because each symbol is unique we cannot access the property
using another symbol with the same description:

```
1  console.log(pterodactyl[Symbol('position')]);
2  // => undefined
```

If everything ended here the world would be perfect, we could
use symbols for data privacy and live happily ever after. However,
there's a drawback: The JavaScript Object prototype provides the
getOwnPropertySymbols method that allows you to get the symbols
used as properties within any given object. This means that after all
this trouble we can access the position property by following this
simple procedure:

```
1  var symbolsUsedInObject = Object.getOwnPropertySymbols(pterodactyl);
2  var position = symbolsUsedInObject[0];
3  console.log(position.toString());
4  // => Symbol(position)
5  // Got ya!
6
7  console.log(pterodactyl[position]);
8  // => {x: 10, y: 10}
9  // ups!
```

So you can think of symbols as a soft way to implement data
privacy, where you give a clearer intent to your code, but where
your data is not truly private. This limitation is why I still prefer
using closures over Symbols.

Concluding

In this chapter you learned the most straightforward way to work
with objects in JavaScript, the object initializer. You learned how
to create objects with properties and methods, how to augment
existing objects with new properties and how to use getters and
setters. We also reviewed how to overload object methods and
ease the repetitive creation of objects with factories. We wrapped
factories with a pattern for achieving data privacy in JavaScript
through the use of closures.

You also learnt about the small improvements that ES6 brings to
object initializers with the shorthand notation for both methods
and properties. We wrapped the chapter with a review of the new
ES6 Symbol type and its usage for attaining a soft version of data
privacy.

```javascript
/*

This must be the weirdest piece of dune man has ever known.
There's two wizards surrounded by a critter, a mouse, a giant
bat, a venomous frog, a monster, a teeny tiny and a giant
spider, a stealthy monster, a crazy monkey, a dark spider, a
sugary critter?, an ooze and a ptero... a pterodactyl
whatever that may be.

*/

randalf.says("And that's how you summon creatures to your cause!"
             + "An army!");

mooleen.says("Ah□□");
mooleen.says("Summon them from where?");

randalf.says("hmm... good question!");
randalf.says("Powerful javascriptmancers can create stuff " +
             "out of nothing");
randalf.says("Initiates summon creatures from..." +
             "wherever creatures come from");

randalf.says("There's a lot of sand here... " + "
             "Why not create a sand golem?");
```

Exercises

Experiment JavaScriptmancer!

You can experiment with these exercises and some possible solutions in this jsFiddle[61] or downloading the source code from GitHub[62].

Create a Sand Golem!

Use an object initializer to create a sand golem. You are welcome to use shorthand syntax if you so choose! It should satisfy the following snippet of code:

```
sandGolem.toString();
// (returns) => Giant Sand Golem
sandGolem.walksTo(1,1);
// => Giant Sand Golem walks to (1,1);
sandGolem.grabs('spider');
// => Giant Sand Golem grabs spider
sandGolem.grabs('monkey', 'venomous frog');
// => Giant Sand Golem grabs monkey and venomous frog
sandGolem.grabbedStuff;
// (returns) => ['spider', 'monkey', 'venomous frog']
```

Solution

```
mooleen.concentrates();

/*
A sudden wind appears from out of nowhere, a small whirlwind
that sucks the sand beside mooleen and grows, and grows, and
```

---

[61]http://bit.ly/javascriptmancy-objects-basics-exercises
[62]https://github.com/vintharas/javascriptmancy-code-samples

```
 6   grows until it becomes and imposing giant figure that vaguely
 7   resembles something human.
 8   */
 9
10   let sandGolem = {
11     position: {x: 0, y: 0},
12     walksTo(x, y){
13       console.log(this + ' walks to (' + x + ',' + y + ')');
14       this.position.x = x;
15       this.position.y = y;
16     },
17     toString(){
18       return 'Giant Sand Golem';
19     },
20     grabbedStuff: [],
21     grabs(...items){
22       this.grabbedStuff.push(...items);
23       console.log(this + ' grabs ' + items.join(' and '));
24     }
25   }
26
27   console.log(sandGolem.toString());
28   // (returns) => Giant Sand Golem
29   sandGolem.walksTo(1,1);
30   // => Giant Sand Golem walks to (1,1);
31   sandGolem.grabs('spider');
32   // => Giant Sand Golem grabs spider
33   sandGolem.grabs('monkey', 'venomous frog');
34   // => Giant Sand Golem grabs monkey and venomous frog
35   console.log(sandGolem.grabbedStuff);
36   // (returns) => ['spider', 'monkey', 'venomous frog']
37
38   mooleen.says('voilⵁⵁ!');
```

How Much More Weight Can it Carry?

By the immutable laws of physics, a sand golem can only lift up to 40 items at once. Create a spaceAvailableOnBoard getter that retrieves the amount of space available in a golem at a given time.

Solution

```
1   let sandGolemImproved = {
2     position: {x: 0, y: 0},
3     walksTo(x, y){
4       console.log(this + ' walks to (' + x + ',' + y + ')');
5       this.position.x = x;
6       this.position.y = y;
7     },
8     toString(){
9       return 'Giant Sand Golem';
10    },
11    grabbedStuff: [],
12    grabs(...items){
13      this.grabbedStuff.push(...items);
14      console.log(this + ' grabs ' + items.join(' and '));
15    },
16    get spaceAvailableOnboard(){
17      const maxSpace = 40;
18      return maxSpace - this.grabbedStuff.length;
19    }
20  }
21
22  sandGolemImproved.grabs('pterodactyl');
23  // => Giant Sand Golem grabs pterodactyl
24  console.log(sandGolemImproved.spaceAvailableOnboard);
25  // => 39
```

Golems for Everyone!

Write a factory function that allows you to create
as many golems as you like. You should be able to
name them during creation, otherwise it will be hard
to keep track of them. You are welcome to use ES6
short-hand syntax if you so choose.

Solution

```
1   function SandGolem(name){
2     return {
3       name,
4       position: {x: 0, y: 0},
5       walksTo(x, y){
6         console.log(this + ' walks to (' + x + ',' + y + ')');
7         this.position.x = x;
8         this.position.y = y;
9       },
10      toString(){
11        return 'Giant Sand Golem (' + name + ')';
12      },
13      grabbedStuff: [],
14      grabs(...items){
15        this.grabbedStuff.push(...items);
16        console.log(this + ' grabs ' + items.join(' and '));
17      },
18      get spaceAvailableOnboard(){
19        const maxSpace = 40;
20        return maxSpace - this.grabbedStuff.length;
21      }
22    };
23  }
24
25  let sand = SandGolem('sand');
26  let dune = SandGolem('dune');
27  let beach = SandGolem('beach');
28  sand.grabs(dune);
29  // => Giant Sand Golem (sand) grabs Giant Sand Golem (dune)
30
31  mooleen.says('hehe that was fun');
```

 ### Hide the Details

Update your sand golem to hide its position and
grabbedStuff from external access.

Solution

```
1   function SandGolem(name){
2     let position = {x: 0, y: 0},
3         grabbedStuff = [];
4     return {
5       name,
6       walksTo(x, y){
7         console.log(this + ' walks to (' + x + ',' + y + ')');
8         position.x = x;
9         position.y = y;
10      },
11      toString(){
12        return 'Giant Sand Golem (' + name + ')';
13      },
14      grabs(...items){
15        grabbedStuff.push(...items);
16        console.log(this + ' grabs ' + items.join(' and '));
17      },
18      get spaceAvailableOnboard(){
19        const maxSpace = 40;
20        return maxSpace - grabbedStuff.length;
21      }
22    };
23  }
24
25  var shy = SandGolem('shy');
26  console.log(shy.position);
27  // => undefined
28  shy.walksTo(1,1);
29  // => Giant Sand Golem (shy) walks to (1,1)
30  console.log(shy.grabbedStuff);
31  // => undefined
32  shy.grabs('ooze');
33  // => Giant Sand Golem (shy) grabs ooze
34
35  randalf.says('Excellent! Now we are ready to start our journey');
36  mooleen.says('Where are we going?');
37  randalf.says('To the north! I have some friends left there');
38  mooleen.says('To the north then...');
39
40  /*
41  And to the north started the weirdest procession anyone has ever
42  seen. Two wizards, a sand golem, sand, dune and beach, shy, a
43  critter, a mouse, a giant bat, a teeny tiny and a giant spider,
44  a crazy monkey...
```

```
45    */
```

Mysteries of the JavaScript Arcana: JavaScript Quirks Demystified

Beware of any assumptions,
distrust any preconceptions,
forgo your experience,
and think with the mind of a beginner.

> \- Appa Ojnh
> The White Sage

```
/*
After weeks of travelling north Mooleen and Randalf arrive to a
green valley surrounded by majestic white-peaked mountains as
far as the eye can see. There's the beginning of a mountain trail
and two persons beside it waiting for them...
*/

randalf.says('Ah... the Misty Mountains. What a beautiful sight!');
randalf.says('Mooleen, I introduce you to zandalf and bandalf');
randalf.says('I trust them like if they were my brothers...');

randalf.says('...because they actually ARE my brothers');
mooleen.says('Ehem... I can see the resemblance');

/*
Randalf, Zandalf and Bandalf look nothing alike. Where Randalf is
tall and spindly, with a carefully trimmed beard and a good
natured resemblance, Zandalf is freakishly small and plump,
and Bandalf is... blue. Literally blue, like the sky in a
clear morning.
*/

randalf.says("Great! While we go up I'd like to tell you something");
randalf.says("I've noticed that some of your incantations have been \
misfiring");
mooleen.says('Misfiring? What? I know what I am doing... most of the\
 time');

randalf.says('So you meant to light that bale of hay on fire?');
mooleen.says('Yeeees');
randalf.says('And the cart beside it?');
mooleen.says('Yeeeeees');
randalf.says('And the two blocks of buildings surrounding it...');
mooleen.says('Yeee....');

randalf.says('What about my finest robes?');
mooleen.says('That was actually on purpose');

randalf.says('Mooleen...');
randalf.says('OK. I see that you are stumbling with some of the ' +
             'quirks and gotchas of JavaScript-mancy');
randalf.says('Let me give you a couple of tips');
```

A Couple of Tips About JavaScript Quirks and Gotchas

While **JavaScript looks a lot like a C-like language, it does not behave like one in many ways.** This, I would say, is the biggest reason why C# developers get so confused when they come to JavaScript.

If you've followed the book closely, you may have noticed that I have decided to call these unexpected behaviors the **JavaScript Arcana.** You have already seen several examples of these shadowy features thus far. Let's make a quick summary of them:

- Function scope and variable hoisting
- Array-like objects
- Function overloading

We'll start this chapter by making a short review of the quirks that you've already learned (repetition is a great tool for learning). And we'll continue by diving deeper into these other parts of the JavaScript Arcana:

- The sneaky this keyword
- Global scope as a default
- Type coercion madness
- JavaScript strict mode

We will focus particularly in the obscure behavior of the this keyword, our most dangerous foe. I expect that what you will learn in this chapter will save you from unmeasurable frustration in the future.

A Quick Refresher of the JavaScript Arcana 101

In *The Basics of JavaScript Functions* we saw how **JavaScript has function scope**. That is, as opposed to C# where every block of code creates a new scope, in JavaScript it is only functions that create new scopes. Every time you declare a variable through the var keyword it is scoped to its containing function. You also learned the concept of hoisting and how the JavaScript runtime moves your variable declarations to the top of a function body. Finally, you discovered how **ES6 brings the let and const keywords that give you the ability to declare block-scoped variables and forget about the headaches of hoisting and function-scoped variables.**

In Function Patterns: Arbitrary Arguments you learned about the arguments object. It can be accessed within every function to retrieve the arguments being passed to that function at runtime. You saw how the arguments object, although it looks like an array, it is actually what we call an array-like object. **Array-like objects can be enumerated, indexed and have a length property but they lack all array methods.** You also discovered **how to convert these objects to actual arrays using Array.prototype.slice (or Array.from)** and how the new **ES6 *rest operator*** solves the arguments issue completely.

In Function Patterns: Overloading you learned how you cannot overload JavaScript functions or methods in the same way that you do in C#. Instead, you can use several patterns to achieve the same effect: Argument inspection, options objects, ES6 default arguments or functional programming with polymorphic functions.

Now that we've warmed up to JavaScript weirdest features let's take a look at the behavior of this.

This, Your Most Dangerous Foe

Experiment JavaScriptmancer!!

You can experiment with all examples in this chapter directly within this jsFiddle[63] or downloading the source code from GitHub[64].

One of the most common problems when a C# developer comes to JavaScript is that it expects this to work exactly as it does in C#. And She or He or Zie will write this common piece of code unaware of the terrible dangers that lurk just one HTTP call away...

```
1    function UsersCatalog(){
2      this.users = [];
3      getUsers()
4
5      function getUsers(){
6        $.getJSON('https://api.github.com/users')
7        .success(function updateUsers(users){
8          this.users.push(users);
9          // BOOOOOOOM!!!!!
10         // => Uncaught TypeError:
11         //    Cannot read property 'push' of undefined
12       });
13     }
14   }
15   var catalog = new UsersCatalog();
```

In this code example we are trying to retrieve a collection of

---

[63]http://bit.ly/javascriptmancy-javascript-arcana
[64]https://github.com/vintharas/javascriptmancy

users from the GitHub API[65]. We perform an AJAX[66] request using jQuery `getJSON` and if the request is successful the response is passed as an argument to the `updateUsers` function.

The example throws an exception `cannot read property 'push' of undefined` which is the JavaScript version of our well known nemesis: The `NullReferenceException` (*we meet again*). Essentially, when we evaluate the `updateUsers` function, the `this.users` expression takes the value of `undefined`. When we try to execute `this.users.push(users)` we're basically calling the method `push` on nothing and thus the exception being thrown.

In order to understand why this is happening we need to learn how `this` works in JavaScript. In the next sections we will do just that. By the end of the chapter, when we have demystified `this` and become this-xperts, you'll be able to understand what is the cause of the error.

JavaScript Meets This

So `this` in JavaScript is weird. Unlike in other languages, **the value of `this` in JavaScript depends on the context in which a function is invoked**. Repeat. The behavior of `this` in JavaScript is not 100% stable nor reliable at all times, **it depends on the context in which a function is invoked**.

This essentially means that depending on how you call a function, the value of `this` inside that function will vary. We can distinguish between these four scenarios:

---

[65]http://bit.ly/github-api

[66]AJAX stands for `Asynchronously JavaScript and XML` and is a technology that allows you to get data from a server even after a web page has already been loaded. The significance and impact of AJAX in modern web development is huge because not only does it let you create highly interactive websites but also deliver a website in chunks as they are needed. Since its inception, browsers have implemented support for AJAX via the XMLHttpRequest object. Because of its complexity, I decided to use the simpler `$.getJSON`. In the near future, you'll be able to do AJAX requests using the improved `fetch` API. Yey!

- this and objects
- this unbound
- this explicitly
- this bound

This And Objects

In the most common scenario for an OOP developer we call functions as methods. That is, we call a function that is a property within an object using the dot notation.

If we have a hellHound spawned in the pits of hell with the ferocious ability of breathing fire:

```
// #1. A function invoked in the context of an object (a method)
var hellHound = {
  attackWithFireBreath: function(){
    console.log(this + " jumps towards you and unleashes " +
                "his terrible breath of fire! (-3 hp, +fear)");
  },
  toString: function (){ return 'Hellhound';}
}
```

When we call its attackWithFireBreath method using the dot notation this will take the value of the object itself:

```
hellHound.attackWithFireBreath();
// => Hellhound jumps towards you and unleashes
//    his terrible breath of fire! (-3 hp, +fear)
// 'this' is the hellHound object
```

Nothing strange here. This is the version of this we know and love from C#. Things get a little bit trickier in the next scenario.

This Unbound

In JavaScript you can do crazy things. Things like invoking a method without the context of the object in which it was originally defined. Since functions are values we can just save the `attack-WithFireBreath` method within a variable:

```
1   // #2. A function invoked without the context of its object
2   var attackWithFireBreath = hellHound.attackWithFireBreath;
```

And invoke the function via the newly created variable:

```
1   attackWithFireBreath();
2   // => [object Window] jumps towards you and unleashes
3   //    his terrible breath of fire! (-3 hp, +fear)
```

Ooops! What did just happen here? `this` is no longer the hell hound but the `Window` object. You may be asking yourself: *What?* And here comes the weird part that you need to remember: **Whenever you invoke a function without an object as context the `this` automatically becomes the `Window` object.**

The Window[67] object in JavaScript represents the browser window and contains the document object model (also known as DOM) an object representation of the elements within a website.

JavaScript Strict Mode

From ES5 onwards you can use strict mode (http://bit.ly/mdn-strict-mode) to get a better experience with JavaScript. Things that cause silent or unexpected errors and can be a headache to debug prior to ES5 throw explicit errors when you enable strict mode.

You can enable strict mode by writing `'strict mode';` at the

---

[67]You can find more information about the Window object and the DOM at MDN (http://bit.ly/mdn-window-object)

top of a JavaScript file or function.

With strict mode enabled the this object in this scenario will get the value of undefined. This will likely cause an error in your code and alert you about this unwanted behavior. Fail early, fail fast and fix your code as soon as possible.

You can learn more about strict mode at the end of the chapter.

As a cool exercise, you can now take that free function and add it to another object zandalf different from the original:

```
// we could add the same method to another object:
var zandalf = {
  toString: function(){return 'zandalf';}
};
zandalf.attackWithFireBreath = attackWithFireBreath;
```

Then call it as a method with the dot notation:

```
zandalf.attackWithFireBreath();
// => zandalf jumps towards you and unleashes
//    his terrible breath of fire! (-3 hp, +fear)
// => 'this' is the jaime object
```

And again, when we invoke the original function in the context of an object, **even when it is another one different from the original, this takes the value of that object**.

Let's make a summary of what you've seen up until now:

1. Call a function in the context of an object and this will take the value of the object
2. Call a function without context and this will take the value of the Window object. Unless you are in *strict mode* in which case it will take the value of undefined.

This Explicitly

All functions in JavaScript descend from the Function prototype[68]. This prototype provides two helpful methods that allow you to explicitly set the context in which to execute a function: call and apply.

Take the attackWithFireBreath function from the last example. This time, instead of calling it directly, we use its call method and pass the object zandalf as an argument:

```
1  attackWithFireBreath.call(zandalf);
2  // => zandalf...
3  // => 'this' is zandalf
```

The object zandalf becomes the context of the function and thus the value of this. Likewise, if we call the apply method on the same function and pass an object hellHound as argument:

```
1  attackWithFireBreath.apply(hellHound);
2  // => hell hound...
3  // => 'this' is hellHound
```

We can verify how the object hellHound becomes the context of the function and the value of this.

But, what happens if the original function has paremeters? Worry not! Both call and apply take additional arguments that are passed along to the original function. Take this function attackMany-WithFireBreath that unleashes a terrible breath of fire on many unfortunate targets:

---

[68]http://bit.ly/mdn-function-prototype

```
1  function attackManyWithFireBreath(){
2    var targets = Array.prototype.slice.call(arguments, 0);
3    console.log(this + " jumps towards " + targets.join(', ') +
4      " and unleashes his terrible breath of fire! (-3 hp, +fear)");
5  }
```

The `call` method let's you specify a list of arguments separated by commas in addition to the value of `this`:

```
1  attackManyWithFireBreath.call(hellHound, 'you', 'me', 'the milkman');
2  // => Hellhound jumps towards you, me, the milkman and unleashes
3  //     his terrible breath of fire! (-3 hp, +fear)
```

Likewise, `apply` takes an array of arguments:

```
1  attackManyWithFireBreath.apply(hellHound, ['me', 'you', 'irene']);
2  // => Hellhound jumps towards me, you, irene and
3  //     unleashes his terrible breath of fire! (-3 hp, +fear)
```

And that's how you can set the value of `this` explicitly. Let's recapitulate what we've learned so far:

1. Call a function in the context of an object and `this` will take the value of the object
2. Call a function without context and `this` will take the value of the `Window` object. Unless you are in *strict mode* in which case it will take the value of `undefined`.
3. Call a function using `call` and `apply` passing the context explicitly as an argument and `this` will take the value of whatever you pass in.

This Bound

As of ES5, the `Function` prototype also provides a very interesting method called `bind`. `bind` lets you create new functions that **always have a fixed context**, that is, a fixed value for `this` [69].

---

[69] Another cool use of `bind` is *partial application*, but we'll take a look at that when we get to the tome of functional programming.

Bind Doesn't Cause Side Effects

It is important to note that bind will not alter the original function at all. It will return a new function that is bound to the object given as an argument.

Let's use bind to set a fixed value for this in our original attackWithFireBreath function. bind will return a new function attackBound that will have this with a value of our choosing. In this case, it will be hellHound:

```
1  // As of ES5 we can bind the context of execution of a function
2  // FOR EVER
3  attackBound = attackWithFireBreath.bind(hellHound);
```

After using bind, the value of this is bound to the hellHound object even if you are not using the dot notation:

```
1  attackBound();
2  // => Hellhound jumps towards you and unleashes
3  //    his terrible breath of fire! (-3 hp, +fear)
4  // `this` is Hellhound even though I am not using the dot notation
```

Moreover, if you assign the attackBound method to another object and call it using the dot notation, the attackBound method is executed in the context of the original object hellHound. That is, after binding a function to a context with bind, the context will remain the same even after assigning the function to another object:

```
1   // the function is bound even if I give the function to another obje\
2   ct
3   zandalf.attackBound = attackBound;
4
5   zandalf.attackBound();
6   // => Hellhound ...
7   // `this` is Hellhound even though I am using dot notation
8   // with another object
```

Once a function is bound it is not possible to un-bound it nor re-bind it to another object:

```
1   // You cannot rebind a function that is bound
2   var attackReBound = attackBound.bind(zandalf);
3
4   attackReBound();
5   // => Hellhound ...
6
7   attackBound();
8   // => hellHound ...
```

But you can always use the original unbound function to create new bound versions through subsequent calls to bind with different contexts:

```
1   // But you can still bind the original
2   var attackRebound = attackWithFireBreath.bind(zandalf);
3   attackRebound();
4   // => zandalf...
```

Concluding This

In summary, this can take different values based on how a function is invoked. It can:

- Be an object if we call a function within an object with the dot notation

- Be the Window object or undefined (*strict mode*) if a function is invoked by itself
- Be whichever object we pass as argument to call or apply
- Be whichever object we pass as argument to bind.

If now that you are a *this-xpert* we go back to the original example you will be able to spot the problem at once. Since the updateUsers function is a callback, it is not invoked in the context of the UsersCatalog object. Callbacks are invoked as normal functions, and thus in the context of the Window object (or undefined in *strict mode*). Because of this, the value of this within updateUsers wouldn't be catalog but undefined[70].

Because this is not the catalog object, it doesn't have a users property and thus the resulting cannot read property of undefined error:

```
1   function UsersCatalog(type){
2     this.users = [];
3     getUsers()
4
5     function getUsers(){
6       $.getJSON('https://api.github.com/users')
7       .success(function(users){
8         this.users.push(users);
9         // BOOOOOOOM!!!!!
10        // => Uncaught TypeError:
11        //    Cannot read property 'push' of undefined
12        // 'this' in this context is the jqXHR object
13        // not our original object
14      });
15    }
16  }
17  var catalog = new UsersCatalog();
```

---

[70]In this particular case however, because we are using *jQuery* to perform an AJAX request, the value of this is *jQuery* jqXHR object, an object that represents the AJAX request itself (we can assume that *jQuery* calls the updateUsers callback in the context of a jqXHR object).

You can solve this issue in either of two ways. You can take advantage of JavaScript support for closures, declare a self variable that *"captures"* the value of this when it refers to the UsersCatalog object and use it within the closure function as depicted below (a very common pattern in JavaScript):

```
1   function UsersCatalogWithClosure(){
2     "use strict";
3     var self = this;
4
5     self.users = [];
6     getUsers()
7
8     function getUsers(){
9       $.getJSON('https://api.github.com/users')
10      .success(function(users){
11        self.users.push(users);
12        console.log('success!');
13      });
14    }
15  }
16  var catalog = new UsersCatalogWithClosure();
```

Or you can take advantage of bind and ensure that the function that you use as callback is bound to the object that you want:

```
1   //#2. Using bind
2   function UsersCatalogWithBind(){
3     "use strict";
4
5     this.users = [];
6     getUsers.bind(this)();
7
8     function getUsers(){
9       $.getJSON('https://api.github.com/users')
10      .success(updateUsers.bind(this));
11    }
12
13    function updateUsers(users){
14      this.users.push(users);
```

```
15      console.log('success with bind!');
16    }
17  }
18  var catalog = new UsersCatalogWithBind();
```

Later within the book, you'll see how **ES6 arrow functions** can also lend you a hand in this type of scenario.

Global Scope by Default and Namespacing in JavaScript

As you will come to appreciate by the end of the book, JavaScript has a minimalistic design. It has a limited number of primitive constructs that can be used and composed to achieve higher level abstractions and other constructs that are native to other languages. One of these constructs are **namespaces**.

What about ES6 Modules?

ES6 comes with modules which make this section somewhat obsolete. However, while we have now native modules there is no standard module loader yet. That is, we have a way to define modules but not a way to load them in the browser.

In order to do that you'll need to setup a front-end build pipeline with one of the existing community-driven module loaders which is not a trivial thing to do at this point. Because of that, **some of you may still appreciate this simple way to define your own namespaces.**

The remainder of this section will continue discussing *namespaces* in the absence of modules. Later in the series you'll learn everything about modules and how they help you manage, encapsulate and distribute your code.

Since we do not have the concept of *namespaces*, variables that are declared in a JavaScript file are part of the global scope where they are visible and accessible to every JavaScript file within your application. Yey! Party!

```
1  var dice = "d12";
2  dice;
3  // => d12
4  window.dice
5  // => d12
6  // ups... we are in the global scope/namespace
```

The problems with global variables are well known: they tightly couple different components of your application and they can cause name collisions. Imagine that you have several JavaScript files declaring variables with the same names but performing different tasks. Or imagine importing third party libraries that could overwrite your own variables. **Chaos and destruction!!** Because of these problems we want to completely avoid the use of global variables, yet we lack support for *namespaces* in JavaScript... *What to do?*

We can use objects to emulate the construct of namespaces. A commonly used pattern is depicted below where we use what we call an IIFE[71] (immediately invoked function expression) to create/augment a namespace:

---

[71]http://en.wikipedia.org/wiki/Immediately-invoked_function_expression

```
1   // IIFE - we invoke the function expression as soon as we declare it
2   (function(armory){
3       // the armory object acts as a namespace
4       // we can add properties to it
5       // these would constitute the API for
6       // the 'armory' module/namespace
7       armory.sword = {damage: 10, speed: 15};
8       armory.axe = {damage: 15, speed: 8};
9       armory.mace = {damage: 16, speed: 7};
10      armory.dagger = {damage: 5, speed: 20};
11
12      // additionally you could declare private variables and
13      // functions as well
14
15  // either augment or create the armory namespace
16  }(window.armory = window.armory || {} ));
17
18  console.log(armory.sword.damage);
19  // => 10
```

An immediately-invoked function expression is just that, a function expression that you invoke immediately. **By virtue of being a function it creates a new scope where you can safely have your variables and avoid name collisions with the outside world.** If you were to declare a variable with the same name of an existing variable in an outer scope, the new variable would just shadow the outer variable.

By immediately invoking the function you can extend the window.armory object with whichever properties you desire, creating a sort of public API for the armory object that becomes a namespace or module. A container where you can place properties and functions and expose them as services for the rest of your application.

We will come back to *namespacing* and higher level code organization in JavaScript within the tome on JavaScript modules.

Type Coercion Madness

In the basic ingredients of javascript-mancy you learned a little bit about type coercion in JavaScript. You learn how JavaScript provides the == and != **abstract equality operators** that let you perform loose equality between values and the === and !== operators that perform strict equality.

By using the first set of operators JavaScript will try to coerce the types being compared to a matching type before performing the comparison, whilst the second set of operators expect a matching type. You also learned how type coercion creates the concept of *falsey* and *truthy* by assigning true and false to different values and types when being converted to boolean.

I thought it would be interesting for you to learn a little bit more about this JavaScript feature and about its possible pitfalls.

JavaScript was designed to be an accessible language[72], a language that even a layman, someone with no prior programming experience could use to create interactive websites. A welcoming language that would help anyone to write their own web applications and solve their own problems. You can see this vision clearly in many of the features of JavaScript, even in some of the most controversial ones. If you think about it from this perspective, it doesn't feel so weird that the following statement evaluates to true:

```
1   > 42 == '42'
2   // => true
```

For is not 42 equal to '42'? Don't both refer to the same number? Does it really matter that they have different types? And so we have implicit conversion of types.

In my experience, taking advantage of type coercion usually results in more terse code:

---

[72]Check this awesome jsJabber chapter to learn more about the origins of JavaScript from the very illustrious Brendan Eich http://bit.ly/js-origin.

```
1   // as opposed to (troll !== null && troll !== undefined)
2   > if (troll) {
3       // do stuff
4   }
```

Taking advantage of the strict equality usually results in more correct, less bug-prone code:

```
1   > if (troll !== null && troll !== undefined){
2   // do stuff
3   }
```

In the first case the condition will be satisfied as long as troll has a truthy value: It could be an object, an array, a string, a number different than 0. In the second case, the condition will be satisfied whenever troll is not null nor undefined (so even it troll is equal to 0 as opposed to the previous example). **Expressiveness or correctness, choose the one that you prefer.**

The truthy and falsey values for the most common types are as follow (note how we use the !! to explicitly convert every value to booleans). Both arrays and objects are truthy, even when they are empty:

```
1   > !![1,2,3]
2   // => true
3   > !![]
4   // => true
5   > !!{message: 'hello world'}
6   // => true
7   > !!{}
8   // => true
```

A non-empty string is truthy while an empty string is falsey:

```
1   > !!"hellooooo"
2   // => true
3   > !!""
4   // => false
```

Numbers are truthy but for 0 that is falsey:

```
1   > !!42
2   // => true
3   > !!0
4   // => false
```

undefined and null are always falsey:

```
1   > !!undefined
2   // => false
3   > !!null
4   // => false
```

Using JavaScript in Strict Mode

From ES5 onwards you can use strict mode[73] to get a better experience with JavaScript. One of the main goals of strict mode is to prevent you from falling into common JavaScript pitfalls by making the JavaScript runtime more proactive in throwing errors instead of causing silent ones or unwanted effects.

Take the example of the value of this in callbacks. Instead of setting the value of this to the Window object, when you use **strict mode** the value of this becomes undefined. This little improvement prevents you from accessing the Window object or extending it by mistake, and will alert you with an error as soon as you try to do it. **Short feedback loops and failing fast are sure recipes for success.**

Other improvements that come with *strict mode* are:

---

[73]http://bit.ly/mdn-strict-mode

- trying to create a variable without declaring it (with var, let or const) will throw an error. Without strict mode it will add a property to the Window object.
- trying to assign a variable to NaN, or to a read-only or non-writable property within an object throws an exception
- trying to delete non-deletable properties within an object throws an exception
- trying to have duplicated names as arguments throws a syntax error
- and more explicit errors that will help you spot bugs faster

Additionally with strict mode enabled the JavaScript runtime is free to make certain assumptions and perform optimizations that will make your code run faster. If you want to learn more about the nitty-gritty of strict mode I recommend that you take a look at the MDN (Mozilla Developer Network)[74], the best JavaScript resource in the web.

Enabling Strict Mode

You can enable strict mode by writing 'strict mode'; at the top of a JavaScript file. This will enable strict mode for the whole file:

```
1   'strict mode';
2   // my code ...
3   var pouch = {};
```

Alternatively, you can use the *strict mode* declaration at the top of a function. This will result in the *strict mode* only being applied within that function:

---

[74]http://bit.ly/mdn-strict-mode

```
1   (function(){
2     'strict mode';
3     // my code ...
4     var bag = {};
5
6   }());
```

Wrapping your *strict mode* declarations inside a function will prevent the *strict mode* from being applied to code that may not be prepared to handle *strict mode*. This can happen when concatenating *strict mode* scripts with *non-strict mode* scripts like external third party libraries outside of your control.

ES6 modules always use strict mode semantics.

Concluding

In this chapter you learned about the weirdest bits of JavaScript, the mysterious JavaScript Arcana. You started the chapter by reviewing parts of the JavaScript Arcana that you read about in previous chapters: function scope and variable hoisting, array-like objects and function overloading.

You continued taking a look at the sneaky this keyword, and understood how its value depends on the context in which a function is executed:

- If you invoke a function as a method using the dot notation, the this value will be the object that holds that method.
- If you call a function directly the value of this will be the Window object (or undefined in strict mode).
- If you call a function using either call, apply or bind, the value of this will be set to the object that you pass as argument to either of these functions.

- You can use `bind` to create a new version of a function that is bound to a specific object. That is, in that new funtion `this` becomes the object for all eternity.

You saw how JavaScript assumes global scope by default and how you can achieve a similar solution to namespaces by using objects to represent them and organize your code. You examined the concept of IIFE (Immediately Invoked Function Expression) and how you can use it to create an isolated scope to declare your variables and add them to a namespace object.

After that you reviewed type coercion in JavaScript to finally wrap the chapter examining **strict mode**, a more restricted version of JavaScript that attempts to help you find bugs faster by failing more loudly.

```
/*
The small group starts walking up the mountain trail slowly.
The path becomes narrower and steeper as they gain altitude,
the air colder and crispier until it starts snowing. All of
the sudden the group is surrounded by a thick mist that removes
any sense of time or orientation.

The group continues walking for what feels like an eternity.
Suddenly Bandalf stops. This makes Zandalf crash into him,
Randalf into Zandalf and Mooleen into Randalf, Zandalf and
Bandalf. Ordinarily this wouldn't have been a problem if it
weren't for the six sand golems, the crazy monkey, the
pterodactyl and the dozen of creatures that were following
right behind.
*/

mooleen.says("That was awkward");
bandalf.says("We're here!");

/*
As it by art of magic the mist starts disolving revealing
an inmense cavern.
*/

randalf.says("Welcome to The Caves of Infinity, " +
             "headquarters of the Resistance, last remnant " +
```

```
                "of the High Order of JavaScript-mancy")
    randalf.says("Now we'll start your real training");

    mooleen.says("Super");
```

Exercises

 Experiment JavaScriptmancer!

You can experiment with these exercises and some possible solutions in this jsFiddle[75] or downloading the source code from GitHub[76].

Find The Bug! Get the JavaScript-NomiCon!

The following piece of code has a bug. Fix the problem and gain access to the oh-so-powerful JavaScript-NomiCon! The most valued treaty of JavaScriptmancy known to men, elves, dwarves and gnomes alike:

```
1   function LibraryOfTheHighOrder(){
2     this.books = [];
3
4     this.summonBooks = function(){
5       $.getJSON('https://api.myjson.com/bins/3tp73')
6         .then(function updateBooks(books){
7           this.books.push(...books);
8           // caBOOOOOOM!!!!
9           // ERROOOOORRRR!!!
10          // Cannot read property push of undefined
11          for(let book of books){
12            console.log(book.name + ": " + book.type);
13          }
14        });
15    };
16  }
17  var library = new LibraryOfTheHighOrder();
18  library.summonBooks();
```

Solution

```
1   function LibraryOfTheHighOrder(){
2     this.books = [];
3
4     this.summonBooks = function(){
5       $.getJSON('https://api.myjson.com/bins/3tp73')
6         .then(function updateBooks(books){
7           this.books.push(...books);
8           for(let book of books){
9             console.log(book.name + ": " + book.type);
10          }
```

```
11          }.bind(this));
12      };
13  }
14  var library = new LibraryOfTheHighOrder();
15  library.summonBooks();
16  // => JavaScript-NomiCon: treaty of the dark and arcane arts
17  //      of JavaSCript-mancy
18  //  30 minute meals with Jamie Oliver: comfort food that
19  //      you can cook at home!
20  //  Pride and Prejudice: Novel
21
22  mooleen.says('Yes! Pride and Prejudice! I love that one!');
```

Protect The Library From Name Collisions!

Protect the library from name collisions by creating a new namespace called javascriptmacy.

If you are planning on using ES6 modules you can safely ignore this exercise.

Solution

```
1   (function(javascriptmancy){
2       javascriptmancy.LibraryOfTheHighOrder = LibraryOfTheHighOrder;
3
4       function LibraryOfTheHighOrder(){
5         this.books = [];
6         this.summonBooks = function(){
7           $.getJSON('https://api.myjson.com/bins/3tp73')
8             .then(function updateBooks(books){
9                this.books.push(...books);
10               for(let book of books){
11                 console.log(book.name + ": " + book.type);
12               }
13             }.bind(this));
14       };
```

```
15      }
16    }(window.javascriptmancy = window.javascriptmancy || {}));
17    var li = new window.javascriptmancy.LibraryOfTheHighOrder();
18    console.log(li);
19    // => LibraryOfTheHighOrder {books: Array[0]}
```

There's a Hard To Detect Bug In This Snippet! Strict Mode To the Rescue!

Enable strict mode in this function and find out the error

```
1    (function(){
2       secretBook = 'Diary of Mooleen';
3    }());
```

Solution

```
1    (function(){
2      "use strict";
3      secretBook = 'diary of mooleen';
4      // => Uncaught ReferenceError: secretBook is not defined;
5      // We were adding a property to the window object!!! :O
6    }());
```

A Guide to Strings, Finding the Right Words and Proper Spell Intonation

Klaatu...
verata...
n...
Necktie.
Nectar. Nickel. Noodle.

    - Ash
    Epic Hero of Ages

```
/*

Days and weeks pass and Mooleen continues training in the magic arts
of JavaScriptmancy. One fine morning...

*/

randalf.says('Excellent!');
randalf.says('The next step of your training is to do The Trials');
randalf.says('Completing The Trials will make you ' +
             'a true JavaScript-mancer');

mooleen.says('What are The Trials?');
randalf.says('The first rule of The Trials: ' +
             'You do not talk about The Trials');

mooleen.says('All right but where do I start?');
randalf.says('The second rule of The Trials: ' +
             'You do not talk about the Trials');
mooleen.says('Aaaaah');

/*

Randalf starts doing very weird gestures with his face. It looks
like he is getting a stroke... or wait... it looks like he's
pointing to somewhere...

*/

mooleen.picksUp(pieceOfScrappedPaper);
randalf.says('Aha! I see that you have found the first clue! ' +
             'Impressive!');

mooleen.reads(pieceOfScrappedPaper);
// => To Start The Trials Find The Right Words You Must
```

Find the Right Words You Must

Experiment JavaScriptmancer!!

You can experiment with all examples in this chapter directly within this jsBin example[77] or downloading the source code from GitHub[78].

The use of words, text and text manipulation is commonplace in applications today. Often times applications will provide some sort of user interface as a way to allow user interaction. This UI will contain a myriad of textual information in various forms like labels, tooltips, help texts, text-based content, etc. Even applications that don't expose a user interface will often log information to the filesystem or to analytics services for troubleshooting and monitoring.

JavaScript, like many other languages, has a primitive type that catters to all your text representation and manipulation needs, the string. In this chapter you'll learn all you need to know about strings in JavaScript and the exciting new features that come with ES6: template literals and tags.

Let's start with the basics first!

The Basic Of Strings

You create a string by either using single ' or double quotes ".

---

[77]http://bit.ly/javascriptmancy-strings
[78]https://github.com/vintharas/javascriptmancy

```
1   // you can create a string using double quotes
2   > typeof "Klaatu... verata... n... Necktie. Nectar. Nickel. Noodle."
3   // => string
4
5   // or using single quotes
6   > typeof 'Klaatu... verata... n... Necktie. Nectar. Nickel. Noodle.'
7   // => string
```

You will often use a single quoted ' string to include " double quotes inside the string and vice versa:

```
1   // you'll often use a ' to escape "
2   > "Ya ain't gonna need that fairy dust!"
3   // => ya ain't gonna need that fairy dust!
4
5   // and vice versa
6   > 'it was, in essence, a sophisticated heat beam which we called a "\
7   laser".'
8   // => it was, in essence, a sophisticated heat
9   //     beam which we call a "laser".
```

You can concatenate two strings using the + operator:

```
1   > "Three rings " + "for the elves"
2   // => three rings for the elves
```

The + operator is often used to inject values within a string and thus create text based on data:

```
1   > var conan = {toString: function() {return 'Conan, the cimmerian';}}
2   > conan + " was a famous hero of a past age"
3   // => Conan, the cimmerian was a famous hero of a past age
```

You can also create multiline strings using the same operator:

```
1  > "There are few men with more blood on their hands than me. " +
2  "None, that I know of. " +
3  "The Bloody-Nine they call me, my enemies, and there's a lot of 'em"
4  // => "There are few men with more blood on their hands than me.
5  //     None, that I know of. The Bloody-Nine they call me, my
6  //     enemies, and there's a lot of 'em"
```

Or, alternatively, with a backslash at the end of each line \:

```
1  > "There are few men with more blood on their hands than me.\
2  None, that I know of.\
3  The Bloody-Nine they call me, my enemies, and there's a lot of 'em"
4  // => "There are few men with more blood on their hands than me.
5  //     None, that I know of. The Bloody-Nine they call me, my
6  //     enemies, and there's a lot of 'em"
```

Additionally, you can insert new lines using the newline character '\n':

```
1  > "There are few men with more blood on their hands than me.\n None,\
2  that I know of.\n The Bloody-Nine they call me, my enemies, and the\
3  re's a lot of 'em"
4  // => "There are few men with more blood on their hands than me.
5  //     None, that I know of.
6  //     The Bloody-Nine they call me, my enemies, and there's a
7  //     lot of 'em"
```

As you may have deduced from the previous example, JavaScript uses the backslash '\' as escape character:

```
1  > "\""
2  // => "
3  > '\''
4  // => '
```

Now that you've got a better grasp of strings in JavaScript, let's take a look at the different operations you can perform on them.

Are Strings Arrays of Characters?

JavaScript strings are not arrays of characters, they behave more like array-like objects. They have a length property, they can be enumerated and indexed but they lack most of the methods of an array. They are also immutable.

> Just like in C#, strings are immutable. Performing operations on a string doesn't change the current string but creates a new one. Attempting to change the value of a string, for instance, by trying to replace the value at an specific index will be ignored.

```
1   var justDoIt = 'Just DO IT!';
2
3   // they have a length property
4   console.log('length of justDoIt: ' + justDoIt.length);
5   // => length of justDoIt: 11
6
7   // they can be enumerated
8   for (var c in justDoIt) console.log(justDoIt[c]);
9   // => J
10  // => u
11  // => etc
12
13  // they don't have array methods
14  console.log(justDoIt.forEach)
15  // => undefined
```

Even though strings are not arrays, you can use some of the array functions on a string by borrowing them from Array.prototype. For instance, you can traverse each character in a string using forEach:

```
1  > Array.prototype.forEach.call(justDoIt,
2                        function(c){console.log(c);})
3  // => J
4  // => u
5  // => etc...
```

Or inject an arbitrary string between each character with `join`:

```
1  Array.prototype.join.call(justDoIt, '--')
2  // => J--u--s--t-- --D--O-- --I--T--!
```

However, if we try to use `reverse` it throws an error:

```
1  Array.prototype.reverse.call(justDoIt);
2  // BOOM!
3  // TypeError: cannot assign to read only property '0'....
```

The error message gives us some hints as to why `reverse` doesn't work: The implementation of reverse is trying to do an in-place string reversal. Because strings are immutable, attempting to replace the first character in a string with the last one causes an error and therefore the `"cannot assign to read only property '0'"`.

Remember, you can use any array methods on strings as long as they don't attempt to mutate the original string.

Performing Operations with strings

In addition to these array methods, the string type also provides its own series of methods to help you perform the most common text operations.

You can concatenate strings with `concat` just like you did with the + operator:

```
1  > String.prototype.concat('hello my nemesis', 'we meet again')
2  // => hello my nemesis we meet again
3
4  > justDoIt.concat(' - Shia Labeaouf')
5  // => Just DO IT! - Shia Labeaouf
```

You can obtain an uppercase or lowercase version of an existing string using toUpperCase and toLowerCase:

```
1  console.log(justDoIt.toUpperCase());
2  // => JUST DO IT!
3
4  console.log(justDoIt.toLowerCase());
5  // => just do it!
```

You can extract a character at a specific position with chartAt:

```
1  > justDoIt.charAt(0)
2  // => j
```

The indexOf method returns the position of the first occurrence of a piece of text within a string.

```
1  > justDoIt.indexOf('DO')
2  // => 5
```

You'll often see it used to find out whether a piece of text exists in a string by comparing it to -1:

```
1  // indexOf returns `-1` when it can't find the piece of text
2  > justDoIt.indexOf('DO') !== -1
3  // => true
4  > justDoIt.indexOf('Sand castle') !== -1
5  // => false
```

Alternatively you can use the search method. It is an enhanced version of indexOf that allows you to specify what you are looking for using a regular expression:

```
1  > justDoIt.search(/DO/)
2  // => 5
```

match is, in turn, an enhanced version of search that lets you find
multiple matches within a string according to a regular expression
of your choice:

```
1  > justDoIt.match(/DO/)
2  // => ["DO"]
3
4  > justDoIt.match(/DO.*/)
5  // => ["DO IT!"]
```

The replace method lets you replace a piece of text with another
one of your own choosing:

```
1  > justDoIt.replace('DO IT!', 'DANCE!')
2  // => Just DANCE!
```

Since replace also allows for regular expressions, you can match
all occurrences of a substring and replace them at once. Just use the
g flag (which stands for *global*):

```
1  > 'a dragon is a creature that can breathe fire'
2    .replace(/a /g, 'the ')
3  // => the dragon is the creature that can breathe fire
```

The substr and substring methods let you extract bits of text from
an array by specifying indexes. The former expects the *start index*
and the *length* of the substring whilst the latter expects the *starting*
and *ending indexes*:

```
1  // String.prototype.substr(startIndex, length)
2  > 'a dragon is a creature that can breathe fire'.substr(2, 6)
3  // => dragon
4
5  // String.prototype.substring(startIndex, endIndex)
6  > 'a dragon is a creature that can breathe fire'.substring(2, 6)
7  // => drag
```

You can split a string in several pieces using the split method. The resulting pieces of splitting the string are returned as items of an array:

```
1  > 'a dragon is a creature that can breathe fire'.split(' ');
2  // => ["a", "dragon", "is", "a", "creature", "that",
3  //    "can", "breathe", "fire"]
```

The split and join methods make it dead easy to convert a string into an array and *vice versa*. Using them will allow you to take advantage of both the string and array methods without limitations. You have a string and want to use the Array.prototype.map method? Convert it into an array via split, perform whichever operations you need and then use join to get your string back.

```
1  > 'a dragon is a creature that can breathe fire'.split(' ')
2    .join(' ');
3  // => 'a dragon is a creature that can breathe fire'
```

New String Features in ES6

ES6 brings a lot of exciting new features to strings:

- Several new helpful methods like startsWith and endsWith.
- A complete overhaul of how we define strings in JavaScript with **Template Literals**[79]. Template Literals provide a much

---

[79] *Template literals* are also known as *String Templates*

better support for string interpolation, multiline strings, HTML-friendly strings and the ability to create reusable string formatters called **tags**.

ES6 Brings Some New String Methods

After reading the previous sections you may have missed three methods you often use in C#: Contains, StartsWith and EndsWith. Well, worry no more because ES6 brings all these new methods to JavaScript strings:

The startsWith and endsWith methods work just like in C#. The first one verifies whether a string starts with a given substring and the latter checks whether or not a string ends with a given piece of text:

```
1  > 'thunder and lightning!'.startsWith('thunder')
2  // => true
3  > 'thunder and lightning!'.endsWith('lightning!')
4  // => true
```

The includes method performs the same function as C# Contains by checking whether or not a piece of text is contained within a string:

```
1  > 'thunder and lightning!'.includes('thunder')
2  // => true
3  > 'thunder and lightning!'.includes('lightning!')
4  // => true
5  > 'thunder and lightning!'.includes('and')
6  // => true
```

Note how using the includes method provides a much better developer experience and readable code than the indexOf method from previous sections.

Finally, ES6 brings the repeat method that allows you to create a new string by repeating an existing string a specific number of times:

```
1   > 'NaN'.repeat(10) + ' BatMan!'
2   // => NaNNaNNaNNaNNaNNaNNaNNaNNaNNaN BatMan!
```

The Awesomeness of ES6 Template Literals

ES6 template literals provide a new and very powerful way of working with strings. You can create a string using a template literal by wrapping some text between backticks:

```
1   > `Rain fire and destruction upon thy enemies!`
2   // => Rain fire an destruction upon thy enemies!
```

Template literals let you use both single and double quotes freely without the need to escape them:

```
1   > `Rain fire n' destruction upon thy "enemies"!`
2   //=> Rain fire n' destruction upon thy "enemies"!
```

One of the greatest strengths of template literals is that you can inject values in a very straightforward and readable fashion. By using the notation ${target} inside the template literal you can include the value of the variable target in the resulting string. This is also know as **string interpolation**:

```
1   let target = 'Sauron', spell = 'balefire'
2   console.log(`Blast ${target} with ${spell}!`)
3   // => blast Sauron with balefire!
4
5   // prior to ES6 we would've needed to write:
6   // 'blast' + target + 'with' + spell
```

You can include any variable that is accessible within the scope where the template literal is declared. Say goodbye to concatenating strings and variables with the + operator. Bye and farewell!

Additionally, you are not limited to using variables when doing string interpolation. **You can use any valid JavaScript expression.** For instance, you could call a function:

```
1   function calculateDamage(modifier){
2     return Math.round(modifier*Math.random())
3   }
4   console.log(`Blast ${target} with ${spell} making
5             ${calculateDamage(10)} damage`)
6   // => Blast Sauron with balefire making 4 damage
```

Or perform arithmetics:

```
1   console.log(`1 + 1 is not ${1+1} ===> SYNERGY!!!`);
2   // => 1 + 1 is not 2 ===> SYNERGY!!!
```

Another great improvement from template literals over vanilla strings are multiline strings. With template literals, if you want to have a multiline string, you just write a multiline string. It's that easy:

```
1   let multiline = `I start in this line,
2   and then I go to the next,
3   because there are few things in life,
4   that I like best`
5   console.log(multiline);
6   // => I start on this line,
7   // and then I go to the next...
```

Tags

Tags are a very interesting feature of template literals. They allow you to customize how a specific template literal gets parsed into a string.

To apply a tag you prepend its name to the template literal:

```
1   // appreciate how the orcSpeech tag appears before
2   // the string template
3   let clothes = 'boots';
4   let orcLikesBoots = orcSpeech`I like those ${clothes} that you're we\
5   aring!`
```

In this example we have created a tag orcSpeech to parse any piece of speech into the way orcs speak (who I've heard speak numerous times). When we evaluate the resulting string we can verify how the tag has transformed the original text into garbled orc speech:

```
1   console.log(orcLikesBoots);
2   // => I like thossse bootsss that you'rre wearring!
```

How did that happen? Well, a tag is merely a function and what you see above is the result of calling that function with the string literal as input.

More specifically, a tag function takes each string literal of a template and each substitution (the ${} tokens) and returns the parsed string after composing literals and substitution together:

```
1   function orcSpeech(literals, ...substitutions){
2     // do your magic
3     // return parsed string
4   }
```

In the previous example the literals and substitutions would be:

```
1   literals => "I like those", " that you're wearing"
2   substitutions => ${clothes}
```

The implementation of the orcSpeech tag function could look like this:

```
1   function orcSpeech(literals, ...substitutions){
2     console.log(literals); // => ['I like those ',
3                            //      ' that you're wearing']
4     console.log(substitutions); // => ['boots']
5
6     let phrase = literals[0];
7     substitutions.forEach(function(s, idx){
8       phrase += `${s}${literals[idx+1]}`
9     });
10
11    return phrase.replace(/s/g, 'sss').replace(/r/g, 'rr')
12  }
```

Where we compose literals and substitutions and then replace s and r with sss and rr respectively giving the original sentence that rough touch characteristic of orcs, goblins and other creatures of darkness.

```
1   console.log(orcLikesBoots);
2   // => I like thossse bootsss that you'rre wearring!
```

When the tag is applied to a template literal like you saw above, the effect is the same as that of calling the tag function with the literals and substitutions. So this down here would be the same:

```
1   let orcLikesBoots =
2       orcSpeech`I like those ${clothes} that you're wearing!`
```

As calling orcSpeech as a function:

```
1   let orcLikesBoots =
2       orcSpeech(['I like those ', " that you're wearing!"], 'boots');
```

In addition to what you've seen thus far, tags also give you the possibility to access the raw string literals. Having access to raw literals lets you customize even how you parse special characters such as *end of line* /n, *tabs* /t, etc.

We can illustrate this with an example of a hypothetical orc-SpeechRaw tag:

```
1  function orcSpeechRaw(literals, ...substitutions){
2    console.log(literals.raw); // => ['I like those ',
3                               //       ' that you're wearing']
4    console.log(substitutions); // => ['boots']
5
6    let phrase = literals.raw[0];
7    substitutions.forEach(function(s, idx){
8      phrase += `${s}${literals.raw[idx+1]}`
9    });
10
11   return phrase.replace(/s/g, 'sss').replace(/r/g, 'rr')
12 }
```

The literals array exposes a raw property that contains the same information than the literals array but in raw format. If you take a look at the output of the *non-raw* tag orcSpeech:

```
1  console.log(
2    orcSpeech`I like those ${clothes}\n\n that you're \twearing!`)
3  // => ["I like those ", "
4  //
5  // that you're  wearing!"]
6  // ['boots']
7  // I like thossse bootsss
8  //
9  // that you'rre  wearring
```

You'll be able to appreciate how the special characters have been transformed into whitespace. If you then take a look at the output of the *raw* tag orcSpeechRaw:

```
1  console.log(
2    orcSpeechRaw`I like those ${clothes}\n\n that you're \twearing!`)
3
4  // => ["I like those ", "\n\n that you're \twearing!"]
5  // ["boots"]
6  // "I like thossse bootsss\n\n that you'rre \twearring!"
```

You'll see how the special characters are available in the `literals.raw` array.

In summary, **tags give you the opportunity of creating reusable formatting functions or even small text manipulation DSL's (Domain Specific Languages) for your web applications.** For instance, an interesting application of tagged template literals could be building your own HTML templating engine:

```
1  let inventory = [
2    {name: 'rusty sword', price: 2},
3    {name: 'health potion', price: 10},
4    {name: 'medallion of Valor', price: 300}
5  ];
6
7  console.log(ul`
8  ${inventory.map(function(item){
9    return li`${item.name}: ${item.price} silvers`
10 })}`)
11 // => "<ul>
12 // <li>rusty sword: 2 silvers</li>
13 // <li>health potion: 10 silvers</li>
14 // <li>medallion of Valor: 300 silvers</li>
15 // </ul>"
```

Where we would create a `ul` and `li` tags that would be an extension over the more generic `html` tag:

```
1   function html(literals, ...substitutions){
2     let phrase = literals[0];
3     substitutions.forEach(function(s, idx){
4
5       // if array convert to string
6       if (Array.isArray(s)) s = s.join('\n');
7
8       phrase += `${s}${literals[idx+1]}`;
9       // you could also add some special characters processing
10      // for parsing non HTML compliant characters like &
11    });
12    return phrase;
13  }
14
15  function ul(literals, ...substitutions){
16    return `<ul>${html(literals, ...substitutions)}</ul>`;
17  }
18
19  function li(literals, ...substitutions){
20    return `<li>${html(literals, ...substitutions)}</li>`;
21  }
```

The code when applying the templating engine could be simplified
further if we used ES6 *arrow functions* which we'll cover in the next
chapter. But there's nothing preventing us from taking a sneak-peek
right?

```
1   ul`${inventory.map(item => li`${item.name}:${item.price} coins`)}`
```

Beautiful!

String Cheatsheet

Basics

Basics	description
`'a string','"a string"`	Create a string
`"Y'all", 'the "laser"'`	Escape single and double quotes
`"You are: " + status`	Concatenate strings and values using +
`"lalalala too long" + "lala"`	Concatenate for multiline strings
`"lalalala too long\` `  lala"`	Create multiline strings using \ at the end of each row
`"this is\n a new line"`	Special characters start with \

String Methods

String Methods	description
`concat(str1, str2, ...)` `-"this is".concat(" excellent")`	Concatenate strings `-"this is excellent"`
`toUpperCase()` `-"abracadabra".toUpperCase()`	Uppercase all characters in a string `-"ABRACADABRA"`
`toLowerCase()` `-"SHAZAM!".toLowerCase()`	Lowercase all characters in a string `-"shazam"`
`charAt(position)` `-"Just DO IT!".charAt(0)`	Get character at given position `-"J"`
`indexOf(string)` `-"JUST DO IT!".indexOf("DO")`	Gets position of the first occurrence of a string `-5`
`search(regExp)` `-"JUST DO IT!".search(/DO/)`	Gets position of the first occurrence of a regular expression
`match(regExp)`	Find strings matching a regex

String Methods	description
- `"JUST DO IT!".search(/DO.*/)`	- `['DO', 'DO IT']`
`replace(str or regex, str)`	Find and replace using a string or regex
- `"JUST DO IT!".replace('DO IT!', 'DANCE!')`	- `"JUST DANCE!"`
`split(separator)`	Separate string into an array of items using a separator
- `"JUST DO IT".split(" ")`	- `["JUST", "DO", "IT"]`

ES6 String Methods

String Methods	description
`startsWith(str)`	Check whether a string starts with some text
- `"JUST DO IT".startsWith("JUST")`	
`endsWith(str)`	Check whether a string ends with some text
- `"JUST DO IT".endsWith("IT")`	
`includes(str)`	Check whether a string contains some text
- `"JUST DO IT".includes("DO")`	
`repeat(times)`	Create a new string by repeating the current string N times
- `"Na".repeat(3)`	- `"NaNaNa"`

ES6 Template Literals

Template Literals	description
`` `new literal` ``	Create template literal - `"new literal"`
`` `I have ${coins} coins` ``	Variable interpolation - `"I have 10 coints"`
`` `I have ${1+1} coins` ``	Evaluate expressions - `"I have 2 coins"`
`` li`purse` ``	Use of tags - `"<li>purse</li>"`

Concluding

And we got to the end! In this chapter you learned a ton about strings in JavaScript, you saw how strings are a primitive type which behave in a very similar way to C# strings. They are immutable and performing operations on them or changing them in some fashion results in a new string being created.

Strings behave like array-like objects and although they don't have array methods, you can apply the non-destructive array methods on them by virtue of using `call` and `apply`. In addition to this, strings have a lot of methods that you can use to perform operations like concatenation, matching, searching, extracting and replacing pieces of text.

ES6 brings new string methods like `startsWith` and `endsWith` but more importantly it comes with a new way to work with strings in the form of template literals. Template literals are a great improvement over vanilla strings because they let you inject values within strings in a very straightforward fashion and make creating multiline strings seamless. Tags are a great companion to template literals that let you customize how a template literal is parsed into a string opening an endless world of possibilities when it comes to text manipulation in JavaScript.

```
mooleen.says('Abracadabra!');
// nothing happens

mooleen.says('42!');
// nothing

mooleen.says('By the Power of Grayskull, I HAVE THE POWER!!!');
// still nothing

mooleen.says('Dammit! What can it be?!');
```

Exercises

Experiment JavaScriptmancer!

You can experiment with these exercises and some possible solutions in this jsFiddle[80] or downloading the source code from GitHub[81].

Word Barrage!

Create a multiline string (a string that spans several lines) in three different ways

Solution

```
1   let magicWords1 = "Roses are grey, " +
2   "Violets are grey, " +
3   "I'm a dog";
4
```

---

[80]http://bit.ly/javascriptmancy-strings-exercises
[81]https://github.com/vintharas/javascriptmancy-code-samples

```
5    let magicWords2 =  "Roses are grey,\
6    Violets are grey,\
7    I'm a dog";
8
9    // this keeps whitespace
10   let magicWords3 = `Roses are grey,
11   Violets are grey,
12   I'm a dog`;
```

Rack Your Brains!

Mooleen has no idea what the magic words could be so she starts thinking, and reflecting, racking her brains for a long, long time. Write a function that fulfills the following snippet using ES5:

```
1    rackBrains(12);
2    // => mooleen racks her brains for 12 long minutes
```

Solution

```
1    function rackBrains(minutes){
2      console.log('Mooleen racks her brain for ' + minutes + ' long minu\
3    tes');
4    }
5    rackBrains(12);
6    // => Mooleen racks her brain for 12 long minutes
```

Rack Your Brains With ES6!

Update the rackBrains function to use ES6 template literals.

Solution

```
1   function rackBrainsES6(minutes){
2     console.log(`Mooleen racks her brain for ${minutes} long minutes`);
3   }
4   rackBrainsES6(12);
5   // => Mooleen racks her brain for 12 long minutes
```

 ## Create The Moolen DSL with Tags!

Use tags to create a Mooleen Domain Specific Language. It should work like this:

```
1   console.log(rackBrains`for 15 minutes`);
2   // => mooleen racks her brains for 12 long minutes
3   console.log(says`what is going on?`);
4   // => mooleen says: "What is going on?"
```

Solution

```
1   function rackBrains(literals, ...substitutions){
2     let phrase = literals[0];
3     substitutions.forEach(function(s, idx){
4       phrase += `${s}${literals[idx+1]}`
5     });
6     return `Mooleen racks her brains ${phrase}`;
7   }
8
9   function says(literals, ...substitutions){
10    let phrase = literals[0];
11    substitutions.forEach(function(s, idx){
12      phrase += `${s}${literals[idx+1]}`
13    });
14    return `Mooleen says: ${phrase}`;
15  }
```

```
16
17   console.log(rackBrains`for 15 minutes`);
18   // => mooleen racks her brains for 12 long minutes
19   console.log(says`what is going on?`);
20   // => mooleen says: "What is going on?"
```

Count the Occurrences!

Create a count function that counts the ocurrence of a piece of text in a string and uses at least one string method.

Solution

```
1    function count(phrase, text){
2      return phrase.match(new RegExp(text, 'g')).length;
3    }
4    let phrase = "in this city, in this land, there's no place for you";
5    let inCount = count(phrase, "in");
6    console.log(`There are ${inCount} 'in' in the phrase`);
7    // => There are 2 'in' in the phrase
8
9    mooleen.says('Wait... I got it!');
10   mooleen.says('Klaatu barada nikto!!');
11   /*
12     Mooleen is now standing in the middle of a spindly stone bridge
13     with seemingly no end and no beginning.
14   */
15   gort.says('Welcome to The Trials!');
```

Upgrading Your Everyday JavaScript Magic With ES6 - Destructuring

There's always a better way
to solve a problem
You just haven't found it...

...yet

- Torvik Knivsa
  Alchemist

```
mooleen.says('Yes!!!');
mooleen.says('Wait... This is really creepy...');

gort.says('Welcome to The Trials!');

mooleen.says(`Did you know that I'm afraid of heights?`);

gort.says('Welcome to The Trials!');

/*

Mooleen approaches Gort who remains completely still with
a very inhuman smile in his face. She extends her arm to touch
him but her hand slips right through gort. Suddenly he vanishes.

*/

mooleen.says(`Hmm... Alright, I suppose I'll just walk to the
             right... or left`);
/*
Mooleen walks for about 30 seconds when suddenly gort appears
right in front of her.
*/

gort.says(`Welcome to this interactive tutorial by @vintharas!`);
gort.says('Say `Start` to start the tutorial');

mooleen.says('Ehem... Start?');

gort.says(`Welcome to the Future! ECMAScript 6!`);
```

Welcome to the Future! ECMAScript 6

Welcome back JavaScriptmancer! So far in this first part of the book you've seen several great ES6 features:

- In The Basics Of JavaScript Functions you learned about the new let and const keyword that let you declare block scoped variables.

- In Useful Function Patterns: Default Parameters you saw how ES6 brings default parameters to JavaScript. They have a very similar syntax to C# and let you use any valid expression as a default value, even objects and functions.
- In Useful Function Patterns: Multiple Arguments you found out about *rest* parameters. They work just like C# `params` and let you define functions that take an arbitrary number of arguments.
- In On the Art of Summoning Servants and Critters, Or Understanding The Basics of JavaScript Objects you discovered how ES6 simplifies object initializers with the shorthand syntax (both for properties and methods). You also learned about ES6 *symbols* and how they can help you with data privacy.
- In A Guide to Strings, Finding the Right Words and Proper Spell Intonation you dived into ES6 Template Literals and learned how they revolutionize the way we work with strings in JavaScript. You also took a look at tags and the new string methods.

In this and the upcoming chapters we will introduce other great ES6 features that you can use in your everyday JavaScript: destructuring, arrow functions and the spread operator. It's time to upgrade your JavaScript wizardry to ES6!

Destructure All The Things!

Experiment JavaScriptmancer!!

You can experiment with all examples in this chapter directly within this jsBin example[82] or downloading the source code from GitHub[83].

---

[82]http://bit.ly/javascriptmancy-es6-destructuring
[83]https://github.com/vintharas/javascriptmancy-code-samples

ES6 comes with a very handy new feature called *destructuring*. *Destructuring* lets you extract parts of information from within objects and other data structures in a very natural and concise manner.

Destructuring Objects

In the simplest of use cases, you can initialize variables from properties of objects using the following syntax:

```
1  let pouch = {coins: 10};
2  let {coins} = pouch;
```

This is equivalent to:

```
1  let coins = pouch.coins;
```

Using *destructuring* in a real world example is not very different. Imagine that you have a cimmerian barbarian that is yearning to improve his JavaScript skills. Let's call him conan:

```
1   let conan = {
2         firstName: 'Conan',
3         lastName: 'the barbarian',
4         height: 178,
5         weight: 90,
6         email: 'conan.thecimmerian@akilonia.com',
7         toString() {
8             return this.firstName;
9         }
10      };
```

We can create a javascriptmancyCourse object that allows anyone, not just barbarians, to learn some javascript by using a helpful signUp method:

```
1   let javascriptmancyCourse = {
2       signUp(person){
3           let {firstName, lastName} = conan;
4           console.log(`Thank you ${firstName}, ${lastName}!!
5   You've successfully signed up to our very special JavaScript course!
6   Welcome and prepare to learn some JavaScript!`);
7   }};
8
9   javascriptmancyCourse.signUp(conan);
10  // => Thank you Conan, the barbarian!!
11  //     You've succesfully signed up to our very special
12  //     JavaScriptmancy course!
13  //     Welcome and prepare to learn some JavaScript!
```

The `let {firstName, lastName} = conan` lets us extract the information necessary from the conan object and have it ready for processing in a terse single statement. If you appreciate writing beautiful code it doesn't get better than this.

And there's more! You are not limited to using variables that have exactly the same names than the properties within the original object. You can take advantage of a slightly more advanced *destructuring* syntax to map an object property to a different variable:

```
1   let { lastName:title } = conan;
```

This is equivalent to:

```
1   let title = conan.lastName;
```

So that lastName is the name of the *origin* property and title is the name of the *destination* variable. Additionally, if you try to extract a property that doesn't exist in the source object, the newly created variable will be undefined:

```
1    // let pouch = {coins: 10};
2    let {bills} = pouch;
3    console.log(bills);
4    // => undefined
```

To prevent this from happening you can use default values in tandem with *destructuring* syntax. With this powerful combination, if an object doesn't have a given property, your variable still gets a default value instead of undefined.

```
1    // let pouch = {coins: 10};
2    let {bills=10} = pouch;
```

Using defaults with *destructuring* as depicted above will ensure that you'll never be poor and enjoy those illusory 10 bills even when they are not in your pouch. Magic!

Yet another mighty feature of *destructuring* is the ability to extract properties that are deep within an object. Imagine that you have one of those useful bags that have infinite pockets and you want to reach for your tobacco pouch:

```
1    let bag = {
2        leftPocket: {
3            tobaccoPouch: ['pipe', 'tobacco']
4        },
5        rightPocket: [pouch],
6        interior: ['10 pieces of dried meat', 'toilet paper', 'leprechau\
7    n']
8    };
```

Well you can create a new tobbacoPouch variable using destructuring. It's this easy:

```
1   let {leftPocket: {tobbacoPouch}} = bag;
2
3   console.log(`Let's see what I've got in my tobaccoPouch:
4     ${tobaccoPouch}`);
5   // => Let's see what I've got in my tobaccoPouch: pipe,tobacco
```

You can read this like *go into the* leftPocket *grab the* tobaccoPouch *and put it in its own separate variable.*

Again if the property you are trying to extract doesn't exist you'll get undefined:

```
1   let {leftPocket: {secretPouch}} = bag;
2   console.log(`Let's see what I've got in my secret pouch:
3     ${secretPouch}`);
4   // => Let's see what I've got in my secret pouch: undefined
```

But beware, because if there is a missing property in the object graph on the way to the specific property you want, the *destructuring* will result in a SyntaxError:

```
1   let {centralPocket: {superSecretPouch}} = bag;
2   // => SyntaxError:
3   //    Cannot read property 'superSecretPouch' of undefined
```

In this previous example the centralPocket property doesn't exist in the bag object. This means that the JavaScript runtime cannot traverse the object to get to the superSecretPouch and thus you get the SyntaxError as a result.

And now that we're talking about errors and problems, let's take a look at something that you cannot do with destructuring, something that has bitten me repeatedly: Extracting a property into an existing variable. No, this here won't work:

```
1   // let pouch = {coins: 10};
2   let money = 0;
3   {money} = pouch;
```

Yes, I know... But don't be sad. The happy news is that you can also use all you've learned thus far with arrays! Wiii! Let's destructure!

Destructuring Arrays

Destructuring arrays is just as easy as destructuring objects. Instead of using curly braces {} though, you'll use the more familiar array square brackets []:

```
1   let [one, two, three] = ['goblin', 'ghoul', 'ghost', 'white walker'];
2   console.log(`one is ${one}, two is ${two}, three is ${three}`)
3   // => one is goblin, two is ghoul, three is ghost
```

In this example you see how we extract the first three elements of the array and place them in three distinct variables: one, two and three. The fourth element in the array, the scary white walker remains unreferenced by any variable.

You can also jump places within the array:

```
1   let [firstMonster, , , fourthMonster] =
2     ['goblin', 'ghoul', 'ghost', 'white walker'];
3   console.log(`the first monster is ${firstMonster}, the fourth is
4     ${fourthMonster}`)
5   // => one is goblin, two is ghoul, three is ghost
```

Destructuring arrays comes very handy when you want to get the first element of an array in a very *readable* and *intuitive* fashion:

```
1   let [first] = ['goblin', 'ghoul', 'ghost', 'white walker'];
2   console.log(`first is ${first}`)
3   // => first is goblin
```

Which you can combine with the *rest operator* like this:

```
1   let [first, ...rest] = ['goblin', 'ghoul', 'ghost', 'white walker'];
2   console.log(`first is ${first} and then go all the rest: ${rest}`)
3   // => first is goblin and then go all the rest ghoul, ghost,
4   //    white walker
```

Unfortunately this trick doesn't work for the last element of the array because the *rest operator* is greedy. It wants to extract all items in the array and therefore [...initialOnes, last] wouldn't do the job.

You could be a super crafty fox and do the following:

```
1   let [last] = Array
2       .from(['goblin', 'ghoul', 'ghost', 'white walker'])
3       .reverse();
4   console.log(`last is ${last}`);
5   // => last is whiteWalker
```

Beautiful[84]! Another use case for *array destructuring* is to swap the values of two variables:

---

[84]The next step would be to create two methods first and last that would encapsulate these two implementation and extend the Array.prototype object. Soon we will take a look at that within the OOP section of the book.

```
1  console.log(`first is ${first}, last is ${last}`);
2  // => first is goblin, last is white walker
3
4  [first, last] = [last, first];
5
6  console.log(`but wait! Now first is ${first}, last is ${last}`)
7  // => but wait! Now first is white walker, last is goblin
```

Finally, you can enjoy the versatile *defaults* when performing *array destructuring* as well:

```
1  let [aMonster, anotherMonster, yetAnotherMonster='cucumber']
2      = ['goblin', 'ghoul'];
3  console.log(`We've got a monster that is a ${aMonster},
4  another that is ${anotherMonster}, and yet another one
5  that is a ${yetAnotherMonster}`);
6  // => We've got a monster that is a goblin, another that
7  //    is ghoul, and yet another one that is a cucumber
```

Because we try to extract three elements from an array that only has two the yetAnotherMonster variable would get a value of undefined. The use of a default prevents that and ensures that the variable has a safe value of cucumber. Because nothing speaks of safety like a cucumber.

Destructuring Function Arguments

In Useful Function Patterns: Default Parameters you briefly saw how destructuring can be useful when used within the parameter list of a function.

```
1   // With destructuring we can unpack the direction from
2   // the incoming object and use it right away
3   let randalf = {
4       toString(){ return 'Randalf the Mighty'; },
5       castIceCone(mana, {direction}){
6           console.log(`${this} spends ${mana} mana
7               and casts a terrible ice cone ${direction}`);
8       }
9   };
10
11  let options = { direction: 'towards Mordor'}
12  randalf.castIceCone(10, options);
13  // => Randalf the Mighty spends 10 mana and
14  //     casts a terrible ice cone towards Mordor
```

The principle is the same but the *destructuring* process happens in a more indirect fashion. One piece of the destructuring is the object being passed as an argument to a method, in this case `options`:

```
1   randalf.castIceCone(10, options);
```

And the other bit is the *destructuring* syntax with the specific variables as part of the method signature {direction}:

```
1       castIceCone(mana, {direction}){
```

Just like normal *destructuring* it also works with arrays:

```
1   function castMiniIceCone(mana, [target, ...others]){
2      var caster = this || 'God almighty';
3      console.log(`${caster} spends ${mana} mana
4   and casts a super teeny tiny ice cone that only reaches
5   ${target} but misses ${others} because it is so tiny and cute`);
6   }
7   randalf.castMiniIceCone = castMiniIceCone;
8   randalf.castMiniIceCone(10, ['giant', 'troll', 'death knight']);
9   // => Randalf the Mighty spends 10 mana
10  //     and casts a super teeny tiny ice cone that only reaches
11  //     giant but misses troll,death knight because it is so
12  //     tiny and cute
```

And you can use any of the features you've learned in this section for both object and array parameters: defaults, nested properties, jumping over array items, etc.

Concluding

In this chapter we did a brief review of all the ES6 features that you've learned so far: let, const for block scoped variables, *default parameters*, *rest parameters* which work like C# params, shorthand syntax for object initializers, symbols, template literals, tags and the new string methods.

We also dived deeper into *destructuring* and learned how you can use this new feature to easily extract properties from objects and items from arrays. You discovered that you can use *destructuring* within the arguments of a function and how to combine *destructuring* and *default values* when the property you are trying to extract doesn't exist within an object or array.

```
gort.says(`And that's all you need to know about ES6 destructuring`);
gort.says(`Would you like to attempt your luck with the exercises?`);
gort.says(`Say 'yes' to start the exercises`);

mooleen.says('Yes!');
```

```
gort.says('What do I have in my back pocket?');

mooleen.says('Your humanity?');

gort.says('"Your humanity?" is incorrect');
/*
gort says the "Your humanity?" part with Mooleen's voice
which gives her the jeeper creepers.
*/

gort.says(`You have *two* tries left. After that you'll be obliterat\
ed`);
gort.says('Thank you for playing!');

mooleen.says('Obliterated?');
gort.says('"Obliterated?" is incorrect');

gort.says(`You have *one* try left. After that you'll be obliterated\
`);
gort.says('Thank you for playing!');
```

Exercises

Experiment JavaScriptmancer!

You can experiment with these exercises and some possible solutions in this jsFiddle[85] or downloading the source code from GitHub[86].

---

[85]http://bit.ly/javascriptmancy-destructuring-exercises
[86]https://github.com/vintharas/javascriptmancy-code-samples

You Have One Try Left!

Use ES6 Destructuring to find out what gort has in his back pocket

```
1   let gort = {
2     name: 'Gort',
3     title: 'the android',
4     backPocket: 'cucumber'
5   };
```

Solution

```
1   let {backPocket} = gort;
2
3   mooleen.says(`It's a ${backPocket}!!`);
4   // => Mooleen says: It's a cucumber!!
5
6   gort.says('Correct!');
7   gort.says('What is at the end of this corridor? Turn north? Turn eas\
8   t?');
```

What is at The End of This Corridor?

Use ES6 Destructuring to find out what lies beyond at the end of the corridor, then to the north and then to the east. Save the solution in a variable called destiny.

```
1    let map = {
2      startOfTheCorridor: 'an infinite wall of blackness',
3      endOfTheCorridor: {
4        north: {
5          east: 'A white house, with a boarded front door'
6        }
7      }
8    };
```

Solution

```
1    let { endOfTheCorridor: { north: { east:destiny }}} = map;
2    mooleen.says(`It's ${destiny}!!`);
3    // => It's A white house, with a boarded front door!!
4
5    gort.says('Excellent! You are on a streak!');
6    gort.says('For the last test in this tutorial');
7    gort.says('What is the name of the second book in this bookshelf?')
8
9    /* A bookshelf materializes from thin air */
```

The Second Book in The BookShelf

Use ES6 Destructuring to find out which is the second book in the bookshelf:

```
1  let bookshelf = [
2      'Dungeons and Dragons 2nd Ed',
3      'The Blade Itself',
4      'The Silmarillion',
5      'Mistborn',
6      'The Wheel of Time'];
```

Solution

```
1  let [,book,] = bookshelf;
2  mooleen.says(`The name of the book is ${book}!`);
3  // => The name of the book is The Blade Itself!
4
5  gort.says('Congratulations! You have completed this tutorial!');
6  gort.says(`Say 'next' to continue or 'try again' to repeat`);
7
8  mooleen.says(`I think I'll go with NEXT, thank you very much`);
```

Upgrading Your Everyday JavaScript Magic With ES6 - Arrow Functions

Speak less.
That way there's less chance
that you'll say something stupid.

Think about that,
when you craft your next spell.

- Kyeich Chir
Guardian of the word

```
gort.says('Welcome to Tutorial number 2! Arrow Functions!');
gort.says('The only functions that go straight to the mark!');

/*... silence ...*/

gort.says(`...because they're... terse... and... arrows?`);

mooleen.slowClaps();
mooleen.says('ha ha')

gort.says(`My creator had a special sense of humor.`);

mooleen.says('Please be quick.')
mooleen.says('Before I choose to be obliterated on purpose.');

/*
    The white house vanishes to reveal a shooting range.
*/

gort.says('Behold! The Arrow Function!')
```

Behold! The Arrow Function!

Experiment JavaScriptmancer!!

You can experiment with all examples in this chapter directly within this jsBin example[87] or downloading the source code from GitHub[88].

Arrow functions are one of my favorite features in ES6. They give you a beautiful and terse way to write JavaScript functions which is reminiscent of C# lambda expressions.

Here you have a vanilla JavaScript function expression:

---

[87]http://bit.ly/javascriptmancy-es6-arrow-functions
[88]https://github.com/vintharas/javascriptmancy-code-samples

```
1   let createWater = function (mana){
2       return `${mana} liters of water`;
3   }
```

And here you have an equivalent version as an **arrow function**:

```
1   let createWater = mana => `${mana} liters of water`;
```

If you call any of these functions you'll get the same result:

```
1   console.log(createWater(10));
2   // => 10 liters of water
```

Let's examine the *arrow function* in closer quarters. You may have noticed that it doesn't have any `return` statement. And that's because in its simplest incarnation, the *arrow function* has an implicit `return` that returns whichever expression is to the right of the fat arrow =>. Note that this notation is only valid when an *arrow function* has a single statement.

Like in C#, you'll often see *arrow functions* used in conjunction with array methods such as `filter` (the JavaScript version of *LINQ*'s Where):

```
1   let monsters = ['orc chieftain', 'orc grunt', 'small orc', 'goblin'];
2   let orcs = monsters
3     .filter(m => m.includes('orc'));
4   console.log(orcs);
5   // => ["orc chieftain", "orc grunt", "small orc"]
```

You can define *arrow functions* with any arbitrary number of arguments. For instance, you can have no arguments at all:

```
1   let helloMiddleEarth = () => "hello Middle Earth!";
2
3   console.log(helloMiddleEarth());
4   // => hello Middle Earth!
```

Or one:

```
1   let frodo = {
2     toString(){ return 'Frodo'},
3     destroyTheOneRing() {
4       console.log(`${this} throws the one ring into the entrails of Mo\
5   unt Doom`);
6     },
7     hideFrom(enemy, how) {
8       console.log(`${this} hides from the ${enemy} ${how}`);
9     }
10  };
11
12  let destroyDaRing = (hobbit) => hobbit.destroyTheOneRing();
13
14  destroyDaRing(frodo);
15  // => Frodo throws the one ring into the entrails of Mount Doom
```

Two:

```
1   let nazgul = {
2     toString(){ return 'scary nazgul';}
3   };
4   let useElvenCloak = (hobbit, enemy)
5       => hobbit.hideFrom(enemy, 'with an elven cloak');
6
7   useElvenCloak(frodo, nazgul);
8   // => Frodo hides from the scary nazgul with an elven cloak
```

Or as many arguments as you want using the *rest syntax*:

```
1  useElvenCloak = (hobbit, ...enemies)
2    => hobbit.hideFrom(enemies, 'with an elven cloak');
3  useElvenCloak(frodo, nazgul, 'orc', 'troll');
4  // => Frodo hides from the scary nazgul,orc,troll with an elven cloak
```

Because they are just functions you can also use defaults:

```
1  destroyDaRing = (hobbit=frodo) => hobbit.destroyTheOneRing();
2  destroyDaRing();
3  // => Frodo throws the one ring into the entrails of Mount Doom
```

And *destructuring*:

```
1  let companyOfTheRing = {
2    smartestHobbit: frodo,
3    wizard: 'Gandalf',
4    ranger: 'Aragorn',
5    // etc
6  };
7  destroyDaRing =
8    ({smartestHobbit}) => smartestHobbit.destroyTheOneRing();
9
10 destroyDaRing(companyOfTheRing);
11 // => Frodo throws the one ring into the entrails of Mount Doom
```

If the body of your *arrow function* has more than one statement then you'll need to wrap it inside curly braces just like you would do in C#:

```
1   let eatRation = (hobbit, rations) => {
2     let ration = rations.shift();
3     if (ration) {
4       hobbit.hp += ration.hp;
5       console.log(`${hobbit} eats ${ration} and ` +
6                     `recovers ${ration.hp} hp`);
7     } else {
8       console.log(`There are no rations left! We're all gonna die!!`);
9     }
10  }
11
12  let rations = [{
13    name: 'sandwich',
14    hp: 5,
15    toString(){ return this.name;}
16  }];
17
18  eatRation(frodo, rations);
19  // => Frodo eats sandwich and recovers 5 hp
```

Additionally, when you have more than one statement you'll need to return a value explicitly:

```
1   let carveWood = (wood, shape) => {
2     console.log(`You carve a piece of ${wood} into a ${shape}`);
3     return {name: shape, material: wood};
4   }
5   let pipe = carveWood('oak', 'pipe');
6   // => You carve a piece of oak into a pipe
```

An *arrow function* can also return an object via the object initializer syntax. When doing so, you'll need to wrap it inside *parentheses*. That way the JavaScript runtime will be able to understand that it is an object and not a block of code:

```
1   let createHealthPotion = () => ({
2     name: 'potion of health',
3     hp: 10,
4     toString(){
5       return `${this.name} (+${this.hp}hp)`;
6     }});
7   let healthPotion = createHealthPotion();
8   console.log(healthPotion.toString());
9   // => potion of Health (+10 hp)
```

In summary, *arrow functions* are awesome. Using arrow functions you'll be able to write much terser code and still get to use features like destructuring or defaults. But as functions themselves they are a little bit special, and when I say a little I mean **a lot**.

Arrow Functions Arcana

Indeed, though they seem like regular functions, *arrow functions* have their quirks:

- They don't have this
- They don't have an arguments object
- You cannot use bind, apply and call to set the context in which they are evaluated
- You cannot use new nor super

This may be surprising but if you take a look at the ECMA-262 specification[89], that is, JavaScript's own specification, you'll read the following:

14.2.16 Arrow Functions - Runtime Semantics: Evaluation

---

[89]Find out more about arrow functions within the spec at http://bit.ly/es6-spec

An *ArrowFunction* does not define local bindings for arguments, super, this, or new.target. Any reference to arguments, super, this, or new.target within an *ArrowFunction* must resolve to a binding in a lexically enclosing environment. Typically this will be the Function Environment of an immediately enclosing function.

But what does it exactly mean for arrow functions not to have their own version of this nor arguments?

It means that when you refer to this or arguments within an *arrow function* you are actually referring to this or arguments in the enclosing environment. Let's clarify this with an example.

Let's say that we have gollum that wants to be pleasant to you just before he stabs you in the back and steals your wedding ring. If we use normal functions to define his greetings:

```
1   let gollum = {
2     name: 'Golum! Golum!',
3     toString(){ return `${this.name}!!!`;},
4     saysHi(){
5       console.log(`Hi! I am ${this}`);
6       setTimeout(function(){
7         console.log(`${this} stabs you in the back and
8   steals your wedding ring while saying 'My Preciouuuuuus'`)
9       },/*waitPeriodInMilliseconds*/ 500);
10    }
11  };
```

And then call the function saysHi:

```
1   // call it in the context of the gollum object
2   gollum.saysHi();
3   // => Hi! I am Gollum! Gollum!!!!
4   // => "[object Window] stabs you in the back and
5   //     steals your wedding ring while saying 'My Preciouuuuuus'"
```

As we expected, gollum happily salutes us. Then, after a short while, he returns and stabs us in the back. The only problem being that it is no longer gollum but the Window object. This is nothing new. We learned about this strange behavior of this in Mysteries of the JavaScript Arcana. But what happens if we use an *arrow function* instead of a normal function?

```
1    // what happens if we use an arrow function instead?
2    let gollumWithArrowFunctions = {
3      name: 'Golum! Golum!',
4      toString(){ return `${this.name}!!!`;},
5      saysHi(){
6        console.log(`Hi! I am ${this}`);
7        setTimeout(() =>
8          console.log(`${this} stabs you in the back and
9   steals your wedding ring while saying 'My Preciouuuuuus'`)
10       ,/*waitPeriodInMilliseconds*/ 500);
11     }
12   };
```

Notice how we have rewritten the saysHi function to use an *arrow function* within setTimeout instead of a normal function. If we call it:

```
1    gollumWithArrowFunctions.saysHi();
2    // => Hi! I am Gollum! Gollum!!!!
3    // => Golum! Golum!!!! stabs you in the back and
4    //     steals your wedding ring while saying 'My Preciouuuuuus'
```

The *arrow function* guarantees that the right version of this is used. *What is happening?* **Because the *arrow function* doesn't have its** own version of `this` it accesses the `this` defined by the `saysHi` method (effectively behaving like a closure). Because `saysHi` was called using the dot notation `gollumWithArrowFunctions.saysHi` then the object itself is the value of `this` and thus everything works yey! And we die an ignominious death at *Gollum's* hands. No!

What are the consequences of this? Well, the most exciting consequence of an *arrow function* not having its own `this` is that it makes them *more resistant* to the `this` problems you saw in Mysteries of the JavaScript Arcana (they are more resistant but not bullet proof as you'll see later in this chapter).

Let's bring this concept home with another example, the same one we used in Mysteries of the JavaScript Arcana:

```
1   function UsersCatalogJQuery(){
2     "use strict";
3     var self = this;
4
5     this.users = [];
6     getUsers()
7
8     function getUsers(){
9       $.getJSON('https://api.github.com/users')
10      .success(function updateUsers(users){
11        // console.log(users);
12        // console.log(this);
13        try {
14          this.users.push(users);
15        } catch(e) {
16          console.log(e.message);
17        }
18        // BOOOOOOOM!!!!!
19        // => Uncaught TypeError:
20        //     Cannot read property 'push' of undefined
21        // 'this' in this context is the jqXHR object
22        // not our original object
23        // that's why we usually use a closure here instead:
24        // self.products = products;
25      });
26    }
```

```
27    }
28    var catalog = new UsersCatalogJQuery();
```

Again, if you take advantage of *arrow functions* and substitute the updateUsers function expression for an *arrow function* you'll solve the problem. And in a more elegant way than binding the function explicitly (with bind) or using a closure (var self = this). You can appreciate that elegance in this example below:

```
1    function UsersCatalogJQueryArrowFunction(){
2      "use strict";
3      this.users = [];
4      this.getUsers = function getUsers(){
5        $.getJSON('https://api.github.com/users')
6        .success(users => this.users.push(users)); // arrow function
7        // this is mostly equivalent to:
8        // .success(function(users){
9        //            return this.users.push(users);}.bind(this))
10     };
11
12     this.getUsers();
13   }
14   var catalog = new UsersCatalogJQueryArrowFunction();
```

Arrow Functions And This Gotchas

Now that we've learned about the good parts of the *arrow function* and how it can help us write terser code and avoid some problems with the this keyword let's take a look at its darker sides: when an *arrow function* doesn't behave like a function.

Let's start with the not having this and when it can become a problem.

Beware of Using Arrow Functions With Object Literals

My first thought when I learned about arrow functions was: *Awesome! Now I can use arrow functions everywhere!* And so I wrote this:

```
1  let raistlin = {
2    name: 'Raistlin',
3    toString(){ return this.name;},
4    deathRay: () =>
5      console.log(`${this} casts a terrible ray of deaaaath!`)
6  }
```

To my surprise, when I tried to have `raistlin` cast an evil death ray this is what happened:

```
1  raistlin.deathRay();
2  // => [object Window] casts a terrible ray of deaaaath!
```

The *arrow function*, which we had thought impervious to `this` problems before, now reveals us the classic `this` issue.

What is happening here? Well, if you remember from the previous section *arrow functions* don't have `this`. Because of that, when you try to access `this` inside an *arrow function* you're referring to the `this` of the outer scope. In the case of an object literal, the `this` from the outer scope is no other than the `Window` object. Again, the rules we learned about `this` in Mysteries of the JavaScript Arcana don't apply to *arrow functions* and calling an *arrow function* using the dot notation doesn't evaluate it in the context of the object. **So remember, be wary of using arrow functions as properties of object literals.**

You Can't Bind Arrow Functions

You cannot use `bind` with arrow functions. If you are brave enough to try to bind an *arrow function* to an object you'll be sorely disappointed because it won't work.

Let's illustrate it with an example:

```
1   let saruman = {
2     name: 'Saruman, the White',
3     toString(){ return this.name;},
4     raiseUrukhai(){
5       console.log(`${this} raises a Urukhai from the pits ` +
6                     ` of Isengard`);
7       return {name: 'Uruk', hp: 500, strength: 18};
8     },
9     telekineticStaffAttack: () =>
10      console.log(`${this} uses his staff to throw
11  you across the room "telekinetically" speaking`)
12  }
```

Behold saruman! Another epic javascriptmancer. He has a couple of methods that show his magic prowess. One `raiseUrukhai` is a regular function, the other `telekineticStaffAttack` uses an *arrow function*. If we call these methods using the dot notation:

```
1   saruman.raiseUrukhai();
2   // => Saruman, the White raises a Urukhai from the pits of Isengard
3
4   saruman.telekineticStaffAttack();
5   // => [object Window] uses his staff to throw
6   //    you across the room "telekinetically" speaking
7   //    this would be undefined instead of Window if we used
8   //    strict mode
```

Again, just like we saw in the previous section, when we call `telekineticStaffAttack` method the `this` gets evaluated as `Window`. But let's say that we want to solve it as we are accustomed to by using `bind`.

If we use `bind` to bind these two methods to a different object:

```
1   // if we try to bind these two methods to a new object
2   let boromir = {name: 'Boromir of Gondor',
3                     toString(){return this.name;}};
4   let raiseUrukhaiBound = saruman.raiseUrukhai.bind(boromir);
5   raiseUrukhaiBound();
6   // => Boromir of Gondor raises a Urukhai from the pits of Isengard
```

We can appreciate how we can bind a normal function but when we try to bind an *arrow function* nothing happens:

```
1   let telekineticStaffAttackBound =
2       saruman.telekineticStaffAttack.bind(boromir);
3
4   telekineticStaffAttackBound();
5   // => undefined uses his staff to throw
6   //    you across the room "telekinetically" speaking
7   //    didn't work, not telekinetic staff attack for Boromir
```

Since an *arrow function* doesn't have this it makes no sense to bind it.

Even though **arrow functions are not the same as bound functions**, once an *arrow function* is declared and encloses its nearest this it pretty much behaves in the same way as a *bound function*. Let's illustrate this idea with some code:

```
1   // this is a constructor function
2   let Warg = function(name, size){
3     this.name = name;
4     this.size = size;
5     this.name = '${name}, the ${size} warg`;
6     // wargs don't bark, they wark
7     this.wark = () => console.log(`${name} warks!: Wark! Wark! );
8     this.jump = (function(){
9       console.log(`${name} jumps around`);
10    }).bind(this);
11  }
12
13  // here we are creating a new object using the new operator
14  let willyTheWarg = new Warg('willy', 'litte');
```

In this example we are using a *constructor function* and the *new* keyword to instantiate a fiery warg. Even though we haven't seen any of these concepts yet because I am reserving them for the OOP section of the series, they are still the best way to exemplify the similar behavior of *arrow functions* and *bound functions* (I hope you'll forgive me).

Essentially you use the new keyword to instantiate new objects via *constructor functions*. When you apply the *new* keyword on any function the JavaScript runtime instantiates an object {}, sets it as the this value of the function, then evaluates the function and finally returns it. This is useful because it is the this value that the wark method is going to enclose and safeguard for the rest of the program execution.

After creating willyTheWarg we got ourselves an *arrow function* wark and a bound function jump. If we execute any of them we will be able to appreciate how this refers to the warg itself:

```
1   // this is an arrow function
2   willyTheWarg.wark();
3   // => willy, the litte warg warks!: Wark! Wark!
4
5   // and this is the bound function
6   willyTheWarg.jump();
7   // => willy jumps around
```

This is the expected behavior, but *what happens if we are mean and take these functions away from willyTheWarg?*

Well the *bound function*, as we learned in Mysteries of the JavaScript Arcana, will still have willyTheWarg as its context:

```
1  let jump = willyTheWarg.jump;
2  jump();
3  // => willy, the litte warg warks!: Wark! Wark!
4
5  let goblin = {jump: jump};
6  goblin.jump();
7  // => willy, the litte warg warks!: Wark! Wark!
```

And the *arrow function* behaves in exact the same way. Instead of being explicitly bound to willyTheWarg it is implicitly bound by the closure over the this variable:

```
1  let wark = willyTheWarg.wark;
2  wark();
3  // => willy, the litte warg warks!: Wark! Wark!
4
5  goblin.wark = wark;
6  goblin.wark();
7  // => willy, the litte warg warks!: Wark! Wark!
```

This similar behavior and the fact that neither *bound* nor *arrow* functions can be *bound* (re-bound in the case of the *bound* function) makes both types of function practically identical in this situation. The only difference being that *bound* functions don't need a closure, you can just bind a normal function to whatever object you want by just calling the bind method. *Arrow functions*, on the other hand, can be seen to be *implicitly bound* to their enclosing context by virtue of the closure.

You Can't Use Apply or Call on Arrow Functions

In addition to bind, **you cannot use call nor apply on an *arrow function* to change its context**. If you remember Mysteries of the JavaScript Arcana, you can use call and apply to explicitly set the context in which a function is executed, that is, the value of this:

```
1   let caragor = {toString(){return 'scary caragor';}}
2   let howl = function({times}){
3     console.log(`${this} howls to the moon ${times} times!`);
4   }
5   // a normal function let's you set its context explicitly via apply \
6   or call
7   howl.apply(caragor, [{times: 3}]);
8   // => scary caragor howls to the moon 3 times!
9   howl.call(caragor, {times: 4});
10  // => scary caragor howls to the moon 4 times!
```

But if you try to use either `apply` or `call` with an *arrow function*, the context that you pass as argument will be completely ignored:

```
1   // an *arrow function* completely ignores the value of `this` passed\
2    as argument
3   willyTheWarg.wark.apply(caragor);
4   // => willy, the litte warg warks!: Wark! Wark!
5   willyTheWarg.wark.call(caragor);
6   // => willy, the litte warg warks!: Wark! Wark!
```

In the example above you can easily appreciate how instead of scary caragor the `${this}` within the `wark` *arrow function* is evaluated as `willy, the little`. This demostrates how *arrow functions* ignore the context when called with either `call` or `apply`.

Arrow Functions Don't Have Arguments Object

Another interesting feature of *arrow functions* is that they don't have arguments object. Just like with `this` if you attempt to access the `arguments` object within an *arrow function* you'll access the arguments of the enclosing environment.

If you remember More Useful Function Patterns - Multiple Arguments every function in JavaScript has a `arguments` object that you can use to access which arguments where passed to a function. So if you have a normal function that logs the `arguments` object:

```
1  function rememberWhatISaid(){
2    console.log(`you said: ${Array.from(arguments).join(', ')}`);
3  }
```

You can easily demonstrate how the arguments object collects those arguments being passed to the function:

```
1  rememberWhatISaid('hello', 'you', 'there');
2  // => you said: hello, you, there
3  rememberWhatISaid('supercalifragilisticusespialidosus')
4  // => you said: supercalifragilisticusespialidosus
```

Not so with *arrow functions*:

```
1  let forgetWhatISaid = () => {
2    console.log(`I am going to forget that you said: ${arguments}`);
3  }
4  forgetWhatISaid('I said Wazzaaaaa');
5  // => error ReferenceError: arguments is not defined
```

The arguments variable is not defined and thus we get a ReferenceError. Let's define it and see what happens:

```
1  let arguments = ['trying something crazy'];
2  let forgetWhatISaid = () => {
3    console.log(`I am going to forget that you said: ${arguments}`);
4  }
5  forgetWhatISaid('I said Wazzaaaaa');
6  // => I am going to forget that you said: trying something crazy
```

We can also make the same experiment wrapping an *arrow function* inside another function:

```
1  let createMemoryWisp(){
2    return () => console.log(`*MemoryWisp*: You said...
3  ${Array.from(arguments).join(', ')}`);
4  }
5  let wispRememberThis = createMemoryWisp(1, 2, 3, 4, 'banana!');
6  wispRememberThis('important password', '123456789');
7  // => *MemoryWisp*: You said... 1, 2, 3, 4, banana!
```

So as you can see in both these examples, *arrow functions* don't
have their own arguments object and use the arguments object
of their enclosing environment. But *What if we want to send an
arbitrary number or arguments to an arrow function?* Well, in that
case you should use the *rest operator*:

```
1  function createMemoryWispWithRest(){
2    return (...thingsToRemember) =>
3        console.log(`*MemoryWisp*: You said... ${thingsToRemember.jo\
4  in(', ')}`);
5  }
6  let wispRememberThisAgain = createMemoryWispWithRest();
7  wispRememberThisAgain('important password', '123456789');
8  // => *MemoryWisp*: You said... important password, 123456789
```

In summary, whenever you use arguments inside an *arrow function*
you'll be accessing the enclosing environment's arguments object.
So if you want to send multiple arbitrary arguments to an *arrow
function* use the *rest operator*.

Arrow Functions and the New and Super Operators

The new and super operators are two operators that we will see
in depth in the OOP section of the series. The new operator lets you
create new instances of objects when applied to any function which
will then act as a constructor. The super keyword is new in ES6

and lets you access methods in parent classes within an inheritance chain.

In much the same way as with `bind`, `call` and `apply`, you cannot use `new` nor `super` with an *arrow function*.

Concluding

In this chapter you learned about ES6 *arrow functions* which resemble *lambdas* in C#. *Arrow functions* let you use a terser syntax than the normal function syntax and help you avoid problems with the `this` keyword by using the `this` value of their enclosing environment.

Arrow functions are a little bit special in what regards to `this` since they are the only *functions* in JavaScript that don't have their own `this` value. Because of this characteristic you cannot use `bind`, `call` or `apply` to specify the context in which an *arrow function* will be evaluated. In a similar fashion you cannot use the `new` and `super` operators with an *arrow function*.

Additionally, *arrow functions* don't have their own `arguments` object, if you try to access `arguments` inside an *arrow function* you'll access the `arguments` object within the enclosing function. This means that if you want for an *arrow function* to take an arbitrary number of arguments you'll need to use the *rest syntax*.

```
gort.says(`And that's all you need to know about ` +
          `ES6 arrow functions`);
gort.says(`Would you like to attempt your luck with the exercises?`);
gort.says(`Say 'yes' to start the exercises`);

mooleen.says('Yes!');
mooleen.says(`I see what you're doing`);
mooleen.says(`you're not gonna catch me again on this one`);

gort.says(`You have *two* tries left. After that you'll be ` +
          `obliterated`);
```

```
gort.says('Thank you for playing!');

mooleen.says(`D'oh!`);

gort.says(`You have *one* try left. After that you'll be ` +
          ` obliterated`);
gort.says('Thank you for playing!');

/* silence */

gort.says(`You shall make a magic bow...`)
```

Exercises

Experiment JavaScriptmancer!

You can experiment with these exercises and some possible solutions in this jsFiddle[90] or downloading the source code from GitHub[91].

You Shall Make a Magic Bow!

Use ES6 Arrow functions to convert this ordinary wooden bow into a magic bow that can pierce the targets in this tutorial.

```
1  let woodenBow = {
2    shoot(target){
3      console.log('You shoot a arrow to the ${target}');
4    }
5  }
```

Substitute the shoot function for an arrow function.

[90]http://bit.ly/javascriptmancy-es6-arrow-functions-exercises
[91]https://github.com/vintharas/javascriptmancy-code-samples

Solution

```
1   let magicBow = {
2     shoot: (target) =>
3         console.log(`You shoot a magic arrow to the ${target}`)
4   };
5   mooleen.weaves('magicBow.shoot("first target")');
6   // => You shoot a magic arrow to the first target
7
8   /* as mooleen shots the target it vanishes in thin air */
9
10  mooleen.says(`ha! Look at that! I'm awesome!`);
11  mooleen.says(`Now there's only one left!`);
12
13  gort.says(`Excellent job!`);
14  gort.says(`You shall make a better bow!`);
15
16  mooleen.says(`But this bow is awesome!`);
17  gort.says(`Can you pierce these with that bow?`);
18
19  /* All of the sudden 5 more targets materialize from thin air */
20
21  mooleen.says('Really?');
```

 ## You Shall Make a Better Bow!

Improve your bow to be able to shoot elemental arrows to multiple targets. You should be able to satisfy the following interface:

```
1   elementalBow.shoot('fire', 'target 1');
2   // => you shoot a fire arrow to target 1
3   elementalBow.shoot('ice', 'target 2', 'target 3');
4   // => you shoot a ice arrow to target 2 and target 3
```

Solution

```
1  let elementalBow = {
2    shoot: (element, ...targets) =>
3      console.log(`you shoot a ${element} arrow to ` +
4                  `${targets.join(' and ')}`)
5  };
6
7  mooleen.weaves(`elementalBow.shoot('fire', 'target 1', 'target 2',
8                  'target 3', 'target 4' , 'target 5')`);
9  // => you shoot a fire arrow to target 1
10       and target 2 and target 3 and target 4 and target 5
11
12 mooleen.says(`That's how I roll`);
13
14 gort.says('Congratulations! You have completed this tutorial!');
15 gort.says(`Say 'next' to continue into the last and most difficult t\
16 rial`);
17
18 mooleen.says(`NEEEEXT!!!`);
```

Upgrading Your Everyday JavaScript Magic With ES6 - The Spread Operator

Learn to recognize beauty in code,
it will make the task of coding
a pleasure in itself,
it will make you appreciate code
in a whole different way.

- Zazongel emjia
Bard and Poet

```javascript
gort.says('Welcome to Tutorial number 3! The Spread Operator!');
gort.says('This is the Final Trial To Become a JavaScriptmancer')

mooleen.says('Awesome!')

/*
    The shooting range disappears...
    The sky remains though...
    sky upwards...
    sky downwards...
    Mooleen begins to fall...
*/

mooleen.says('What!? Aaahhhhhhh!!!');

gort.says('Ready To Spread Your Wings?')
```

Ready To Spread Your Wings?

In More Useful Function Patterns: Multiple Arguments you learned about *rest parameters*, a new ES6 feature, that lets you define functions with an arbitrary number of arguments just like params in C#.

The *spread* operator works sort of in an opposite way to the *rest* operator. Where the *rest* operator takes a variable number of arguments and packs them into an *array*, the *spread* operator takes and *array* and **expands** it into its compounding items.

In this chapter you'll see several recipes that will help you write better code by taking advantage of the spread operator like, for instance, concatenating arrays.

Use the Spread Operator to Seamlessly Concatenate Arrays

 ### Experiment JavaScriptmancer!!

You can experiment with all examples in this chapter directly within this jsBin example[92] or downloading the source code from GitHub[93].

You can use the *spread operator* to easily concatenate *arrays* with each other. Let's say that we want to collect our most terrible enemies for later reference. We have an array knownFoesLevel1 and another array newFoes with newly acquired enemies (because you can never have enough enemies):

```
let knownFoesLevel1 = ['rat', 'rabbit']
let newFoes = ['globin', 'ghoul'];
```

Since it's easier to manage one collection than two, we want to merge these two collections into one single *array*. Where you would have used the concat method in ES5:

```
let knownFoesLevel2 = knownFoesLevel1.concat(newFoes);
console.log(knownFoesLevel2);
// => ["rat", "rabbit", "globin", "ghoul"]
```

In ES6 you can use the *spread* operator to achieve the same result with a much clearer syntax:

---

[92]http://bit.ly/javascriptmancy-spread-operator
[93]https://github.com/vintharas/javascriptmancy

```
1  let knownFoesLevel2WithSpread = [...knownFoesLevel1, ...newFoes];
2  console.log(knownFoesLevel2WithSpread);
3  // => ["rat", "rabbit", "globin", "ghoul"]
```

You can even mix *arrays* and singular items:

```
1  let undead = ['zombie', 'banshee', 'vampire', 'skeleton'];
2  let knownFoesLevel3 = [...knownFoesLevel2, 'troll', 'orc',
3                         ...undead];
4  console.log(knownFoesLevel3);
5  // => ["rat", "rabbit", "globin", "ghoul", "troll",
6  //     "orc", "zombie", "banshee", "vampire", "skeleton"]
```

Easily Use Apply With the Spread Operator

Another useful use case of the *spread operator* is as an alternative syntax to Function.prototype.apply.

In Mysteries of the JavaScript Arcana you learned about how you can use the apply function to explicitly set the context (this) in which a function is executed. You also learned how apply expects an *array* of arguments as second parameter and how when the function is finally invoked each element within the *array* is passed as a separate argument to the original function.

Well the *spread operator* let's you call an arbitrary function with an *array* of arguments in a better way than apply does.

Let's say that you are working on a spell to command your minions with random actions because being too predictive is boring and you appreciate the wild factor. You express these random actions as *arrays*: ['minion1', 'action', 'minion2']

```
1  let action = ['hobbit', 'attacks', 'rabbit'];
```

Now let's say that you have a function of your own device where you want actions to be done *viciously* (looks like you are in a foul mood today):

```
1  function performActionViciously(agent1, action, agent2){
2      console.log(`${agent1} ${action} ${agent2} viciously`);
3  }
```

Because the action is expressed as an *array* but the performAction-Viciously function expects a separate series of arguments you need a way to adapt these two disparate elements.

Prior to ES6 you would have used the apply function:

```
1  performActionViciously.apply(/* this */ null, action);
2  // => hobbit attacks rabbit viciously
```

Where you would need to fill in the context in which the function will be executed for the apply method to work (that is, the value of this).

With ES6 you can use the *spread operator* to easily perform an action:

```
1  // let action = ['hobbit', 'attacks', 'rabbit'];
2  performActionViciously(...action);
3  // => hobbit attacks rabbit viciously
```

No need to set the context in which the function is executed and the resulting code is much concise with the omission of apply.

Now you may be asking yourself: *Why don't I make the performActionViciously function take an array as argument and forget all this spread operator nonsense?* Well, you could do that. But what happens when you have *no control* over the function being called?

Take console.log. Imagine that, instead of performing these actions *viciously*, you just want to log them. Because console.log takes an arbitrary number of arguments and you have an array, you need some way to adapt the array to the expected signature. Again, prior to ES6 you would use `apply`:

```
1  // console.log expects something like this
2  // console.log(a1, a2, a3, a4, etc)
3  console.log.apply(/* this */ console.log, action);
4  // => 'hobbit', 'attacks', 'rabbit'
```

With ES6 and the *spread operator* you can simplify the code sample above greatly:

```
1  console.log(...action);
2  // => 'hobbit', 'attacks', 'rabbit'
```

Another example in which the *spread operator* comes handy is when we want to extend an existing *array* with another *array*. In the olden days we would have written:

```
1  let anotherAction = ['jaime', 'cleans', 'the dishes'];
2  let moreThingsToClean = ['the toilet', 'the hut', 'the stables'];
3  Array.prototype.push.apply(anotherAction, moreThingsToClean);
4  console.log(anotherAction);
5  // => ['jaime', 'cleans', 'the dishes', 'the toilet',
6  //      'the hut', 'the stables'];
```

With the *spread operator* it's as easy as:

```
1  anotherAction.push(...moreThingsToClean);
```

In summary, *do you have some variable as an array and need to apply it to a function that takes separate arguments?* **Use the spread operator.**

Converting Array-likes and Collections Into Arrays

Another interesting application of the *spread* operator is to convert *array-like objects* into *arrays*.

If you remember More Useful Function Patterns: Multiple Arguments, *array-like* objects are a special type of object that can be indexed, enumerated, has a *length* property but doesn't have any of the methods of an *array*. Some examples of *array-like* objects are the arguments object inside functions or the list of DOM[94] nodes that result when using document.querySelector.

Let's imagine that we have a web-based user interface, a form, to help us create minions based on some characteristics that we can type manually (*for even wizards can benefit from web interfaces*). It could look like this:

```
1   <form action="post" id="minion">
2     <label for="name">Name:</label>
3     <input type="text" name="name" value="Orc">
4
5     <label for="class">Class:</label>
6     <input type="text" name="class" value="Warrior">
7
8     <label for="strength">Strength:</label>
9     <input type="number" name="strength" value="18">
10
11    <button>Save</button>
12  </form>
```

When you click on the Save button we want to store these values and create a new minion that will serve us for eternity. So we add an event handler saveMinion that will be called when the form is submitted:

---

[94]The DOM or Document Object Model is an object representation of a website where each HTML element is represented by an object called a node.

```
1   // select the form element with the id of minion
2   let form = document.querySelector('form#minion');
3
4   // when submitting the form we will call the saveMinion function
5   form.addEventListener('submit', saveMinion);
```

In the example above we use the document.querySelector method to select the form element that represents the actual form on the web page. After that, we call the addEventListener method to register a saveMinion event handler for the submit event of the form. Whenever the user clicks on the Save button, the form will be submitted and the saveMinion method will be called.

The next step would be to extract the values from the inputs above. *How can we go about that?* Well, we can select all the inputs within the form and extract the values that we or another wizards have typed in.

```
1   function saveMinion(e){
2     let inputs =  form.querySelectorAll('input'),
3         values = [];
4
5     for (let i = 0; i < inputs.length; i++) {
6       values.push(inputs[i].value);
7     }
8
9     console.log(values);
10    // => ["Orc", "Warrior", "18"]
11
12    // TODO: createMinion(values);
13
14    // this just prevents the form from being submitted via AJAX
15    e.preventDefault();
16  }
```

So we use the form.querySelectorAll('input') method to select all input elements within the form. This method returns an *array-like* object of nodes. Because it has a *length* property we can use a simple *for* loop and a new array `values` to collect the values. After that we can create our brand new minion with the extracted values.

But, is there a better way to collect these values? What about converting the `inputs` *array-like* object to an *array* and using the helpful *array* methods instead of the *for* loop? *Spread operator* to the rescue!

```
function saveMinionWithSpread(e){
  let values = [...form.querySelectorAll('input')]
    .map(i => i.value);

  console.log(values);
  // => ["Orc", "Warrior", "18"]

  // TODO: createMinion(values);

  // this just prevents the form from being submitted via AJAX
  e.preventDefault();
}
```

By converting the *array-like* to an *array* using the *spread operator* we can use *array* functions such as `map` and write more beautiful code! `map` works just like *LINQ*'s `Select` and let's you perform transformations on each item of a collection. In this case we just transform a collection of elements into values. Awesome right?

In addition to *array-like* objects you can use the *spread operator* to convert any iterable object to an array. For instance a `Set` (a collection of unique items):

```
1  // You can also convert any iterable into an array using spread
2  let exits = new Set(['north', 'south', 'east', 'west']);
3
4  console.log(exits);
5  // => [object Set]
6
7  console.log([...exits]);
8  // => ['north', 'south', 'east', 'west];
```

Or a `Map` (like a C# `Dictionary`):

```
1   let box = new Map();
2   box.set('jewels', ['emerald', 'ruby']);
3   box.set('gold coins', 100);
4
5   console.log(box);
6   // => [object Map]
7
8   console.log([...box]);
9   // => [["jewels", ["emerald", "ruby"]], ["gold coins", 100]]
10  // in this case we get an array of key-value pairs
```

Spread Lets You Combine New and Apply

The *spread* operator also lets you combine the `new` operator with the ability to `apply` arguments to a function. That is, the ability to instantiate objects using a *constructor function* while, at the same time, adapting an array of arguments into a *constructor function* that expects separate arguments.

Let's continue the example from the previous section where we extracted the characteristics of our minion from an *HTML form*. To refresh your memory the form looked like this:

```
1   <form action="post" id="minion">
2     <label for="name">Name:</label>
3     <input type="text" name="name" value="Orc">
4
5     <label for="class">Class:</label>
6     <input type="text" name="class" value="Warrior">
7
8     <label for="strength">Strength:</label>
9     <input type="number" name="strength" value="18">
10
11    <button>Save</button>
12  </form>
```

The next natural step would be to create a new minion using those characteristics and the following *constructor function*:

```
1   function Minion(name, minionClass, strength){
2     this.name = name;
3     this.minionClass = minionClass;
4     this.strength = strength;
5     this.toString = function(){
6       return `I am ${name} and I am a ${minionClass}`;
7     }
8   }
```

If we were to use pure ES5 we would need to unwrap the values before we use them:

```
1   var newMinion = new Minion(values[0], values[1], values[2]);
```

With ES6 we can combine new with the *spread* operator to get this beautiful piece of code:

```
1   let newMinion = new Minion(...values);
```

The full code example could look like this:

```
1    // add event handler for the form submit event
2    form.addEventListener('submit', saveMinionForReal);
3
4    function saveMinionForReal(e){
5      let values = [... form.querySelectorAll('input')]
6        .map(i => i.value);
7      console.log(values);
8      // => ["Orc", "Warrior", "18"]
9
10     // create minion with the values
11     let newMinion = new Minion(...values);
12     console.log(`Raise and live my minion: ${newMinion}!!!`)
13     // => Raise and live my minion: I am Orc and I am a Warrior!!!
14
15     // saveNewMinion(newMinion);
16
17     e.preventDefault();
18   }
```

In the example above we first extract the values from the form and then we use them to create a newMinion object by applying both the new and the *spread* operators at once.

Concluding

In this chapter you learned about the ES6 *spread* operator and how it works in sort of the opposite way to the *rest* operator. Instead of grouping separate items into an array, the *spread* operator expands arrays into separate items.

You learned how you can use it in many scenarios usually resulting in more readable code: to easily concatenate arrays, as a substitute for apply, to convert *array-like* objects and even other iterables to arrays and, finally, to combine the new operator with apply.

This chapter wraps the first tome of JavaScriptmancy! Great job JavaScriptmancer! Time to *spread* your wings and dive into the mysteries of data structures in JavaScript!

```
/*
Mooleen keeps falling and falling, she breaks through a sea
of clouds, and to her horror she sees the ground below
approaching... very... very fast.
*/

gort.says(`And that's all you need to know about ` +
        `ES6 spread operator`);
gort.says(`Would you like to attempt your luck with the exercises?`);
gort.says(`Say 'yes' to start the exercises`);

mooleen.says(`F***** offf!!!!`)

gort.says(`You have *two* tries left. After that you'll ` +
        ` be obliterated`);
gort.says('Thank you for playing!');

mooleen.says(`Oh my god, are you kiddin' me right now?`);

gort.says(`You have *one* try left. After that you'll ` +
        `be obliterated`);
gort.says('Thank you for playing!');

/* silence */

gort.says(`You are going to need some wings to get out of this one`)
```

Exercises

 ## Experiment JavaScriptmancer!

You can experiment with these exercises and some possible solutions in this jsFiddle[95] or downloading the source code from GitHub[96].

---

[95]http://bit.ly/javascriptmancy-es6-spread-operator-exercises
[96]https://github.com/vintharas/javascriptmancy-code-samples

You Are Going to Need Some Wings To Get Out of This One

Time is of the essence. Unless you create some wings for Mooleen she'll encounter a horrible death at the hands of gravity. Use the ES6 spread operator to gather all these wings from diverse birds together in one single array!

```
1   let scatteredFeathers = ['dove feather', 'colibri feather'];
2   let aGoldenFeather = 'golden feather';
3   let eagle = {
4       hp: 50,
5       description: 'a majestic eagle',
6       inventory: ['25 eagle feathers']
7   };
```

Solution

```
1   mooleen.says('feathers... feathers... really? Poor eagle...')
2
3   let feathersForMagicWings = [...scatteredFeathers, aGoldenFeather,
4                                ...eagle.inventory];
5
6   mooleen.says(`Voila!` +
7               ` Here are the feathers ${feathersForMagicWings}`);
```

Now Fly!

Use the spread operator to create a new pair of wings using the Wings spell below. Remember to use the new operator to create the new wings:

```
1   function Wings(peacefulBirdFeather, quickestFlappingBirdFeather,
2                   goldenFeather, eagleFeathers){
3     if (peacefulBirdFeather !== 'dove feather' ||
4         quickestFlappingBirdFeather !== 'colibri feather' ||
5         goldenFeather !== 'golden feather' ||
6         !eagleFeathers.includes('eagle'))
7       throw new Error(`You don't have all the ingredients needed!!!`);
8
9     console.log('A beautiful pair of translucent' + '
10                 magic wings suddenly appear in your back!');
11
12     this.fly = function(){
13       console.log('You soar into the air like a majestic eagle');
14     };
15   }
```

Solution

```
1   let magicWings = new Wings(...feathersForMagicWings);
2   // => A beautiful pair of translucent magic wings suddenly
3   //    appear in your back!
4   magicWings.fly();
5   // => You soar into the air like a majestic eagle
6
7   /*** mooleen starts flying and barely misses the dusty earth ***/
8   mooleen.says('Phewwwww!!!');
9
10  gort.says('Congratulations!')
11  gort.says(`Now you're a full-fledged JavaScriptmancer!`)
12  gort.says('Welcome to the order master!');
13
14  /* gort vanishes */
15
16  mooleen.says('Wait... How do I get back?');
```

Tome I.II
JavaScriptmancy and Data Structures

JavaScript Arrays: The All-in-one Data Structure

Remember,

Grasp the subject,
and the words will follow.

Have the argument clear in your mind,
and the words will flow naturally.

Focus on the data structures first,
and your code will be cleaner.

> \- Svotarld Siunl
> Sage

```javascript
/*
After some getting used to and two or three near death experiences
Mooleen makes it back to The Caves of Infinity.
*/

randalf.says("I see you've won your wings." +
             "Congrats JavaScript-mancer!");
mooleen.says("They'll come handy when I decide to get " +
             "the hell out of here");

randalf.says("Indeed they will. But you're not ready yet.");
mooleen.says("Really?");

randalf.says("Really. You still lack one of the most " +
             "important elements!");
mooleen.says("A battle axe?");

randalf.says("A wand! Staff! Or a Schepter! And you get " +
             "to choose your own!")
randalf.says("Or as they say, the wand will choose you...");

mooleen.says("Are there any battle-axe-shaped wands?");

randalf.says("There might... Follow me to the armory!")

/*
Apparently the armory means a room filled with immense, massive,
unending quantities of shit... err... diverse items in different
degrees of decomposition.
*/

mooleen.says("I reckon JavaScript-mancers aren't known for their" +
             " tidiness, are they?");
randalf.says("What? This is in perfect order");
randalf.says("it's just... an interesting sorting mechanism");
mooleen.says("the not-giving-a-f*** sorting mechanism?")

randalf.says("Ehem... " +
             "We'll just need to make sense of all these items");
```

We'll Just Need To Make Sense of All These Items

For a very long time (up until the year 2015 and the advent of ES6) the only data structure available in JavaScript was the array. This was not a big problem for the hordes of JavaScript developers because JavaScript's array is an array, a list, a queue, a stack and, in addition, provides similar functionality to LINQ. Sounds interesting? Let's have a look.

JavaScript's Array

Experiment JavaScriptmancer!!

You can experiment with all examples in this chapter directly within this jsBin[97] or downloading the source code from GitHub[98].

The easiest way to create an array in JavaScript is to use the array literal:

```
1  var rightPocket = [];
2  console.log('This is what I have in my right pocket: ' +
3    rightPocket);
4  // => This is what I have in my right pocket:
```

Although you can use the Array constructor as well:

---

[97]http://bit.ly/javascriptmancy-arrays
[98]https://github.com/vintharas/javascriptmancy-code-samples

```
1   var leftPocket = Array();
2   console.log('And this is what I have in my left pocket: ' +
3     leftPocket);
4   // => And this is what I have in my left pocket:
```

Which unfortunately is a little bit inconsistent. For instance, you can use the Array constructor with one single argument to create an array of an arbitrary size:

```
1   console.log(Array(1));
2   // => [undefined]
3   console.log(Array(3));
4   // => [undefined, undefined, undefined]
```

Or you can use it with more than one argument to create an array that will contain the arguments that you pass in (just like [ ]):

```
1   console.log(Array(1, 2, 3));
2   // => [1, 2, 3]
```

As you would expect from any array worth its salt, you can set items in the array by index:

```
1   rightPocket[0] = 'bearded axe';
2   leftPocket[0] = '10 gold coins';
3
4   console.log('right pocket: ' + rightPocket);
5   // => right pocket: bearded axe
6   console.log('left pocket: ' + leftPocket);
7   // => left pocket: 10 gold coins
```

And you can also retrieve these items by indexing the array:

```
1  console.log('I have a ' + rightPocket[0] + 'in my right pocket. ' +
2    'I am maniac... and I have to patent this pants...');
3  // => I have a bearded axe in my right pocket.
4  //     I am maniac... and I have to patent this pants...
```

Arrays have a dynamic size and they grow as you add new elements to them. You can access the size of an array using its `length` property:

```
1  console.log('The size of my right pocket is: ' + rightPocket.length);
2  // => The size of my right pocket is: 1
3  rightPocket[1] = "orb of power";
4  console.log('And now it is: ' + rightPocket,length);
5  // => And now it is 2
```

Specially interesting is the fact that JavaScript allows you to have elements of disparate types within the same array:

```
1  var leatherBag = ['20 gold coins',
2    {name: 'wand of invisibility',
3     charges: 1,
4     toString(){return this.name;}}];
5  console.log('You examine your leather bag and find: ' + leatherBag);
6  // => You examine your leather bag and find: 20 gold coins,wand of i\
7  nvisibility
```

An Extremely Flexible Data Structure

The Array was the sole data structure available in JavaScript for a long time and, as such, it grew to provide a lot of functionality to cover most of the use cases that you usually run into when writing JavaScript applications. It is somewhat of an all-purpose collection.

For instance, it can work as a *stack* (*LIFO - Last In First Out*) if you use the methods `push` and `pop`. These methods add and remove elements from the end of the array respectively:

```
1  rightPocket.push('chewing gum');
2  console.log('You get the ' + right.Pocket.pop());
3  // => You get the chewing gum
```

It can work as a *queue* (*FIFO - First In First Out*) if you use the method shift to extract an item from the beginning of the array and combine it with push:

```
1  leftPocket.push('cheese sandwich');
2  console.log('You pay the cheese sandwich with ' +
3      leftPocket.shift() + '. That was a pricy sandwich...');
4  // => You pay the cheese sandwich with 10 gold coins.
5  //     That was a pricy sandwich...
```

You can also insert items in the beginning of the array by using the unshift method:

```
1  leftPocket.unshift('beautiful stone');
2  console.log('You examine the ' + leftPocket[0] + ' in wonder.');
3  // => You examine the beautiful stone in wonder.
```

Additionally, both push and unshift let you add multiple items at once:

```
1  leatherBag.push('dried meat', 'white feather');
2  leatherBag.unshift('1 copper coin', 'skeleton skull');
3  console.log('You look inside your leather bag and find: ' +
4              leatherBag);
5  // => You look inside your leather bag and find:
6  //     1 copper coin, skeleton skull, 20 gold coins,
7  //     wand of invisibility, dried meat, white feather
```

Another useful method that lets you remove items from any arbitrary position of an array is the splice method. It has many use cases:

```
1  var firstItem = leatherBag.splice(/* start */ 0,
2                            /* numberOfItemsToRemove */ 1);
3  console.log('extracted first item => ' + firstItem);
4  // => extracted first item => 1 copper coin
5
6  // you can use negative indexes to start from the end of the array
7  var lastItem = leatherBag.splice(-1, 1);
8  console.log('extracted last item => ' + lastItem);
9  // => extracted last item => white feather
10
11  var someRandomItemsInTheMiddle = leatherBag.splice(1, 2);
12  console.log('extracted items in the middle => ' +
13              someRandomItemsInTheMiddle);
14  // => extracted items in the middle => 20 gold coins,
15  //                                      wand of invisibility
```

`splice` can even insert items at a given point:

```
1  console.log(rightPocket);
2  // => ["bearded axe", "orb of power"]
3
4  // let's add a couple of items in between the axe and the orb
5  // splice(startIndex, numberOfItemsToRemove, item1, item2, etc...)
6  rightPocket.splice(1, 0, "candlestick", "yerky");
7  console.log(rightPocket);
8  // => ["bearded axe", "candlestick", "yerky", "orb of power"]
```

or remove items and insert items at once:

```
1  // splice(startIndex, numberOfItemsToRemove, item1, item2, etc...)
2  let candle = rightPocket.splice(1, 1, "secret message", "wax");
3  console.log(rightPocket);
4  // => ["bearded axe", "secret message", "wax", "yerky",
5  //      "orb of power"]
```

Sorting Arrays

Arrays offer a couple of methods that let you sort the elements they contain. The first one that you need to consider is the sort method which takes a comparing function as argument. Let's sort our potions:

```
function Potion(name, quantity){
  return {
    name,
    quantity,
    toString(){return `(${this.quantity}) ${this.name}`;}
  };
}

var potionsCase = [
  Potion('potion of firebreathing', 2),
  Potion('potion of vigor', 1),
  Potion('potion of major healing', 3),
  Potion('potion of cure poison', 1)
];
// the compare function f(a,b) should return:
// < 0 if a < b
// 0 if a === b
// > 0 if a > b
potionsCase.sort((p1,p2) => p1.quantity - p2.quantity);
console.log("You examine your potion case closely... " +
            potionsCase);
// => You examine your potion case closely...
//    (1) potion of cure poison,
//    (1) potion of vigor,
//    (2) potion of firebreathing,
//    (3) potion of major healing,
```

And it looks like you need to buy some more of that curing poison because you never know what may be waiting to bite you behind that next corner. The comparing function compare(a,b) is expected to return:

- 0 when a and b are considered equal
- < 0 when a < b
- > 0 when a > b

Another fact that is important to remember is that the sort method does in-place sorting so your original array will reflect the changes after being sorted.

The second array method related to sorting is the reverse method. This method reverses the position of all items within the array and does so in-place:

```
console.log("Let's see what I can sell... " +
            potionsCase.reverse());
// => Let's' see what I can sell...
//    (3) potion of major healing,
//    (2) potion of firebreathing,
//    (1) potion of cure poison,
//    (1) potion of vigor
```

Safe Array Methods

All these methods that we have seen up until now mutate the array itself. This means that using them will change the inner contents of the array where the method is called. Let's look at some safe methods now, methods that don't change the original array.

The concat method lets you concatenate two arrays together and returns the resulting array:

```
// concatenate arrays with concat
var superPocket = rightPocket.concat(leftPocket);
console.log(superPocket);
// => ["bearded axe", "secret message", "wax", "yerky",
//     "orb of power", "beautiful stone", "cheese sandwich"]
```

The join method allows you to join the elements of an array to form a string using an arbitrary separator of your choice:

```
1   function beautifyPocket(pocket){
2     return pocket.join('\n=============\n');
3   }
4   console.log(`You examine your inventory: \n
5   ${beautifyPocket(rightPocket)}`);
6   // => You examine your inventory:
7   //
8   //    bearded axe
9   //    =============
10  //    secret message
11  //    =============
12  //    wax
13  //    =============
14  //    yerky
15  //    =============
16  //    orb of power
```

The indexOf method returns the position of an item within an array:

```
1   var indexOfBeardedAxe = rightPocket.indexOf('bearded axe');
2   console.log('The bearded axe is at position: ' + indexOfBeardedAxe);
```

It is often used to find out whether or not an array contains a given item like this:

```
1   // indexOf returns -1 when it can't find an item
2   if (rightPocket.indexOf('red stone') === -1)
3   {
4     console.log("You don't have a precious red stone in your pocket");
5   }
```

indexOf returns the first ocurrence of an item in an array, alternatively you can use lastIndexOf to find the last ocurrence of an item.

The last safe array method is slice which is a non-destructive alternative to splice. This being JavaScript we couldn't have a similar signature. Instead of working with the *start index* and the *number of items* to remove, the slice method expects the start and end of the subarray to extract:

```
1   console.log('leather bag has ' + leatherBag.length + ' items: ' +
2              leatherBag);
3   // => leather bag has 2 items: skeleton skull,dried meat
4
5   // let's be god and reproduce the dried meat
6   console.log(leatherBag.slice(/* start */ 1, /* end */ 3));
7   // => ['dried meat']
8   // Note how slice extracts up to but not including the end
9
10  // we still have two items in the original array
11  console.log('leather bag has ' + leatherBag.length + ' items: ' +
12             leatherBag);
13  // => leather bag has 2 items: skeleton skull,dried meat
```

slice also supports negative indices which represent starting counting from the end of the array. The end parameters is also optional, so we can extract a new array containing only the last item from the original array pretty easily:

```
1   var lastItem = leatherBag.slice(-1);
2   console.log(lastItem);
3   // => ["dried meat"]
```

Iterating an array

Prior to ES6, JavaScript offered two ways in which to iterate over the elements of an array: the for/in loop and the Array.prototype.forEach method.

The for/in loop is a JavaScript construct that lets you iterate over the properties[99] of any object. In the case of an array, these properties are the indices of the array:

---

[99]The for/in loop let's you iterate over all the *enumerable* properties of an object. Later in this section of the book you'll learn more about the concept of enumerability and how it differs to the concept of iterability introduced in ES6.

```
1   console.log('You examine your inventory: ');
2   for(var index in leatherBag){
3     console.log(leatherBag[index]);
4   }
5   // => You examine your inventory:
6   //     skeleton skull"
7   //     dried meat"
```

The forEach method offers a better developer experience to iterating as it gives you each item of the array directly:

```
1   console.log('You examine your inventory.... closer: ')
2   leatherBag.forEach(function(item) {
3     console.log('You examine ' + item + ' closely');
4   });
5   // => You examine your inventory.... closer:
6   //     You examine skeleton skull closely
7   //     You examine dried meat closely
```

And, additionally, it gives you access to each index and the array itself:

```
1   console.log('You examine your inventory.... veeery closely: ')
2   leatherBag.forEach(function(item, index, array) {
3     console.log('You examine ' + item + ' closely (' +
4               (index+1) + '/' + array.length + ')');
5   });
6   // => You examine your inventory.... veeery closely:
7   //     You examine skeleton skull closely (1/2)
8   //     You examine dried meat closely (2/2)
```

ES6 generalizes the concept of iterability in JavaScript through the addition of the iterator protocol and the for/of loop:

```
1  console.log('You look at the stuff in your bag:');
2  for(let item of leatherBag){
3    console.log(item);
4  }
5  // => You look at the stuff in your bag:
6  //    skeleton skull
7  //    dried meat
```

JavaScript Arrays and LINQ

If you thought that everything you've seen thus far was everything there was about JavaScript arrays you're in for a treat, because *Wait! There is more!*.

One of my favorites features of the JavaScript array is that it comes with a set of methods that are very similar to .NET LINQ. Yes, you read it. Isn't that absolutely awesome? I devote a whole chapter to the Array's LINQ-like methods in the functional programming tome of this series, but here's a small appetizer.

```
1  var shop = [
2    {name: 'sword of truth', type: 'sword', damage: 60, price: 1000},
3    {name: 'shield of stamina', type: 'shield', defense: 50,
4     price: 500, modifiers: [{value: 2, characteristic: 'stamina'}]},
5    {name: 'minor potion of healing', type: 'potion', price: 1,
6     effects: [{value: 10, characteristic: 'hitPoints'}]},
7    {name: 'grand potion of healing', type: 'potion', price: 7,
8     effects: [{value: 50, characteristic: 'hitPoints'}]}
9  ];
10
11 console.log('The shopkeeper looks at you greedily and tells you:');
12 console.log('*These are the potions we have today sir...' +
13             'they are the best in the kingdowm!*');
14 var potions = shop
15         .filter(item => item.type === 'potion')
16         .map(potion => potion.name);
17 for(let potion of potions){
18     console.log(potion);
19 }
```

```
20   // => The shopkeeper looks at you greedily and tells you:
21   //    *These are the potions we have today sir...
22   //     they are the best in the kingdowm!*
23   //    minor potion of healing
24   //    grand potion of healing
```

I used *arrow functions* in this example to give you a feeling of familiarity between the `Array.prototype` LINQ-like methods and LINQ, but you must know that most of these methods are available in ES5 and work just as well with normal function expressions.

```
1   var totalPrice = shop
2       .map(function(item){return item.price;})
3       .reduce(function(total, itemPrice){
4          return total + itemPrice;
5       }, /* initialTotal */ 0);
6   console.log('The total price of the items is ' + totalPrice +
7            ' silvers');
8   // => The total price of the items is 1508 silvers
```

Other ES6 and ES7 Features

In addition to formalizing the concept of iteration in Arrays, ES6 brings several new helpful methods that will make operating on Arrays and Array-likes easier.

The `Array.from` method let's you create an array from any `array-like` and iterable object. It is ES6's solution to the commonplace practice of using `Array.prototype.slice` in ES5 to convert array-likes into proper arrays:

```
1  // (in this case it'd better to use the rest syntax ...items)
2  function sortItems(){
3    var items = Array.from(arguments);
4    return items.sort();
5  }
6  console.log(sortItems('mandragora', 'amber', "elf's tongue"));
7  // => ["amber", "elf's tongue", "mandragora"]
```

Any object that can be iterated over can be converted into an array using Array.from. For instance, a Map:

```
1  var library = new Map();
2  library.set('horror', ['It', 'The thing', 'horrors of Swarland']);
3  library.set('love', ['Romance and Betrayal', 'Beauty I']);
4  library.set('history', ['The fall of the Kraagg Empire']);
5
6  console.log('Welcome to the library of Anriva!' +
7             ' These are our most valuable books');
8  Array.from(library)
9      .forEach(keyValuePair => {
10   console.log(keyValuePair);
11 });
12 // => ["horror", ["It", "The thing", "horrors of Swarland"]]
13 //    ["love", ["Romance and Betrayal", "Beauty I"]]
14 //    ["history", ["The fall of the Kraagg Empire"]]
```

Array.from also takes a second optional argument, a map function that just like LINQ's Select let's you transform each element within the source array into something else of your own choosing:

```
1   function sortItemsProperty(selector, ...args){
2     var items = Array.from(args, selector);
3     return items.sort();
4   }
5
6   console.log(sortItemsProperty(i => i.price,
7     {name: 'mandragora', price: 2},
8     {name: 'amber', price: 10}));
9   // => [10, 2]
```

The `Array.isArray` method provides a more convenient and safer [100] way to check whether an object is an array or not. Prior to ES6 we used to use the following approach:

```
1   console.log('Shop is an array: ' + (shop instanceof Array));
```

With `Array.isArray` it's more straightforward:

```
1   console.log('Shop is an array: ' + Array.isArray(shop));
```

The `Array.of` method lets you create an array from a variable number of arguments and is equivalent to `[]`:

```
1   let ingredients = Array.of('bat wings', 'unicorn horn',
2                               'sesame seeds');
3   // => ['bat wings', 'unicorn horn', 'sesame seeds']
```

Why would you want to use `Array.of` instead of `[]` then? There is a corner case application where `Array.of` is essential, **when creating Array subclasses**:

---

[100]See bit.ly/javascriptmancy-is-this-an-array for more info on why instanceof is not a safe way to determine that an object is an array.

```
1   class ItemsArray extends Array{
2     price(){
3       return this.map(i => i.price).reduce((a, p) => a + p, 0);
4     }
5   }
6   // how can you instantiate an array of ItemsArray in a consistent way
7   let itemsArray = ItemsArray.of(
8     {name: 'bat wings', price: 10},
9     {name: 'unicorn horn', price: 10000},
10    {name: 'sesame seeds', price: 1}
11  )
12  console.log(`the price of all your wares is ` +
13              `${itemsArray.price()} golden coins`);
14  // => the price of all your wares is 10011 golden coins
```

`Array.prototype.copyWithin()` provides a way to copy items within the same array, that is, pick a portion of an array and copy it within the same array. Let's illustrate it with an example:

```
1   [1, 2, 3, 4, 5].copyWithin(/* target index */ 0,
2                              /* start */ 3, /* end */ 4);
3   // copies the items between indexes 3 and 4 => the item 4
4   // into the index 0 of the array
5   // [4, 1, 3, 4, 5]
6
7   // if you leave the end out, it defaults to the length of the array
8   [1, 2, 3, 4, 5].copyWithin(/* target index */ 0, /* start */ 3);
9   // [4, 5, 3, 4, 5]
```

`Array.prototype.fill()` provides a convenient way to fill an existing array with a specific item:

```
1   // [].fill(item, start=0, end=this.length)
2   [1, 2, 3].fill(':)');          // [':)', ':)', ':)']
3   [1, 2, 3].fill(':)', 1);       // [1, ':)', ':)']
4   [1, 2, 3].fill(':)', 1, 2);    // [1, ':)', 3]
```

New Array methods in ES7

ES7, while being a very small incremental release of JavaScript, brings a very convenient way to check whether an item exists within an array, the `Array.prototype.includes()` method:

```
1  if (!rightPocket.includes('red stone'))
2  {
3    console.log("You don't have a precious red stone in your pocket");
4  }
```

This provides a much better developer experience than the `indexOf` method that we saw previously in this chapter:

```
1  // indexOf returns -1 when it can't find an item
2  if (rightPocket.indexOf('red stone') === -1)
3  {
4    console.log("You don't have a precious red stone in your pocket");
5  }
```

In addition to providing which item within the array you are looking for, you can specify an starting index for the search:

```
1  let herbs = ['sage', 'salvia', 'aloe vera'];
2  console.log('Is sage the last item in my herb poach?:',
3     herbs.includes('sage', herbs.length);
4  // => is sage the last item in my herb poach? : false
```

Array Cheatsheet

Basics	description
[]	Create an empty array
[1, 2, 3]	Create an array
Array(n)	Create array with n undefined elements
Array(1, 2, 3)	Equivalent to [1, 2, 3]

Array Unsafe Methods ES5

method name	superpower
`Array.prototype.push(n1, n2...)` - `[].push(1)` - `[].push(1, 2, 3)`	Append item to the end of an array
`Array.prototype.pop()` - `let n = [1].pop()`	Remove item from the end of an array
`Array.prototype.shift()` - `let n = [1].shift()`	Remove item from the beginning of an array
`Array.prototype.unshift(n1, n2...)` - `[].unshift(1)` - `[].unshift(1, 2, 3)`	Insert item to the beginning of an array
`Array.prototype.splice(start, length, n1, n2)` - `[1,2].splice(0, 1)` - `[1,2].splice(-1, 1)` - `[1,2,3,4].splice(1,2)` - `[1,2].splice(0, 1, 'ash')` - `[1,2,3,4].splice(1,2, 'ash', 'gold')`	Remove items from any arbitrary position and insert new ones - remove first item - remove last item - remove two items in the middle - change first item for 'ash' - change two middle items from 'ash' and 'gold'
`Array.prototype.sort(compareFn)` - `[1,2,3].sort()` - `[1,2,3].sort((a,b) => a-b)`	Sort array - sort according to character UNICODE code point value - sort numbers - $a > b \Rightarrow$ return > 0 - $a < b \Rightarrow$ return < 0 - $a === b \Rightarrow$ return 0
`Array.prototype.reverse()` . - `[1,2,3].reverse()`	Reverse order of items within an array

Array Safe Methods ES5

method name	superpower
`Array.prototype.concat(arr)` - `[1,2,3].concat([5,6])`	Concatenates two arrays
`Array.prototype.join(separator)` - `[1,2,3].join(', ')`	Join items of the array using a separator - `"1, 2, 3"`
`Array.prototype.indexOf(n)` - `[1,2,3].indexOf(1)` - `[1,2,3].indexOf(55)`	Returns index of the first ocurrence of an item within an array - returns -1 if the item is not in the array
`Array.prototype.lastIndexOf(n)` - `[1,1,1].lastIndexOf(1)` - `[1,1,1].lastIndexOf(22)`	Returns index of the last ocurrence of an item within an array - returns -1 if the item is not in the array
`Array.prototype.slice(start, end)` - `[1,2,3].slice(1,2)` - `[1,2,3].slice(1)` - `[1,2,3].slice(-1)`	Returns subarray between start and end indexes. end indexed item is not included. - returns [2] - returns [2, 3] - returns [3]

Iterating Arrays

method	superpower
`for/in` loop - `for(var i in arr)`	Loops over the indexes of an array
`for/of` loop - `for(let i of arr)`	Loops over the items of an array
`Array.prototype.forEach`	Loops over the items of an array

method	superpower
- `arr.forEach(doSomething)`	

Array LINQ-like Methods

- See to Chapter LINQ chapter in the Functional Programming Tome of the Series.

New Array Methods in ES6

method name	superpower
`Array.from` - `Array.from(arguments)`	Convert any iterable in an array. Also works on array-likes.
`Array.isArray(obj)` - `Array.isArray([1,2,3])`	Check whether an object is an array.
`Array.prototype.of()` - `MyArray.of(1,2,3)`	Instantiate a new array. Useful when subclassing `Array`
`Array.prototype.copyWithin(target, start, end)` - `[1,2,3].copyWithin(0, 1, 2)`	Copy array subset in place, that is, within the same array. - [2,2,3]
`Array.prototype.fill(item, start, end)` - `[1,2,3].fill(1)` - `[1,2,3].fill(1,2)` - `[1,2,3].fill(1,1,2)`	Fill array with items -[1,1,1] -[1,2,1] -[1,1,3]

ES7

method name	superpower
`Array.prototype.includes(item, start)`	Check whether an array contains an `item`

method name	superpower
- `[1,1,1].includes(2)`	

Concluding

JavaScript's array is an all-purpose collection, a extremely and versatile data structure that will cover most of you application needs. You can use it as a stack, a queue, a list, you can easily perform destructive and non-destructive operations on it. It also has support for LINQ-like functionality that will make working with collections of items a breeze.

Even though JavaScript's array is awesome, there's a couple of use cases that are best suited for other data structures: storing items by an arbitrary key and managing collections of unique items. And that's what we will learn in the next two chapters since both `Maps` (like a `Dictionary<T,T>`) and `Sets` are two new data structures available from *ES6* onwards.

```
/* 4 hours later... */

randalf.says("I'm convinced there were some wands here...");

mooleen.says("Perhaps there were... some eons ago.");

randalf.says("Ok, I have an idea!")
randalf.says("Let's start collecting everything that " +
             "looks like a wand");
randalf.says("You can never trust magic items as you well know");
randalf.says("It could pretty much look like anything");
```

Exercises

Experiment JavaScriptmancer!

You can experiment with these exercises and some possible solutions in this jsFiddle[101] or downloading the source code from GitHub[102].

Let's Go Through All These Boxes

There's numerous boxes with all kind of things. Use array functions to find wands and put them in yet another box. Wands are any object that has a type property with a value of 'wand'.

```
1   let blueBox = ['feather', 'ring',
2       'rotten piece of meat', 'wooden stick',
3       {name: 'wand', type: 'wand', power: 10}];
4   let redBox = [{name: 'bronze sword', type: 'sword', damage: 30},
5       {name: 'iron shield', type: 'shield', defense: 20},
6       {name: 'battle axe', type: 'wand', power: 150}];
7   let greenBox = ['bundle of hair that looks suspicious',
8       {name: 'helmet', type: 'helmet', defense: 10},
9       {name: 'dark schepter', type: 'wand', power: 100},
10      {name: 'firestaff', type: 'wand', power: 120},
11      {name: 'vanilla popsicle', type: 'wand', power: 20}];
```

Solution

```
1   function getMeWandzSpell(...boxes){
2     let wands = [];
3     for(let box of boxes){
4       for(let item of box){
```

---

[101]http://bit.ly/javascriptmancy-arrays-exercises
[102]https://github.com/vintharas/javascriptmancy-code-samples

```
5          if (item.type === 'wand') wands.push(item);
6        }
7     }
8     return wands;
9   }
10
11  let wands = getMeWandzSpell(blueBox, redBox, greenBox);
12  console.log(`${wands.map(w => w.name)}`);
13  // => wand,battle axe,dark schepter,firestaff,vanilla popsicle
14
15  mooleen.says('done!');
```

 ## Now Perfect it With LINQ... Err... Array.Prototype Methods!

Use `Array.prototype` methods like `reduce` and `filter` to perfect the pervious function!

This may be hard if you haven't worked with LINQ or functional programming before so don't fret if you can't solve it yet. We'll cover LINQ and functional programming in depth in the functional programming tome of this series.

Solution

```
1  function getMeWandzSpellWithLINQ(...boxes){
2    return boxes
3      .reduce((items, box) => [...items, ...box], [])
4      .filter(item => item.type === 'wand');
5  }
6
7  let wandsLinq = getMeWandzSpellWithLINQ(blueBox, redBox, greenBox);
8  console.log(`${wandsLinq.map(w => w.name)}`);
9  // => wand,battle axe,dark schepter,firestaff,vanilla popsicle
```

```
10
11    mooleen.says('Check that out! Much better right?');
```

Find The Most Powerful Wand!

Use whichever array methods you've learned to find the most powerful wand (that with the highest power value).

Hint: sort

Solution

```
1   const sortByPower = (wand, anotherWand) =>
2                       wand.power - anotherWand.power;
3   const sortByPowerDescending = (wand, anotherWand) =>
4                       -1 * sortByPower(wand, anotherWand);
5
6   function findTheMostPowerfulWand(wands){
7     const sortedWands = wands.sort(sortByPowerDescending);
8     const [mostPowerfulWand] = sortedWands;
9     return mostPowerfulWand;
10  }
11
12  let mooleensWand = findTheMostPowerfulWand(wands);
13  console.log(`Behold Mooleen, this is your wand!` +
14              ` The ${mooleensWand.name}!!!!`);
15  // => Behold Mooleen, this is your wand! The battle axe!!!!
16
17  mooleen.says('Yeeeees!!!!');
18  randalf.says("I so didn't see this coming");
19  mooleen.says('I knew it! It was meant to be!');
20
21  randalf.says('All right, all right. Now you are ready!');
22  mooleen.says('To find my way home?');
23
24  randalf.says('No! To save Asturi!');
```

Organizing Your Data With ES6 Maps

It is unknown who designed the first map.

But it is said that he got tired of traversing
a whole array of shoes every time he decided
to go for a walk.

- Ckor Srich
Royal Buffoon 2nd Age

```
randalf.says('Now you are a JavaScript-mancer!');
randalf.says('Well... you are THE JavaScript-mancer! The last one');

mooleen.says("But you? And your brothers?");
randalf.says("We can't use any magic anymore, and without magic...");

randalf.says('...we are pretty wise though');
zandalf.says('...and great conversationalists!');
bandalf.says('...and handsome!');

mooleen.says('Oh my god! Where did you just come from?')
mooleen.says("I haven't seen you in the last... what...");
mooleen.says("5 or 6 chapters of the book?");

bandalf.says("We've been tracking");
zandalf.says("surveilling");
bandalf.says("spying");
zandalf.says("barbacueing");

randalf.says("They have been following and studying Great");
randalf.says('Is time for you to face him and for ever banish him ' +
             'from existence!');
randalf.says('Are you ready?');

mooleen.says('Ready as I am going to be');
randalf.says("Ok, then it's time for us to share the secret bows of \
the order");

randalf.says(`In brightest day, in blackest night,
             No evil shall escape my sight.
             Let those who worship evil's might,
             Beware my power - JavaScript-manciaaay!`);

mooleen.says('Javascript-manciaaay? Really?');
zandalf.says(`We never said we were good poets`);

randalf.says('Ehm...Take a look at these maps...');
```

Take a Look at These Maps

ES6 brings two new data structures to JavaScript, the Map and the
Set. This chapter is devoted to the Map, which is fundamentally a

HashTable. We often refer to it as `Dictionary` in C#. JavaScript's `Map` provides a simple API to store objects by an arbitrary key, a very essential functionality required in many JavaScript programs.

JavaScript's Map

Experiment JavaScriptmancer!!

You can experiment with all examples in this chapter directly within this jsBin[103] or downloading the source code from GitHub[104].

You can create a `Map` in JavaScript using the new operator:

```
1   const wizardsArchive = new Map();
```

Once created the `Map` offers two fundamental methods: `get` and `set`. As you can probably guess using your wizardy intuition, you use `set` to add an object to the `Map`:

```
1   wizardsArchive.set( /* key */ 'jaime', /* value */ {
2       name: 'jaime',
3       title: 'The Bold',
4       race: 'ewok',
5       traits: ['joyful', 'hairless']
6   });
```

And `get` to retrieve it:

---

[103]http://bit.ly/javascriptmancy-data-structures-maps
[104]https://github.com/vintharas/javascriptmancy-code-samples

```
1  console.log('Wizard with key jaime => ', wizardsArchive.get('jaime')\
2  );
3  /* => Item with key jaime =>
4    [object Object] {
5      name: "jaime",
6      race: "ewok",
7      trait: ["joyful", "hairless"]
8    }
9  */
```

This being JavaScript you can use any type as key or value, and the same Map can hold disparate types for both keys and values. Yey! Freedom!:

```
1  wizardsArchive.set(42, "What is the answer to life, the universe and\
2    everything?")
3  console.log(wizardsArchive.get(42));
4  // => What is the answer to life, the universe and everything?
5
6  wizardsArchive.set('firebolt', (target) => console.log(`${target} is\
7    consumed by fire`));
8  wizardsArchive.get('firebolt')('frigate');
9  // => frigate is consumed by fire
```

You can easily find how many elements are stored within a Map using the size property:

```
1  console.log(`there are ${wizardsArchive.size} thingies in the archiv\
2  e`)
3  // => there are 3 thingies in the archive
```

Removing items from a Map is very straightforward as well, you use the delete method with the item's key. Let's do some cleanup and remove those nonsensical items from the last example:

```
1  wizardsArchive.delete(42);
2  wizardsArchive.delete('firebolt');
```

Now that we have removed them, we can verify that indeed they are gone using the has method:

```
1  console.log(`Wizards archive has info on '42': ` +
2                `${wizardsArchive.has(42)}`);
3  // => Wizards archive has info on '42': false
4  console.log(`Wizards archive has info on 'firebolt':
5    ${wizardsArchive.has('firebolt')}`);
6  // => Wizards archive has info on 'firebolt': false
```

And when we are done for the day and want to remove every item at once, the Map offers the clear method:

```
1  wizardsArchive.clear();
2  console.log(`there are ${wizardsArchive.size} wizards in the archive\
3  `);
4  // => there are 0 wizards in the archive
```

Iterating Over the Elements of a Map

Just like with arrays you can iterate over the elements of a Map using the for/of loop:

```
1  // let's add some items back so we have something to iterate over...
2  // the set method is chainable by the by!
3  wizardsArchive
4      .set('jaime', {name: 'jaime', title: 'The Bold', race: 'ewok',
5        traits: ['joyful', 'hairless']})
6      .set('theRock', {name: 'theRock', race: 'giant',
7        traits: ['big shoulders']});
8
9  for(let keyValue of wizardsArchive){
10    console.log(`${keyValue[0]} : ${JSON.stringify(keyValue[1])}`);
11  }
```

```
12  /*
13  "jaime :  {\"name\":\"jaime\", \"race\":\".....
14  "theRock :  {\"name\":\"theRock\", \"race\.....
15  */
```

The default `Map` iterator (also available via the `entries` property) lets you traverse a `Map` using *key-value pairs*. Each pair is an array with two items, the first being the key and the second the value. The example above is equivalent to:

```
1  for(let keyValue of wizardsArchive.entries()){
2    console.log(`${keyValue[0]} : ${JSON.stringify(keyValue[1])}`);
3  }
```

Both examples above are a little displeasing to the eye, aren't they? You can improve them greatly if you use the destructuring syntax to extract the key and the value from the key-value array:

```
1  for(let [key, value] of wizardsArchive){
2    console.log(`${key} : ${JSON.stringify(value)}`);
3  }
```

Much nicer right? Alternatively you can use the `Map.prototype.forEach` method analogous to `Array.prototype.forEach` but with keys and values:

```
1  wizardsArchive.forEach((key,value) =>
2    console.log(`${key} : ${JSON.stringify(value)}`)
3  );
4  // => jaime: {\"name\" ...
5  // => theRock: {\"name\" ...
```

In addition to iterating over *key-value pairs*, you can also traverse the keys:

```
1  console.log(Array.from(wizardsArchive.keys()).join(', '));
2  // => jaime, theRock"
```

And the `values`:

```
1  console.log(Array.from(wizardsArchive.values())
2                 .map(i => i.race).join(', '));
3  // => ewok, giant
```

Both the `keys` and `values` iterators provide a better developer experience in those cases where you just need the keys or the values.

Note that in the examples above we created an `Array` from the `keys` and the `values` iterators and concatenated its elements using `join`. This resulted in us "iterating" over the whole `Map` at once, but we could have just as well used a `for/of` loop and operated on each item separately.

Creating a Map From an Iterable Collection

In addition to creating empty *Maps* and filling them with information, you can create *Maps* from any iterable collection. For instance, let's say that you have an array of wizards:

```
1  let jaimeTheWizard = {name: 'jaime', title: 'The Bold',
2                     race: 'ewok', traits: ['joyful', 'hairless']};
3  let theRock = {name: 'theRock', title: 'The Mighty',
4                  race: 'giant', trait: ['big shoulders']};
5  let randalfTheRed = {name: 'randalf', title: 'The Red',
6                     race: 'human', traits: ['pyromaniac']};
7
8  let wizards = [jaimeTheWizard, theRock, randalfTheRed];
```

And you want to group them by `race` and put them on a dictionary where you can easily find them. You can do that by passing a suitably shaped collection into the `Map` constructor:

```
1   var wizardsByRace = new Map(wizards
2                       .map(w => [/*key*/ w.race, /*value*/ w]));
3
4   console.log(Array.from(wizardsByRace.keys()));
5   // => ["ewok", "giant", "human"]
6   console.log(wizardsByRace.get("human").name);
7   // => randalf
```

The Map constructor expects to find an iterator that goes through key-value pairs represented as an array where the first element is the *key* and the second element is the *value*:

```
1   [[key1, value1], [key2, value2], ...]
```

In the example above we used map over the wizards array to transform each element of the original array into a new one that represents key-value pairs, which are the race of the wizard and the wizard itself.

```
1   [["ewok", jaimeTheWizard], ["giant", theRock],
2    ["human", randalfTheRed]]
```

We could create a helper method toKeyValue to make this transformation easier:

```
1   function* toKeyValue(arr, keySelector){
2     for(let item of arr)
3       yield [keySelector(item), item];
4   }
```

The toKeyValue function above is a generator, a special function that helps you build iterators. You'll learn more about generators later in this tome on data structures. For the time being, you just need to understand that we are transforming each element of an array into a key value pair.

When we call the generator we effectively transform the array into an iterator of key value pairs:

```
1    var keyValues = toKeyValue(wizards, w => w.name)
```

We can pass this new iterator to the to the `Map` constructor and obtain the desired `Map` of wizards:

```
1    var keyValues = toKeyValue(wizards, w => w.name);
2    var wizardsByName = new Map(keyValues);
3
4    console.log(Array.from(wizardsByName.keys()));
5    // => ["jaime", "theRock", "randalf"]
```

We still need to perform the transformation in two separate steps which is not very developer friendly. We can improve this by extending the `Array.prototype` with a `toKeyValue` method:

```
1    Array.prototype.toKeyValue = function* toKeyValue(keySelector){
2      for(let item of this)
3        yield [keySelector(item), item];
4    }
```

This would allow you to rewrite the previous example like this:

```
1    var wizardsByTitle = new Map(wizards.toKeyValue(w => w.title));
2    console.log(Array.from(wizardsByTitle.keys()));
3    // => ["The Bold", "The Mighty", "The Red"]
```

You could even bring it one step further by creating a `toMap` function:

```
1  Array.prototype.toMap = function(keySelector) {
2    return new Map(this.toKeyValue(keySelector));
3  }
4  var wizardsByTitle = wizards.toMap(w => w.title);
5  console.log(Array.from(wizardsByTitle.keys()));
6  // => ["The Bold", "The Mighty", "The Red"]
```

Map Cheatsheet

Basic Operations

Basics	description
var map = new Map()	Create an empty map
var map = new Map(iterator)	Create a map from an iterator
var value = map.get('key')	Get a value from the map by key. If the key is not in the map it returns undefined. The key can be of any type.
map.set('key', 'value')	Add an item to the map. If the key already exists within the map the value is overwritten. The key and value can be of any type. Chainable.
map.delete('key')	Remove item by key if it exists. Returns true if an item has been removed and false otherwise.
map.has('key')	Check whether a key exists in the map. Returns true or false whether the key exists or not respectively.
map.size	Returns the number of items in the map
map.clear()	Remove all items within the map

Iterating a Map

Methods of Iteration	description
map.forEach((key,value,map) ⇒ {})	Iterate over every key value pair within a map
map.entries()	Returns a key/value pair iterator. This is the default iterator in Map.prototype[Symbol.iterator]
map.keys()	Returns a key iterator
map.values()	Returns a values iterator

Concluding

In this chapter you learnt how you can take advantage of the new Map data structure to store data by an arbitrary key of your choice. Map is JavaScript's implementation of a HashTable, or a Dictionary in C#, where you can use any type as key and as value.

You also learnt about the basic operations you can perform with a Map, how you can store, retrieve and remove data, check whether or not a key exists within the Map and how to iterate it in different ways.

```
mooleen.says('So are these maps maps where you find stuff or'
             + ' the data structure?');
bandalf.says('They are both.');

zandalf.says('A Map of maps');

randalf.says('Easily indexable by evil sorcerer');

bandalf.says("We've been working on it for years!");

randalf.says("Just pick what you need and upload it " +
             "to your familiar");
mooleen.says("My what?");
randalf.says("You haven't noticed that 5 pound rat " +
             "on your shoulder?");

/*
```

```
Mooleen slowly turns her head to discover a immense
rat, black as coal, perched on her shoulder.
The scene that would've been disturbing by itself
reaches a whole new level when the rat smiles to Mooleen
in a very human, and at the same time completely inhuman, fashion.
*/

mooleen.says('Sweet mother of...');

rat.says("Hello master...");

mooleen.says('I think I just had a heart attack');

bandalf.says('We all do at some point...');
zandalf.says(`I keep telling you we need to exercise more...`);
bandalf.says(`And that extra serving doesn't help either`);
zanfalf.says(`No it doesn't`);

randalf.says('Familiars!')
randalf.says('They are a great aid to JavaScript-mancers');
randalf.says('You can entrust them with your life');
```

Exercises

Experiment JavaScriptmancer!

You can experiment with these exercises and some possible solutions in this jsFiddle[105] or downloading the source code from GitHub[106].

---

[105]http://bit.ly/javascriptmancy-data-structures-maps-exercises
[106]https://github.com/vintharas/javascriptmancy-code-samples

Upload The Maps To Your Familiar

It is said that a human can only maintain 7 things in short-term memory and although they can maintain much more in the long-term one, it requires time and we need to save the world in the next chapter before we finish the book.

Familiars are great aid to JavaScript-mancers because not only do they help you perform menial tasks, they also have a innate knack for remembering things. Create a Map to hold Great and Great's leaders known locations and give it to your familiar by printing the locations to the console.

Note that these locations are in turn stored in a map that looks like this:

```
1   // Key: Great
2   // Value: {
3   //   minions: ['dragon', 'balrog', '400 orcs' ,'12213 goblins'],
4   //   fortresses: ['Tower of doom', 'Cave of calimity','Beach house'],
5   //   knownLocations: { /* known locations object */ },
6   //   knownWeaknesses: ['mild lactose intolerance']
7   // }
8   // Key: Great lieutenant
9   // Value ....
10  // Key: Sauron
11  // Value ....
12  // etc...
```

You'll first need to create the map representation yourself. In order to find Great's leaders consider that the key contains the string 'Great'.

Solution

```
1   // intelligence Archives gathered by Bandalf and Zandalf
2   let intelligenceArchives = new Map();
3   intelligenceArchives.set('Great lieutenant', {
```

```
4     minions: [],
5     fortresses: [],
6     knownLocations: { toString(){ return 'Beach house';}},
7     knownWeaknesses: ['Allergy to gluten']
8   });
9   intelligenceArchives.set('Great', {
10    minions: ['dragon', 'balrog', '400 orcs' ,'12213 goblins'],
11    fortresses: ['Tower of doom', 'Cave of calimity','Beach house'],
12    knownLocations: { toString(){ return 'Ultrasecret base';}},
13    knownWeaknesses: ['mild lactose intolerance']
14  });
15  intelligenceArchives.set('Sauron', {
16    minions: ['immense army'],
17    fortresses: ['many fortresses'],
18    knownLocations: { /* known locations object */ },
19    knownWeaknesses: ['Hyperopia']
20  });
21
22  // Get the keys
23  let keysThatContainGreat = [...intelligenceArchives.keys()]
24                              .filter(k => k.includes('Great'));
25  console.log('Persons of interest: ', keysThatContainGreat);
26  // Create the new map
27  let knownLocationsKeyValuePair = keysThatContainGreat
28      .map(k => [k, intelligenceArchives.get(k).knownLocations]);
29  let knownLocations = new Map(knownLocationsKeyValuePair);
30
31  for(let [evilDude, location] of knownLocations){
32    console.log(`${evilDude} is in ${location}`);
33  }
34  // => Great lieutenant is in Beach house
35  //    Great is in Ultrasecret base
36
37  rat.says('Understood chief!')
38  mooleen.says(`Then it's time to kick some ass!`);
```

Sets, For When There Can Only Be One

We live in a world
that celebrates personality.

Enjoy your uniqueness,
wear it on your sleeve,
wherever you go.

People will love you for it.

> - Lenrolc Srich
> Be yourself

```
/*
    A dark and secret room,
    in a dark and secret corner,
    of a dark and secret and evil, evil, evil lair.
*/
great.says("Are all of the preparations ready?");

grate.says("Aye master. They're ready. " +
          "Prepared the magical charges m'self");

great.says("Great job Grate.");
great.says("They'll never see it coming hahaha");
great.says("Damn useless band of misfits. A complete waste of air.");

grate.says("Complete waste of space m'lord");

great.says("Have you prepared the remote eye as well?");
great.says("I wouldn't want to miss randalf's face when " +
          "he realizes we've known where they've been " +
          "all along and that he's a goner");
grate.says("Aye sir, I also took care of that personally.");

great.says("Excellent! " +
          "Well bring me some popcorn and let's start the show");
/* grate coughs uncomfortably */
grate.says("Ehem... We're out of popcorn sir");

great.says("Out of popcorn?");
grate.says("Well sir, no farmers, no corn, no popcorn");

great.says("Damn... I did love my popcorn");
grate.says("That you did sir.");

great.says("Well... No way of fixing that right now.");
great.says("Let's just move this lever and...");

/*
Great lifts his arm and his hand slowly approaches the lever that
will mean the destruction of JavaScrip-mancy and the forces of
good for ever...
*/

mooleen.throw({item:'battle axe', target: 'lever'});
// => mooleen throws the battle axe and chops Great's hand

rat.says('Impressive master');
mooleen.says('I know right?' +
```

```
               'I was sooo targeting that hand all along.');

   rat.says("You're one of a kind");
```

You Are One of a Kind

A Set is a data structure used to represent a distinct collection of items where each item is unique and only appears once. This is such a common need that, if you have been working with JavaScript for a little while, chances are that you have needed to roll your own implementation at some point. Well, you'll need to do that no more because ES6 comes with a native Set implementation. Hurrah!!

Working With Sets

Experiment JavaScriptmancer!!

You can experiment with all examples in this chapter directly within this jsBin[107] or downloading the source code from GitHub[108].

You can create a new set using the Set constructor:

```
1  let set = new Set();
```

Or from an iterable collection like an array:

---

[107]http://bit.ly/javascriptmancy-data-structures-sets
[108]https://github.com/vintharas/javascriptmancy-code-samples

```
1  let elementsOfMagic = new Set([
2      'earth', 'fire', 'air',
3      'earth', 'fire', 'water'
4  ]);
5
6  console.log(`These are the elements of magic: ` +
7               `${[...elementsOfMagic]}`);
8  // => These are the elements of magic: earth, fire, air, water
```

As you can appreciate from the example above, the array had a duplicated value of earth that is removed when creating the Set. That's because a Set will automatically remove any duplicated items and only store each specific item once.

You can easily add more items to a Set using the add method:

```
1  elementsOfMagic.add('aether');
2
3  console.log(`More magic!: ${[...elementsOfMagic]}`);
4  // => More magic!: earth, fire, air, water, aether
```

The add method is chainable, so adding multiple new items is very convenient:

```
1  elementsOfMagic.add('earth').add('air').add('water');
```

You can check whether an item exists within a Set by using the has method:

```
1  console.log(`Is water one of the sacred elements of magic?` +
2               ` ${elementsOfMagic.has('water')}`)
3  // => Is water one of the sacred elements of magic? true
```

And you can remove items from a set using delete:

```
1  elementsOfMagic.delete('aether');
2
3  console.log(`The aether element flows like the tides and
4  like the tides sometimes disappears:
5  ${[...elementsOfMagic]}`);
6
7  // => The aether element flows
8  //     like the tides and sometimes disappears:
9  //     earth, fire, air, water
```

Additionally, you can get the number of elements within a set using the `size` property:

```
1  console.log(`${elementsOfMagic.size} are the elements of magic`);
```

And remove all the items from a set using `clear`:

```
1  const castMagicShield = () => elementsOfMagic.clear();
2  castMagicShield();
3
4  console.log(`ups! I can't feel the elements: ` +
5              `${elementsOfMagic.size}`);
6  // => ups! I can't feel the elements: 0
```

If you take a minute to reflect about the Set API and try to remember the Map from the previous chapter you'll realize that both APIs are exceptionally consistent with each other. Consistency is awesome, it will help you learn these APIs in a heartbeat and write less error-prone code.

Let's see how we iterate over the elements of a Set.

Iterating Sets

Just like Map you can iterate over the elements of a Set using the for/of loop:

```
1  elementsOfMagic.add('fire').add('water').add('air').add('earth');
2  for(let element of elementsOfMagic){
3    console.log(`element: ${element}`);
4  }
5  // => element: fire
6  //     element: water
7  //     element: air
8  //     element: earth
```

In this case, instead of key/value pairs you iterate over each item within a Set. Notice how the elements are iterated in the same order as they were inserted. The default iterator for a Set is the values iterator. The next snippet of code is equivalent to the one above:

```
1  for(let element of elementsOfMagic.values()){
2    console.log(`element: ${element}`);
3  }
```

The Set also has iterators for keys and entries just like the Map although you probably won't need to use them. The keys iterator is equivalent to values. The entries iterator transforms each item into a key/value pair where both the key and the value are each item in the Set. So if you use the entries iterator you'll just iterate over [value, value] pairs.

In addition to using either of these iterators, you can take advantage of the Set.prototype.forEach method to traverse the items in a Set:

```
1  elementsOfMagic.forEach((value, alsoValue, set) => {
2    console.log(`element: ${value}`);
3  })
4  // => element: fire
5  //    element: water
6  //    element: air
7  //    element: earth
```

Using Array Methods With Sets

The conversion between Sets to Arrays and back is so straight-forward that using all the great methods available in the Array.prototype object is one little step away:

```
1  function filterSet(set, predicate){
2      var filteredItems = [...set].filter(predicate);
3      return new Set(filteredItems);
4  }
5
6  var aElements = filterSet(elementsOfMagic, e => e.startsWith('a'));
7  console.log(`Elements of Magic starting with a: ${[...aElements]}`);
8  // => Elements of Magic starting with a: air
```

We saw many of these methods in the *Array's chapter* but we will see many more in the functional programming tome where we discover its secret *LINQ-like* abilities.

How Do Sets Understand Equality?

So far you've seen that a Set removes duplicated items whenever we try to add them to the Set. But **how does it know whether or not two items are equal?**

Well... It uses **strict equality comparison** (which you may also know as === or !==). This is important to understand because it poses a very big limitation to using Sets in real world applications

today. That's because even though **strict equality comparison**
works great with numbers and strings, it compares objects by
reference, that is, two objects are only equal if they are the same
object.

Let's illustrate this problematic situation with an example. Let's say
that we have a Set of persons which, of course, are unique entities
(we are all beautiful individual wonders just like precious stones):

```
1   let persons = new Set();
```

We create a person object randalf and we attempt to add it twice
to the Set:

```
1    let randalf = {id: 1, name: 'randalf'};
2
3    persons
4      .add(randalf)
5      .add(randalf);
6
7    console.log(`I have ${persons.size} person`)
8    // => I have 1 person
9
10   console.log([...persons]);
11   // => [[object Object] {
12   //   id: 1,
13   //   name: "randalf"
14   //}]
```

The Set has our back and only adds the person once. Since it is the
same object, using strict equality works in this scenario. However,
what would happen if we were to add an object that we considered
to be equal in our problem domain?

So let's say that in a new and innovative view of the world two
persons are equal if they have the same properties, and particularly
the same id (Imagine randalf meeting randalf from the future, they
are equal, but not the same):

```
1   persons.add({id: 1, name: 'randalf'});
2   console.log(`I have ${person.size} persons?!?`)
3
4   // => I have 2 persons?!?
5   console.log([...persons]);
6   /*
7   *= [[object Object] {
8       id: 1,
9       name: "randalf"
10  }, [object Object] {
11      id: 1,
12      name: "randalf"
13  }]
14  */
```

Well, in that case, the object would be added to the Set and as a result, and for all intents and purposes, we would have the same person twice. Unfortunately there's no way to specify equality for the elements within a Set as of today and we'll have to wait to see this feature introduced into the language some time in the future.

We are free to imagine how it would look though, and something like this would work wonderfully:

```
1   let personsSet = new Set([], p => p.id);
```

In the meantime, if you need to use Set-like functionality for objects your best bet is to use a dictionary indexing objects by a key that represents their uniqueness.

```
1   var fakeSetThisIsAHack = new Map();
2   fakeSetThisIsAHack
3     .set(randalf.id, randalf)
4     .set(1, {id: 1, name: 'randalf'});
5   console.log(`fake set has ${fakeSetThisIsAHack.size} item`);
6   // => fake set has 1 item
```

Sets Cheatsheet

Basic Operations

Basics	description
var set = new Set()	Create an empty set
var set = new Set(iterator)	Create a set from an iterator
set.add('value')	Add an item to the set if it is not in the set already. The items added to the set can be of any type. It uses strict equality comparison to determine that. Chainable.
set.delete('value')	Remove item if it exists. Returns true if an item has been removed and false otherwise.
set.has('value')	Check whether an item exists in the set. Returns true or false whether the key exists or not respectively.
set.size	Returns the number of items in the set
set.clear()	Remove all items within the set

Iterating a Set

Methods of Iteration	description
set.forEach((value,value,map) ⇒ {})	Iterate over every item within a set
set.value()	Returns a value iterator. This is the Set default iterator
set.keys()	Returns a key iterator which just lets you iterate over the items within a set (just like values)

Methods of Iteration	description
set.entries()	Returns a key/value pair iterator which lets you iterate over pairs of value/value for those items within a set

Concluding

The Set is a new data structure in ES6 that lets you easily remove duplicates from a collection of items. It offers a very simple API very consistent with the Map API and it's going to be a great addition to your arsenal and save you the need to roll your own.

Unfortunately, at present, it has a big limitation that is that it only supports strict equality comparison to determine whether two items are equal. Hopefully in the near future we will be able to define our own custom version of equality and that day *Sets* will achieve their true potential. Until then use Set with numbers and strings, and rely on Map when you are working with objects.

```
mooleen.says("Great!! Prepare for your demise!!");

great.says("What!?");
grate.says("Yes ma'am?");

mooleen.says("This is awkward. I'm talking to him");

great.says("You'll die insolent garbage!");
great.says("You think you can just come in here, " +
           "confuse my servant and cut my favorite hand?");
great.says("You pathetic excuse for a wizard?");

great.weaves('Kagebushin-no-jutsu!!');

/*
    A seemingly infinite number of Greats appear out of thin air and
    surround Mooleen and rat.
*/
```

```
mooleen.says('Oh my god, I barely could stand the one.');

/* The greats attack mooleen */
```

Exercises

Experiment JavaScriptmancer!

You can experiment with these exercises and some possible solutions in this jsFiddle[109] or downloading the source code from GitHub[110].

Find the Real Great and Terminate Him For Good

There are way too many of them Greats. Find the real Great using a Set and exterminate him before they all overwhelm you.

```
1  let greatsOnTheLeft = ['great', 'great', 'great', 'great'];
2  let greatsOnTheRight = ['great', 'great', 'great'];
3  let greatsBehind = ['great', 'great'];
4  let greatsInTheFront = ['great'];
5  let greatsInADarkCorner = ['great', {
6      name: 'great',
7      class: 'evil Wizard',
8      toString(){return this.name;}}];
```

[109]http://bit.ly/javascriptmancy-data-structures-sets-exercises
[110]https://github.com/vintharas/javascriptmancy-code-samples

Solution

```
1   function findGreat(suspects){
2      let setToFindGreat = new Set(suspects);
3      console.log(`These are the only ones: ` +
4                     `${[...setToFindGreat.values()]}`);
5      return setToFindGreat;
6   }
7
8   let uniqueGreats = findGreat([...greatsOnTheLeft,
9                      ...greatsOnTheRight, ...greatsBehind,
10                     ...greatsInTheFront, ...greatsInADarkCorner]);
11  // => These are the unique great: great, great
12
13  mooleen.says('Haha got ya!');
14  mooleen.weaves("obliterate(uniqueGreats)");
15  // => Mooleen starts weaving a spell!
16  //     ***obliterate(uniqueGreats)***
17  //     A ray of black matter springs from your fingers,
18  //     impacts great and great and turns them into rubble
19
20  mooleen.says("And that's that");
21  mooleen.says("C'est fini");
```

Book I. Epilogue

```
/*
Mooleen walks out from the darkness of the evil lair into
bright daylight.She looks up into a beautiful and
breathtaking dawn and sighs deeply.
*/

mooleen.sighsDeeply();
mooleen.says("That was a good days work");

rat.says("Indeed it was. I particularly enjoyed " +
         "the hand chopping part");

mooleen.says("Yeah... that was an epic move");

rat.says("What now?");

mooleen.says("I suppose it's time to go home");
mooleen.says("If I can find it");

rat.says("I'm sure Randalf knows where to find it");
mooleen.says("I surely hope so. I miss it.");

rat.says("Where are you from anyway?");

mooleen.says("A place called Earth");
```

As they say, all good things must come to an end. I really hope you have enjoyed reading this book, that you've learned a lot of new stuff and that you're super excited about writing some JavaScript!

Have an awesome day ahead of you!

– Jaime, your most humble servant

P.S. I added a bonus chapter! A preview that introduces you to the world of object oriented programming in JavaScript. Take a look. I think you'll love it.

Tome I.III JavaScriptmancy and OOP: The Path of The Summoner (preview)

The Path of Summoning and Commanding Objects (Also Known as Object Oriented Programming)

Introduction to the Path of Summoning and Commanding Objects (a.k.a. Object Oriented Programming)

 Preview!

This chapter is a preview of my next book about the secret path of summoning and commanding objects in JavaScript, which is to say, object oriented programming. Enjoy it!

A Soft Introduction to OOP in JavaScript

Welcome to *the Path of Summoning*[111] *and Commanding Objects*! In this part of these ancient manuscript you'll learn how you can work with objects in JavaScript, how to define them, create them and even how to interweave them. By the end of this part you'll have mastered Object Oriented Programming in JavaScript and you'll be ready to command your vast armies of objects into victory.

JavaScript OOP story is pretty special. When I started working seriously with JavaScript some years ago, one of my first concerns

---

[111]In Fantasy, Wizards of all sorts and kinds *summon* or *call forth* creatures to act as servants or warriors and follow the wizard commands. As a JavaScript-mancer you'll be able to use Object Oriented Programming to summon your own objects into reality and do with them as you please.

as a C# developer coming to JavaScript was to find out how to write a class. I had a lot of prowess in C# and I wanted to bring all that knowledge and ability into the world of JavaScript, so my first approach was to try to map every C# concept into JavaScript. I saw classes, which are such a core construct in C# and which were such an important part of my programming style at the time, as my secret passage to being proficient in JavaScript.

Well, it took me a long while to understand how to mimic classical inheritance in JavaScript but it was time well spent because along the way I learnt a lot about JavaScript and about the many different ways in which it supports object-oriented programming. This quest helped me look beyond classical inheritance into other OOP styles more adequate to JavaScript where flexibility and expressiveness reign supreme over the strict and fixed taxonomies of classes.

In this part of the book I will attempt to bring you with me through the same journey that I experienced. We will start with how to achieve classical inheritance in JavaScript, so you can get a basic level of proficiency by translating your C# skills into JavaScript and then we will move beyond that into new patterns that truly leverage JavaScript as a language and which will blow your mind.

 ## Experiment JavaScriptmancer!!

You can experiment with all examples in this chapter directly within this jsBin[112] or downloading the source code from GitHub[113].

Let's get a taste of what is in store for you by getting a high level overview [114] of object-oriented programming in JavaScript. If you

---

[112]http://bit.ly/javascriptmancy-oop-introduction

[113]https://github.com/vintharas/javascriptmancy

[114]In this section I am going to make a lot of generalizations and simplifications in order to give a simple and clear introduction to OOP in JavaScript. I'll dive into each concept in greater detail and with an appropriate level of correctness in the rest of the chapters about OOP.

feel like you can't follow the examples don't worry. For in the upcoming chapters we will dive deeper in each of the concepts and constructs used, and we will discuss them separately and at a much slower pace.

C# Classes in JavaScript

A C# *class* is more or less equivalent to a JavaScript *constructor function* and *prototype* pair:

```
1   // Here we have a Minion constructor function
2   function Minion(name, hp){
3     // the constructor function usually defines the data within
4     // a "class", the properties contained within a constructor
5     // function will be part of each object created
6     // with this function
7     this.name = name;
8     this.hp = hp;
9   }
10
11  // the prototype usually defines the methods within a "class"
12  // It is shared across all Minion instances
13  Minion.prototype.toString = function() {return this.name;};
```

The *constructor function* represents how an object should be constructed (*created*) while the *prototype* represents a piece of reusable behavior. In practice, the *constructor function* usually defines the data members within a *"class"* while the *prototype* defines its methods.

You can instantiate a new Minion object by using the new operator on the *constructor function*:

```
1    var orc = new Minion('orc', 100);
2    console.log(orc);
3    // => [object Object] {
4    //   hp: 100,
5    //   name: "orc",
6    //   toString: function () {return this.name;}
7    //}
8
9    console.log(orc.toString())
10   // => orc
11
12   console.log('orc is a Minion: ' + (orc instanceof Minion));
13   // => true
```

As a result of instantiating an orc we get a new Minion object with two properties hp and name. The Minion object also has a hidden property called [[prototype]] that points to its prototype which is an object that has a method toString. This *prototype* and its toString method are shared across all instances of the Minion class.

When you call orc.toString the JavaScript runtime checks whether or not the orc object has a toString method and if it can't find it, *like in this case*, it goes down the *prototype chain* until it does. The *prototype chain* is established by the object itself, its prototype, its prototype's prototype and so on. In this case, the *prototype chain* leads to the Minion.prototype object that has a toString method that would be called and evaluated as this.name (orc).

We can mimic classical inheritance by defining a new *"class"* Wizard and make it inherit from Minion:

```
1   // Behold! A Wizard!
2   function Wizard(element, mana, name, hp){
3     // the constructor function calls its parent constructor function
4     // using [Function.prototype.call] (or apply)
5     Minion.call(this, name, hp);
6     this.element = element;
7     this.mana = mana;
8   }
9
10  // the prototype of the Wizard is a Minion object
11  Wizard.prototype = Object.create(Minion.prototype);
12  Wizard.prototype.constructor = Wizard;
```

We achieve *classical inheritance* by:

1. calling the `Minion` *constructor function* from the `Wizard` *constructor*
2. assigning a `Minion` object (created via `Object.create`) as prototype of the `Wizard` *"class"*

With the *constructor* delegation we ensure that a `Wizard` object has all the properties of a `Minion` object. While with the *prototype chain* we ensure that all the methods in the `Minion` prototype are available to a `Wizard` object.

We can also augment the `Wizard` *prototype* with new methods:

```
1   // we can augment the prototype with a new method
2   // to cast mighty spells
3   Wizard.prototype.castsSpell = function(spell, target){
4     console.log(this + ' casts ' + spell + ' on ' + target);
5     this.mana -= spell.mana;
6     spell(target);
7   };
```

Or even override or extend existing methods within its base *"class"* `Minion`:

```
1    // we can also override and extend methods
2    Wizard.prototype.toString = function(){
3        return Minion.prototype.toString.apply(this, arguments) +
4      ", the " + this.element +" Wizard";
5    };
```

Finally we can verify that everything works as expected by instantiating our very own powerful wizard:

```
1    var gandalf = new Wizard("Grey", /* mana */ 50,
2                            "Gandalf", /* hp */ 50);
3    console.log('Gandalf is a Wizard: ' + (gandalf instanceof Wizard));
4    // => Gandalf is a Wizard: true
5    console.log('Gandalf is a Minion: ' + (gandalf instanceof Minion));
6    // => Gandalf is a Minion: true
7
8    console.log(gandalf.toString());
9    // => Gandalf, the Grey Wizard
10
11   var lightningSpell = function(target){
12     console.log('A bolt of lightning electrifies ' +
13                 target + '(-10hp)');
14     target.hp -= 10;
15   };
16   lightningSpell.mana = 5;
17   lightningSpell.toString = function(){ return 'lightning spell';};
18   gandalf.castsSpell(lightningSpell, orc);
19   // => Gandalf, the Grey Wizard casts lightning spell on orc
20   // => A bolt of lightning electrifies orc (-10hp)
```

As you can see from these previous examples writing *"classes"* prior to *ES6* was no easy feat, it required a lot of moving components and a lot of code. That's why *ES6* brings *classes* along which provide a much nicer syntax to what you've seen thus far. This means that instead of having to handle *constructor functions* and *prototypes* yourself, you get the new `class` keyword that nicely wraps both into a more coherent syntax:

```
1   // this is the equivalent of the Minion
2   class ClassyMinion{
3     constructor(name, hp){
4       this.name = name;
5       this.hp = hp;
6     }
7     toString(){
8       return this.name;
9     }
10  }
11
12  let classyOrc = new ClassyMinion('classy orc', 50);
13  console.log(classyOrc);
14  // => [object Object] {
15  //   hp: 100,
16  //   name: "classy orc"
17  //}
18
19  console.log(classyOrc.toString());
20  // => classy orc
21
22  console.log('classy orc is a ClassyMinion: ' +
23    (classyOrc instanceof ClassyMinion));
24  // => classy orc is a ClassyMinion: true
```

And the extend and super keywords:

```
1   // and this is the equivalent of the Wizard
2   class ClassyWizard extends ClassyMinion{
3     constructor(element, mana, name, hp){
4       // super lets you access the parent class methods
5       super(name, hp);
6       this.element = element;
7       this.mana = mana;
8     }
9     toString(){
10      return super.toString() + ", the " + this.element +" Wizard";
11    }
12    castsSpell(spell, target){
13      console.log(this + ' casts ' + spell + ' on ' + target);
14      this.mana -= spell.mana;
15      spell(target);
```

```
16    }
17  }
```

Where extend lets you establish class inheritance and super lets
you access methods from parent classes. Again, we can verify that
it works just like it did before by instantiating a *classy* wizard:

```
1   let classyGandalf = new Wizard("Grey", /* mana */ 50,
2                            "Classy Gandalf", /* hp */ 50);
3   console.log('Classy Gandalf is a ClassyWizard: ' +
4            (classyGandalf instanceof ClassyWizard));
5   // => Classy Gandalf is a ClassyWizard: true
6   console.log('Classy Gandalf is a ClassyMinion: ' +
7            (classyGandalf instanceof ClassyMinion));
8   // => Classy Gandalf is a ClassyMinion: true
9
10  console.log(classyGandalf.toString());
11  // => Classy Gandalf, the Grey Wizard
12
13  classyGandalf.castsSpell(lightningSpell, classyOrc);
14  // => Classy Gandalf, the Grey Wizard casts lightning
15  //     spell on classy orc
16  // => A bolt of lightning electrifies classy orc(-10hp)
```

**It is important to highlight though that ES6 classes are just
syntactic sugar.** Under the hood, these ES6 classes that you have
just seen are translated into *constructor function/prototype* pairs.

And that is how you mimic classical inheritance in JavaScript. But
let's look beyond it.

OOP Beyond Classes

There are a lot of people in the JavaScript community that claim that
the cause of JavaScript not having a nice way to mimic classical
inheritance, not having classes, is that you were not meant to
use it in the first place. You were meant to embrace *prototypical*

inheritance which is the natural way of working with inheritance in JavaScript, instead of hacking it to make it behave sort of like *classical inheritance.*

In the world of *prototypical inheritance* you only have objects, and particularly objects that are based upon other objects which we call *prototypes.* Prototypes lend behaviors to other objects by means of delegation (via the *prototype chain*) or by the so called *concatenative inheritance* which consists in copying behaviors.

Let's illustrate the usefulness of this type of inheritance with an example. Imagine that, in addition to *wizards,* we also need to have some *thieves* for when we need to use more gentle/shrew hand against our enemies. A ClassyThief class could look something like this:

```
 1  class ClassyThief extends ClassyMinion{
 2    constructor(name, hp){
 3      super(name, hp);
 4    }
 5    toString(){
 6      return super.toString() + ", the Thief";
 7    }
 8    steals(target, item){
 9      console.log(`${this} steals ${item} from ${target}`);
10    }
11  }
```

And let's say that a couple of weeks from now, we realize that it would be nice to have yet another type of minion, one that can both cast spells and steals, and why not? Play some music. Something like a *Bard.* In *pseudo-code* we would describe it as follows:

```
1   // class Bard
2   // should be able to:
3   // - cast powerful spells
4   // - steals many items
5   // - play beautiful music
```

Well we are in a pickle here. *Classical inheritance* tends to build
rigid taxonomies of types where something is a Wizard, something
is a Thief but it cannot be both. *How would we solve the issue of the
Bard using classical inheritance in C#?* Well...

- We could move both castsSpell and steals methods to
  a base class SpellCastingAndStealingMinion that all three
  types could inherit. The ClassyThief would throw an exception when casting spell and so would the ClassyWizard when
  stealing. Not a very good solution (goodbye Liskov principle
  [115])

- We could create a SpellCastingAndStealingMinion that duplicates the functionality in ClassyThief and ClassyWizard
  and make the Bard inherit from it. This solution would imply
  code duplication and thus additional maintenance.

- We could define interfaces for these behaviors ICanSteal,
  ICanCastSpells and make each class implement these interfaces. Nicer but we would need to provide an specific
  implementation in each separate class. No so much code
  reuse here.

So none of these solutions are very attractive, they involve bad
design, code duplication or both. *Can JavaScript helps us to achieve
a better solution to this problem?* **Yes it can**

---

[115]The Liskov substitution principle is one of the S.O.L.I.D. principles of object-oriented
design. It states that derived classes must be substitutable for their base classes. This
means that a derived class should behave as portrayed by its base class and not break the
expectations created by its interface. In this particular example if you have a castsSpell
and a steals method in the base class, and a derived class throws an exception when you
call the steals method you are violating this principle because the derived class breaks the
expectations established by the base class (i.e. that you should be able to use both methods).

Imagine that we broke down all behaviors and encapsulated them
inside separate objects (canCastSpells, canSteal and canPlayMu-
sic):

```
1   let canCastSpells = {
2     castsSpell(spell, target){
3       console.log(this + ' casts ' + spell + ' on ' + target);
4       this.mana -= spell.mana;
5       spell(target);
6     }
7   };
8
9   let canSteal = {
10    steals(target, item){
11      console.log(`${this} steals ${item} from ${target}`);
12    }
13  };
14
15  let canPlayMusic = {
16    playsMusic(){
17      console.log(`${this} grabs his ${this.instrument}` +
18               ` and starts playing music`);
19    }
20  };
21
22  let canBeIdentifiedByName = {
23    toString(){
24      return this.name;
25    }
26  };
```

Now that we have encapsulated each behavior in a separate object
we can compose them together to provide the necessary functionality to a wizard, a thief and a bard:

```
1    // and now we can create our objects by composing
2    // this behaviors together
3    function TheWizard(element, mana, name, hp){
4      let wizard = {element,
5                         mana,
6                         name,
7                         hp};
8      Object.assign(wizard,
9                         canBeIdentifiedByName,
10                        canCastSpells);
11     return wizard;
12   }
13
14   function TheThief(name, hp){
15     let thief = {name,
16                        hp};
17     Object.assign(thief,
18                        canBeIdentifiedByName,
19                        canSteal);
20     return thief;
21   }
22
23   function TheBard(instrument, mana, name, hp){
24     let bard = {instrument,
25                        mana,
26                        name,
27                        hp};
28     Object.assign(bard,
29                        canBeIdentifiedByName,
30                        canSteal,
31                        canCastSpells,
32                        canSteal);
33     return bard;
34   }
```

And in a very expressive way we can see how a wizard is someone
than can cast spells, a thief is someone that can steal and a bard
someone that not only can cast spells and steal but can also play
music. By stepping out of the rigid limits of classical inheritance and
strong typing we get to a place where we can easily reuse behaviors
and compose new objects in a very flexible and extensible manner.

We can verify that indeed this approach works beautifully:

```
1   let wizard = TheWizard('fire', 100, 'Randalf, the Red', 10);
2   wizard.castsSpell(lightningSpell, orc);
3   // => Randalf, the Red casts lightning spell on orc
4   // => A bolt of lightning electrifies orc(-10hp)
5
6   let thief = TheThief('Locke Lamora', 100);
7   thief.steals('orc', /*item*/ 'gold coin');
8   // => Locke Lamora steals gold coin from orc
9
10  let bard = TheBard('lute', 100, 'Kvothe', 100);
11  bard.playsMusic();
12  // => Kvothe grabs his lute and starts playing music
13  bard.steals('orc', /*item*/ 'sandwich');
14  // => Kvothe steals sandwich from orc
15  bard.castsSpell(lightningSpell, orc);
16  // => Kvothe casts lightning spell on orc
17  // =>A bolt of lightning electrifies orc(-10hp)
```

The `Object.assign` in the examples is an *ES6* method that lets you extend an object with other objects. This is effectively the *concatenative prototypical inheritance* we mentioned previously.

> We usually call these objects *mixins*. A *mixin* in JavaScript is just an object that you compose with other objects to provide them with additional behavior or state. In the simplest example of *mixins* you just have a single object extending another object, but there's also functional *mixins*, where you use functions instead. We will cover all these *mixin* patterns in detail later in the book with a deep dive into Object.assign and possible alternatives in ES5.

This object composition technique constitutes a very interesting and flexible approach to object-oriented programming that isn't available in C#. But in JavaScript we can use it even with *ES6 classes*!

Combining Classes with Object Composition

Remember that *ES6 classes* are just syntactic sugar over the existing *prototypical inheritance model*. They may look like *classical inheritance* but they are not. This means that the following mix of *ES6 classes* and *object composition* would work:

```
class ClassyBard extends ClassyMinion{
  constructor(instrument, mana, name, hp){
    super(name, hp);
    this.instrument = instrument;
    this.mana = mana;
  }
}

Object.assign(ClassyBard.prototype,
        canSteal,
        canCastSpells,
        canPlayMusic);
```

In this example we extend the `ClassyBard` prototype with new functionality that will be shared by all future instances of `ClassyBard`. If we instantiate a new *bard* we can verify that it can steal, cast spells and play music.

```
let anotherBard = new ClassyBard('guitar', 100, 'Jimi Hendrix', 100);
anotherBard.playsMusic();
// => Kvothe grabs his lute and starts playing music
anotherBard.steals('orc', /*item*/ 'silver coin');
// => Kvothe steals silver coin from orc
anotherBard.castsSpell(lightningSpell, orc);
// => Kvothe casts lightning spell on orc
// =>A bolt of lightning electrifies orc(-10hp)
```

This is an example of *delegation-based prototypical inheritance* in which methods such as `steals`, `castsSpell` and `playsMusic` are delegated to a single *prototype* object (instead of being appended to each object).

So far you've seen classical inheritance mimicked in JavaScript, *ES6 classes* and object composition via mixin objects, but there's much more to learn and in greater detail! Take a sneak peak at what you'll learn in each of the upcoming chapters:

The Path of the Object Summoner Step by Step

In **Summoning Fundamentals: an Introduction to Object Oriented Programming in JavaScript** you'll start by understanding the basic constructs needed to define and instantiate objects in JavaScript where *constructor functions* and the new operator will join what you've discovered thus far about *object initializers*. You'll review how to achieve *information hiding* and you'll learn the basics of JavaScript *prototypical inheritance* model and how you can use it to reuse code/behaviors and improve your memory footprint. You'll complete the foundations of JavaScript OOP by understanding how JavaScript achieves polymorphism.

In **White Tower Summoning or Emulating Classical Inheritance in JavaScript** you'll use *constructor functions* in conjunction with *prototypes* to create the equivalent of C# classes in JavaScript. You'll then push the boundaries of JavaScript inheritance model further and emulate C# classical inheritance building inheritance chains with method extension and overriding just like in C#.

In **White Tower Summoning Enhanced: the Marvels of ES6 Classes** you'll learn about the new *ES6 Class* syntax and how it provides a much better *class* development experience over what it was possible prior to *ES6*.

In **Black Tower Summoning: Objects Interweaving Objects with Mixins** we'll go beyond classical inheritance into the arcane realm of *object composition* with mixins. You'll learn about the extreme extensibility of object-oriented programming based on object composition and how you can define small pieces of reusable behavior and properties and combine them together to create powerful objects (effectively achieving multiple inheritance).

In **Black Tower Summoning: Safer Object Composition with Traits ** you'll learn about an object composition alternative to mixins called traits. Traits are as reusable and composable as mixins but are even more flexible and safe as they let you define required properties and resolve conflicts.

In *Black Tower Summoning Enhanced: Next Level Object Composition With Stamps ** you'll find out about a new way to work with objects in JavaScript called *Stamps that brings object composability to the next level.

Finally, you'll dive into the depths of **Object Internals** and discover the mysteries of the low level JavaScript Object APIs and the new ES6 Reflection APIs.

Concluding

JavaScript is a very versatile language that supports a lot of programming paradigms and different styles of Object-Oriented Programming. In the next chapters you'll see how you can combine a small number of primitive constructs and techniques to achieve a variety of OOP styles.

JavaScript, like in any other part of the language, gives you a lot of freedom when working with objects, and sometimes you'll feel like there are so many options and things you can do that you won't know what's the right path. Because of that, I'll try to provide you with as much guidance as I can and highlight the strengths and weaknesses of each of the options available.

Get ready to learn some JavaScript OOP!

References and Appendix

Appendix A. Setting Up Your Developing Environment For ES6

The best way to get started with ES6 is by using an interactive online REPL. Here is a list of some of my favorites:

- Babel REPL[116] - **bit.ly/babel-repl**. Babel is a ES6 transpiler that let's you take advantage of ES6 and ESnext features today. It is the *de facto* ES6 transpiler.
- jsBin[117] - **jsbin.com**. JsBin is a very popular web prototyping tool with a customizable set of pans to visualize HTML, CSS, JavaScript, a console and the output.
- jsFiddle[118] - **jsfiddle.net**. JsFiddle is yet another popular prototyping tool that let's you look at your HTML, CSS, JavaScript and output at a glance.
- CodePen[119] - **codepen.io** is a web prototyping tool and community.
- ES6 Katas[120] - **es6katas.org** is a collection of interactive katas to learn ES6.

Using ES6 with Node.js

In addition to using prototyping tools for the web, node.js has great support for ES6 as you can appreciate in these compatibility table[121].

---

[116]http://bit.ly/babel-repl

[117]http://www.jsbin.com

[118]http://www.jsfiddle.net

[119]http://www.codepen.io

[120]http://es6katas.org/

[121]http://kangax.github.io/compat-table/es6/

But it you want to be able to use all features of ES6 and ESnext you can take advatange of babel.js[122] and the `babel-node` REPL.

You can install it using the following command:

```
1   $ npm install -g babel
```

And start it using `babel node`:

```
1   $ babel-node
```

This will open a REPL that has complete support for ES6.

ES6 and Modern Browsers

Modern browsers also have an increasing support for ES6. The ES6 compability table[123] can give you a general idea as to how the efforts from the different vendors are going.

The problem with developing for the browser is that you cannot control the runtime in which your application is running like you do when developing a backend in node.js. This means that you cannot rely on your user's browser having the features that you need or want to use. Because of that, transpiling your application from ES6 to ES5 becomes crucial in these environments to make sure that it works in a myriad of devices and can reach as many users as possible.

There's a wide variety of tools that let you transpile your ES6 code to something that can work on any browser and setup a real world ES6 development environment.

---

[122]https://babeljs.io
[123]https://bit.ly/es6-compatibility

Real-World ES6 Development Environments

The *de facto* standard for transpiling ES6 is babel.js[124]. It is very extensible and can be plugged into any of the modern front-end build pipelines. It uses a plugin system that lets you easily decide which features of ES6 and ESnext you want to enable.

Depending on your build tooling of choice you'll need to follow different steps to start using Babel. You can find numerous and extensive guides for Gulp, WebPack, Grunt, Broccoli, etc at bit.ly/setup-es6[125].

---

[124]babeljs.io
[125]http://bit.ly/setup-es6

Appendix B. Fantasy Glossary

If you are not familiar with the genre of fantasy you may have a hard time understanding some of the words I use in this book. Hopefully this glossary will give you some guidance in this respect.

- **Arcane**: Something that is mysterious or secret. Known or understood by very few people.
- **Alchemy**: A science that was used in the Middle Ages with the goal of changing ordinary metals into gold. Also a power or process that changes or transforms something in a mysterious or impressive way.
- **Cimmerian barbarian**: Barbarian from the extreme confines of Cimmeria.
- **Conan**: "Hither came Conan, the Cimmerian, black-haired, sullen-eyed, sword in hand, a thief, a reaver, a slayer, with gigantic melancholies and gigantic mirth, to tread the jeweled thrones of the Earth under his sandalled feet."
- **Balefire**: Balefire is a weapon of the One Power. When a target is struck with balefire, its thread in the Pattern is destroyed, in an amount proportional to the power of the balefire strike. This translates to both the target's existence, and actions up to a certain point, being retroactively erased.
- **Gandalf**: Mighty wizard that has the magic ability to always be on time.
- **Goblin**: An ugly and sometimes evil creature that likes to cause trouble.
- **Golem**: An artificial creature being endowed with life by magic. It is often associated to different elements and materials: fire, earth, sand, etc.

- **Hobbit**: Hobbits are similar to humans, but about half their size. They're chubby, furry-footed home-bodies with a penchant for dwelling in hollowed out hillsides and a racial talent for burglary.
- **Halfling**: see Hobbit.
- **JavaScript-mancer**: Person that has mastered the art of writing awesome JavaScript and has an intimate knowledge of it.
- **JavaScript-mancy**: The arcane art of using JavaScript to alter the world around you.
- **Kender**: A race of wizened 14-year-olds that, unlike halflings, wear shoes.
- **Mana**: For those of you not familiar with magic, mana can be seen as a measure of magical stamina. As such, doing magic (like summoning minions) spends oneâ€™s mana. An empty reservoir of mana means no spellcasting just as a empty reserve of stamina means no more running.
- **Minion**: Someone who is not powerful or important and who obeys the orders of a powerful leader or boss.
- **Saruman**: Powerful wizard prone who likes white clothing and prone to evil deeds
- **Scepter**: A staff or baton borne by a sovereign as an emblem of authority. It can be imbued in magic powers.
- **Spell**: A spoken word or form of words held to have magic power.
- **Spellcasting (casting)**: Performing magic by reciting a spell.
- **Summon**: To bid a creature to come to your aid with the help of magic. It can also create a creature from nothingness.
- **Troll**: An evil giant creature than inhabitates caves, hills and bridges. Some of them show weakness to sunlight.
- **Teleport**: Transfer ones location by using magic
- **Orc**: A race of human-like creatures, characterized as ugly, warlike, and malevolent.
- **Orb**: A circular object that possess unbound magic power.

- **Wand**: A long, thin stick used by a magician to channel its powers.
- **Weave**: See spellcasting.

References

There's a lot of books that have inspired me while writing JavaScript-mancy. Here is a non exhaustive list of the most influential.

Specifications

- ECMAScript 6 Specification[126]

Books

- JavaScript Allonge - Reginald Braithwaite
- You don't know JS - Kyle Simpson
- Functional JavaScript - Michael Fogus
- Effective JavaScript - David Herman
- Understanding ECMAScript 6 - Nicholas C. Zackas
- Secrets of the JavaScript Ninja - John Resig, Bear Bibeault
- Programming JavaScript Applications - Eric Elliott
- Principles of Object Oriented JavaScript - Nicholas C. Zackas
- Eloquent JavaScript - Adam Freeman
- JavaScript the Good Parts - Douglas Crockford

---

[126]http://www.ecma-international.org/ecma-262/6.0